GLOBAL POLITICAL STUDIES

A CONTRIBUTION TO THE CRITIQUE OF CONTEMPORARY CAPITALISM

THEORETICAL AND INTERNATIONAL PERSPECTIVES

Global Political Studies

Additional books in this series can be found on Nova's website under the Series tab.

Additional e-books in this series can be found on Nova's website under the e-book tab.

GLOBAL POLITICAL STUDIES

A CONTRIBUTION TO THE CRITIQUE OF CONTEMPORARY CAPITALISM

THEORETICAL AND INTERNATIONAL PERSPECTIVES

RAJU J. DAS, PH.D.

nova publishers
New York

For permission to use material from this book please contact us:
Telephone 631-231-7269; Fax 631-231-8175
Web Site: http://www.novapublishers.com

Library of Congress Cataloging-in-Publication Data

ISBN: 978-1-63117-559-6

Published by Nova Science Publishers, Inc. † New York

I wish to dedicate this book to my parents.

They both taught me, through their words and actions, to be sympathetic towards people who live in difficult conditions. And my father, who studied philosophy and mathematics, taught me the value of freedom to think and the idea that one cannot take things at their face value. Both of them taught me to value labor and respect laborers. My mother, who could not always satisfy her need for nutritious food during my childhood, taught me the importance of human need in a way she might not realize. My parents wanted me to be a civil servant to be able to make an immediate difference in the world of poor people. I initially agreed but finally betrayed them. I am grateful to them that they did not insist on what they thought I should be.

CONTENTS

INTRODUCTION

The word 'critique', or 'critical', is everywhere. In the academic world we hear of critical sociology, critical human geography, critical anthropology, critical development studies, and so on. The ubiquity of critique is partly associated with the nature of the contemporary world. It is a world of inequality and insecurity. It is a world, which is experiencing economic, political and ecological crisis. And not surprisingly, it is a world that is characterized by resistance, i.e., resistance against globalization and monopolies, against wars and austerity, against social injustice and cultural oppression. Indeed, the system is haunted by the specter of occupy movements, Arab Springs, and movements against dispossession in its various forms.[1]

While we appear to be living in an age of critique, the quality of the critique of society can generally be a lot better. This book, therefore, deals with the theme of social critique. It is about the critique of the capitalist world, *including* of the operations of capitalism and Leftist political responses to it. And the book is a critique of ideas about that world – particularly, of what are considered progressive critiques of capitalism. Its aim is to clarify, in a very basic way, the contours of what it considers to be genuine critique. Its argument is that critique is a fundamental human activity, and that social science can and must be critical and explanatory (of ideas and the world) at the same time. Social science must be critical of the world because of the contradictions and inadequacies in the world. It must be critical of itself and ideas of 'ordinary people', because these ideas contribute to the reproduction of a world that is inadequate and contradiction-ridden. We live in a world which keeps on creating new needs but which frustrates the satisfaction of these needs on the part of the majority. In fact, the majority cannot even satisfy their very basic needs, in spite of the existence of an adequate amount of resources in society.[2] Such a situation demands that our thinking become critical, genuinely critical. And, human beings have an essential ability to be critical: they are 'homo criticus'. That general ability – that 'species' ability -- must be exercised in a very specific way: the mode of critique must reflect the social contradictions of the world and from the

---

[1] Harvey (2010) discusses many different types of resistance against the system.

[2] In mainstream economics, scholars talk more about wants than needs, and that wants are unlimited, in relations to the resources, which are considered scarce (Dowd, 2002). Indeed, the *raison de tre* of mainstream economics lies in this thesis. It forgets, however, that wants are created and are not naturally unlimited, and that society's resources are abused to satisfy *the wants of the well-off*, the resources that could be used to satisfy *the needs of the majority*. It also forgets that the so-called resource is usually socially engineered through class-mechanisms and associated profit logics: including through the monopolization of resources in the hands of a few.

standpoint of negating those contradictions in order to make our world a better, a more humane, place.

In thinking about critique, several questions come to mind. What does 'critique' or 'critical' really mean? Why is critique necessary, and what makes it possible? What forms does critique take? What are the ingredients of philosophical, theoretical, and practical critiques? The idea of critique of ideas implies that there are inadequate ideas. Where do such ideas – 'ideological ideas' – come from then? What social groups should social critique speak to or target as its main audience, and why? These are the questions that Chapter one deals with, at a very basic level, and without using too many references to the academic literature.

What a body of ideas *is* can be seen in relation to what it *is not*, what it is critical of. So a body of ideas seeking to describe/explain its objects of analysis can be seen *as a critique*.. A specific form of the latter is Marxist critique, which is simultaneously the Marxist theory of society. Given much misunderstanding of this body of work, and given that its categories are essential to correctly comprehend contemporary problems facing the humanity, it is necessary to reassert and rearticulate the central categories of the Marxist critique. If Chapter one talks more about critique of ideas as such (e.g., what are the properties of inadequate ideas?), what is presented in Chapter 2 (Marxist theory/critique) is more about inadequacies of the world itself, in its various dimensions (economic, political, cultural, ecological and spatial).

There are four components of Marxist critique: philosophy (a dialectical and materialist worldview); social theory (historical materialism); political economy; and political practice. Marxist explanatory critique must be dialectical, and materialist (in both philosophical and scientific senses). This critique must be multi-scalar, and especially internationalist, emphasizing the international nature of both capitalism and of the fact that a potentially successful fight against it must be ultimately international in scope. The application of fundamental philosophical and social-theoretical Marxist principles sheds important light on the world we live in and on our history. It is the most fundamental and the most uncompromising form of philosophical, theoretical and practical critique of society.[3] Such a critique can be suitably applied to the world we live in and to the ideas about it, including the proposals for changing it. The Marxist critique is the class-based social critique, one that integrates non-class oppression such as that based on race and gender. It shows that people's fight for autonomy and democracy including gender and racial equality and for democratic transparency cannot but be a part of the fight against capitalism itself. An *implicit* aim of the discussion on the *Marxist* critique is to distinguish it from not only *non*-Marxism but also so-called *post*-Marxism. In the process, it indirectly speaks to some of the unfounded criticisms against Marxist critique/analysis that it is intellectually simplistic/rigid/ reductionist, as economistic, and as race- and gender-blind; it is also wrongly seen as a politically undemocratic project.[4] Those who wish to critique the Marxist critique should have a basic understanding of what that critique really is,[5] and not what one thinks what that critique is.[6]

[3] Eagleton (2012:1) makes this point as well. It is a book worth reading.

[4] The discussion – as Part 1 as a whole and Part 3 -- is pitched at the level of beginning graduate and advanced undergraduate scholars; it is also aimed at any person who seeks to, at least, explore what Marxism is in an open-minded way.

[5] I am consciously using the singular noun. One can say that: there is no such thing as *the* Marxist critique, there are rather Marxist critique*s*. One can say that there is no such thing as Marxism, there are rather Marxism*s*. My criticism of such a position is this: there must be something common to Marxisms or Marxist critiques, which represents different forms of that substance, that essence. Otherwise, what is that thing which has many forms (Marxisms, Marxist critiques)? The unity precedes the difference, partly through which the unity is reproduced.

And those who wish to do some trekking in the vast terrain of the Marxist critique in order to enjoy good health and exercise their muscles, a little map of that terrain may come in handy. Chapter 2 aims to offer this opportunity. There are various ways in which the world in which we live and the ideas about this world have been interpreted. The point of Marxist critique is to seek to change some of these interpretations.

Ideas about critique and the Marxist critique in Chapters 1-2 constitute Part 1 of the book, laying the foundations. These ideas are put into action in Parts 2-3. In Part 2, specific academic *ideas about the world* of capitalism are critiqued. In Part 3, particular *aspects of the capitalist world* are questioned from the standpoint of ideas laid out in Part 1. While Part 2 is more for specialist readers, Part 1 and 3 are more for non-specialists.

The importance of the state to our lives cannot be overemphasized. There have been various interpretations of the state. One of these is from standpoint of post-Marxism. Chapter 3 targets the post-Marxist theory, by taking one representative author (John Hoffman). By critically examining the work of this influential British theorist, this chapter shows on what basis one can offer criticisms of much thinking about the capitalist state, including what appears to be Marxist, and thus it shows how not to think about the state. The chapter argues, more specifically, that the material basis of the political is inadequately theorized.

It is one thing to explore the nature of the political in the abstract. It is another thing to scrutinize it in a concrete context. The next chapter – Chapter 4 – does this. It critically discusses the relation between the political and the economic in a given body of academic work about India. This chapter reveals the deficient ways in which some of the best-known authors, including the Nobel Laureate economist-philosopher, Amartya Sen, imagine the relation between the economic on the one hand and the political, including state policies and democracy on the other, in the context of the world's largest and fastest growing democracy.

There has to be something before it can take different forms. Note that whether what is presented as the Marxist critique represents that common thing – that substance – is a different matter. Besides, what is the substance cannot be seen un-dialectically: that is, the boundary between the substance and what is not it is not a final and absolute one. There will be some gray areas, or a certain degree of 'un-decidability'. One of the ways in which the problem of what is the substance is resolved is the way one resolves the question of whether a man who has a few counts of hair on his head is still bald or not. It is about the law of quantity and quality transformation, which is raised numerous times in the book.

[6] One can see why I would disagree with David Laibman's definition of a Marxist as 'anyone who sincerely believes her/himself to be one' (2007: x). Such a definition would work if we could judge a person by what he/she says about himself/herself. The Marxist label indeed can be used and is used ideologically: X and Y (e.g. *post*-Marxists; supporters of certain types of authoritarian regime) can say they are Marxists while their intellectual and political work has little to do with the substance of Marxism, so by doing this they are bringing disrepute to Marxism, and therefore these people's claim that they are Marxists must be forcefully rejected by Marxists. But I entirely agree with Laibman that one must distinguish between good and bad Marxist work. But then a new question arises which is similar to the one raised in the previous footnote: what is common to both good and bad Marxist work? In any case, the question of what is Marxism and what is not Marxism – and therefore who is Marxist and who is not – cannot be avoided at all. Lenin dealt with the issue of what is Marxism numerous times. A rigorous definition of Marxism is a political necessity, and not just an intellectual one. In the academic world, the question is especially pertinent because of two contradictory tendencies. One is that the academia generally is after fads. Another is that: Marxism is associated with rigor and therefore a certain amount of prestige, which many people seek (including for extra-intellectual reasons), but it is not a fad, because it deals with issues that are not going away – class relations and their adverse effects.. In relation to Marxism, what many in the academia, therefore, do to 'resolve' the contradiction, is this: while chasing the fads of the day, many appropriate some words and concepts from Marxism (these concepts usually do not belong to the core of Marxism and/or are used differently from the way Marxists use them). So what we get is a combination of chasing fads (fashionable trends) and some flirtation with Marxism. The resultant product fits with the following description: *post*-Marxism, which is the form that much of so-called critical scholarship takes now-a-days. I will return to this in the next chapter, although briefly.

Chapter 5 discusses theoretical ideas concerning the question of freedom: to what extent is labor free under capitalism? Much scholarly work, including that of Marx, generally assumes that workers are economically free, i.e., they are free to choose their employers. This chapter, revolving around the theme of workers' freedom, performs a double critique. It examines the work of a powerful Marxist scholar (Tom Brass) on the topic of freedom and unfreedom. It first examines the critique by this scholar of existing work, both Marxist and non-Marxist, on freedom/unfreedom. Then the Chapter subjects his own critical views to a sympathetic critique, which poses several questions. For example, should the issue of freedom of labor be posed at the level of capitalist relation as a whole or at the level of capitalist class-fraction (or, correspondingly, capitalist totality or a part of this totality)? Further, while it is evidently true that labor unfreedom is an *empirical* reality, both in the North and in the South, what *conceptual* implication does it have for what it means for a system to be capitalist? Or, more precisely, if all wage-labor in a society becomes unfree labor, will that society be (seen as) capitalist? The critique also raises questions about the unfreedom/freedom issue and the development of productive forces under the dominace of capitalist class relations.

Whether labor is free or not occupies an important location on the map of the discourse on capitalism. This larger discourse has shed light on the class character of capitalism and how its class relations promote or fetter the process of economic development (i.e., development productive forces). These ideas have been explored in the debate on the transition to capitalism in Europe (as in the *Science & Society* debate as well as in the famous Brenner debate). Usually these ideas concern rural areas. Chapter 6 subjects several significant writings on the development of capitalist relations in rural areas in India and show their theoretical contributions and limitations. It discusses how extant class relations and class struggle affect, directly and/or through state mediation, the emergence of new class alliances and the development of the productive forces. Among the major deficiencies in the selected literature discussed is that it conceptualizes class relations more in terms of development of productive forces than social relations and that it ignores imperialism as a class relation at the international scale. The critique offered in the Chapter suggests that the theoretical parameters of the discussion on development of class relations – and more generally, the debate on fettering of productive forces by social relations – need to be expanded in order epistemologically to accommodate the current impact of imperialism on the rural areas of the less developed world.

As mentioned earlier, we seem to be living in an age of critique. On reason is that we live in a world of growing inequality. Progressive people have been trying to explain inequality, including in newly developing countries or emerging economies, and to suggest proposals for change. Social democracy has been an important explanatory critique here: it seeks to explain the problems of inequality and poverty, and economic development, more generally, in terms of the relation between the state and businesses and the resultant inadequate policies. Social democracy seeks to remedy the situation by suggesting ideas about what the state can do. Much of this discussion goes back to the debates on the developmental state in East Asia. In this literature, some social democratic-minded scholars argued that developmental success was due to an activist state that guided and directed the market and businesses. The larger conceptual-political theory underlying this model has travelled from East Asia to India and other places. Chapter 7 critiques a recent, wide-ranging and well-written book, entitled '*Poverty Amid Plenty in the new India*' written by a Princeton professor, Atul Kohli. Kohli is sympathetic to the East Asian model. Kohli argues that the Indian state is becoming more and more pro-business, but not necessarily pro-market, and that because of this alliance between the state and business, there is an impressive growth but inequality is rising, and that a modest social democracy is a potential solution to the problem. The chapter appreciates the argument about the increasing big business influence on the affairs of the state and its adverse effect on democracy and the poor people. But Kohli's criticism of the state is limited because it is from the standpoint *not* of the working masses and their democratic rights but from the standpoint of weaker sections of the private property-owning class, with their interests rooted regionally and nationally. His criticism is also limited because it is from a social-democratic standpoint according to which conditions of the masses could be improved through state interventions *within capitalism*, and that nothing more is necessary. Kohli's view is part of a larger mode of thinking – 'egalitarian liberalism' -- which argues that substantive egalitarianism can be achieved without transcending the present order itself. The chapter's critique has potentially wider implications for discussion on social democracy as a proposal for change, including in the global periphery. The critique also indicates how not to think about poverty and inequality issues which the world is experiencing now. The critique points to the fact that there is a need for more rigorous class-analysis of the state, society and economic development issues, which has more progressive practical implications than suggested by Kohli's limited critique of inequality and state-business relations. Any knowledge claim that explains social problems merely in terms of inadequate government policies and seek their solution in better policies has not understood the material-class character of policies in particular and of the state in general, and therefore is inadequate.

The Part 3 focuses on the critique, not so much of ideas about the world, but of certain aspects of the world itself, in the light of the ideas explored in Part 1 as well as in Part 2. This world itself is seen in terms of what exists (e.g., neoliberal capitalism and its outcomes for ordinary people) and in terms of how people politically respond to it. Although most of the chapters in Part 3 concern, empirically, the US or India, the ideas explored will have wider implications. Chapters 8, 9 and 10 *p*rovide a critique of 'neoliberalism' as it is played out in India and the USA. Chapter 8 reveals the winners and the losers from the neoliberal-capitalist project, and its impact on the production of social and spatial inequalities in India. It also explores the political possibilities of the neoliberal-capitalist project: what does neoliberalism mean for democratic, agrarian, anti-imperialist, and anti-capitalist revolutions?

Chapters 9 and 10 speak to neoliberal capitalism in the US context, revealing how it is treating the working bodies of ordinary citizens in the US. The commercial conduct of drugs companies shows that science, both in the sense of production of new ideas as well as the material fruits of science (e.g., medicines), has been subordinated to the profit-motive. The example of drug companies in the USA discussed in Chapter 9 sheds light on the state's complicity in this process and state's 'inability' to discipline and punish 'erring' companies. It also briefly discusses the potential effect of all this for the legitimacy of the state itself in the eyes of ordinary citizens. Chapter 10 draws attention to a recurrent phenomenon in the history of the US, the most advanced economy in the world: industrial disasters and absence of work-place safety. More than the 'happenstance', i.e., the negligent behavior of individual firms, what is involved is something *systemic*: the capitalist character of the economy and associated profit logic, all supported by the state.

Neoliberalism, as widely known, is a specific form that capitalism has assumed since the 1970s. Whether in the US or in India, neoliberalism has had two kinds of success. One is political-economic and another is ideological. The political-economic success refers to the transfer of the burdens of the capitalist crisis (of profitability, etc.) on: to the working class in a given place (a class fix), to areas other than the origin of the problems (a spatial fix), and to the environment which is subjected to ruthless degradation and commodification (an ecological fix). And there is a political fix in the form of the direct political attack on organizations of the masses (e.g., unions). Neoliberalism's ideological success has come in at least two forms. One is that: while neoliberalism is supposed to be a system where market relations are freer vis a vis state interventions, all this is in the realm of ideas, and is therefore ideological. By using this ideology, the state has legitimized two opposite tendencies: its very active interventions on behalf of the business class, and its withdrawal of the provision of limited welfare to the masses. The second form of the ideological success of neoliberalism is this: the critique of capitalism as such in media and academia, of the *essence* as such, has been more or less diverted to the critique of the neoliberal *form* of capitalism (and of globalization, the geographical form of contemporary capitalism). Critique of *neoliberalism as capitalism* is not necessarily the same thing as the *critique of capitalism as neoliberalism*. Critique of capitalism as merely neoliberalism is the kind of critique, which seeks to find salvation in a more regulated and more nationally-oriented capitalism. Given neoliberalism's multiple successes, it is an imperative that scholars scrutinize its genuine class character: neoliberalism is an accumulation strategy of the capitalist class and its various competing fractions, a strategy that is articulated, and sought to be implemented, with varying success as a governmental policy. Neoliberalism is more than a form of government intervention.

Anthony Giddens, a long time ago, said something useful: unless one is drunk, one will fight injustice. Indeed. Injustice and the fight for justice form the totality in which we live. No class-system goes un-opposed. The practice and ideology of resistance against neoliberalism and indeed against the capitalist system as such has taken many forms. So, chapters 11-12 turn to two of the important ways in which millions of people have tried to respond to the system. One is the politics of Maoism. Maoist movements have a significant presence in a wide array of countries, including the Philippines, Peru, Nepal and India, and indeed in several advanced countries at a more limited scale (e.g., Canada, and the USA). Chapter 9 offers a critique of the Maoist resistance (in India). This movement is not as radical as it appears to be. Its main problem is its inadequate class analysis, theoretically and politically. In other words: it fails to recognize the nature of dominant class relations as capitalist, so therefore it misses the target. It is, more or less, focused on the rural, and therefore effectively divorced from the urban working class. Besides, a part of the movement conflates the power of arms with the power of words; it turns to the use of force, not recognizing that any movement for change must work on, and change, the current level of consciousness of the masses in order to help them become more class conscious, and that it must engage in the ideological-political organization of the masses as a necessary, time-consuming tool of resistance and struggle against the system.

Neoliberalism is characterized by accumulation by dispossession and accumulation by exploitation. Yet, much of the contestation of neoliberalism and indeed much of 'radical' political activity as such one-sidedly takes the form of resistance around local issues (including dispossession, etc.) and without the goal of transcending the system.

The final Chapter is a critique of the limits of this form of Left (micro-) politics: protest politics. This chapter concludes by making some concrete proposals in terms of what is to be done about the low levels of class-consciousness and mobilization of masses, and indeed about the crisis of the leadership of the masses.

PART 1: LAYING THE FOUNDATIONS

Chapter 1

THINKING CRITICALLY: A CRITIQUE OF CRITICAL THINKING

We hear the word, critique, or 'critical' everywhere. It is used even in business schools: there is indeed such a thing as critical management studies.[7] If business schools can be critical, can others be far behind? In the academic world there are: critical sociology, critical human geography, critical anthropology, critical development studies, critical Asian Studies, and so on. Indeed, with anti-globalization, anti-war, social justice, and Occupy type movements, the business of critique is brisk. Critical social thinking has been institutionalized in the form of several journals whose titles include the word 'critical' or 'critique'.[8] Many books with the title 'critique' are being published. One can name several scholars in the art of critique including: Bello, Bidet, Bourdieu, Badiou, Chomsky, (Susan) George, Habermas, Harvey, Hardt, Klein, Monbiot, Negri, (Arundhati) Roy, Amartya Sen, and Zizek. We indeed seem to be living in an age of critique. Callinicos (2006) declares that a renewal of social critique has happened.[9]

What does critique[10] or critical really mean? According to Raymond Williams (1976: 84-85), 'its predominant general sense' is one of 'fault-finding' or 'at least of negative judgment'. That is, to critique is to find fault with, or to see limitations in, the world, which is a world of unequal social relations. It also means being critical of the ideas about the world, which are inadequate. So, critique is a critique of something, which, more or less, exists independently of the critic/scholar (at a given point in time), i.e., critique of social practices and relations in society. And, critique is also the critique of ideas (of lay people and scientists themselves) about social practices and relations and about how these ideas are arrived at.[11] So critique has a dual character. What needs to be emphasized here is the fact that: critique means not only critique of ideas on the ground that these are false or inadequate, but also

---

[7] Conscious (=conscientious) capitalism, capitalism with a humane face, is presumably born out of such things as critical business studies.

[8] See alternative press index (http://www.altpress.org/mod/apc_directory/index.php) for a list of many of these journals and magazines.

[9] He adds that this critique has been more from a non-Marxist standpoint than from a Marxist one. In this context, see Therborn (2008) on Marxist and 'not-so-Marxist Left'.

[10] 'Critique' and 'criticism' are used interchangeably here.

[11] Both forms are related. Critique of ideas is, more or less, critique of ideas about the world, or of ideas about ideas about the world. And, the world can be critiqued through words (or through word-like medium such as painting).

critique of the material conditions which produce – support or underlie -- these false/inadequate ideas, which, in turn, help in the reproduction of those conditions.

Critique is a fundamental human practice. It has a long history, which will not be discussed here, a history, which, in the western world, starts with Kant and Hegel.[12] There are also multiple approaches to critique, informed by different philosophical-social-theoretical traditions. Foucault (1997) describes critique as 'the art of not being governed quite so much' (p. 45; 47), including not being governed by pastoral power. Society needed to govern people, and people wanted to escape this process, i.e., governmentalization (p. 43-44), giving rise to critique or 'critical attitude as virtue' (43). This is not an unimportant point given increasing governmental power over citizens in their everyday lives. From a more general perspective, Butler (2002) argues that critique is always a critique of some specific aspects of society -- instituted practice, discourse, episteme and institution. She further says that critique loses its character when it is abstracted from its operation and made to stand alone as a purely generalizable [i.e., philosophical] practice. Yet, she does agree that it is possible to make *some* generalizations, in a philosophical sense, about the practice of critique. This is partly the goal of this chapter, but at a *very* basic level.

Marx's life-long friend, Engels, who wrote much philosophical material, said: '[T]he criticism of existing society… [is] the main task of any investigation of social questions'.[13] Marx was, of course, a master of the art of critique, who was initially influenced by Hegel and Feuerbach. Many books by Marx contained the word critique. The subtitle of his most famous book, *Capital* was: 'A critique of political economy'. He stressed the need for paying attention 'to the theoretical existence of man [sic], and therefore to make religion, science, etc., the object of our criticism'.[14] Lenin also paid much attention to critique, whether in his philosophical work or in his sociological and political analysis.

Scarcity of Genuine Critique

Indeed, while many people accept the need for being critical, the actual situation with respect to social critique must not be seen uncritically. That is: the appearance that there is much critical work going on needs to be critiqued.[15] One may have seen numerous research

[12] There is a large amount of literature on critique (including some that is cited here. Not all of this literature – not even a very large chunk of this -- is discussed in this chapter, the purpose of which is only to provide a *very* basic and preliminary discussion on the topic, partly from the standpoint of how to do critique. Those who wish a more advanced treatment of the topic of critique may want to first consult with the literature on the philosophy of sciences (e.g. Benton and Craib, 2011; Boyd, et al, 1991; Keat and Urry, 2012; Kincaid, 1996; Sayer, 1992; 2000). In terms of individual writers on the art of critique, the works of Kant (*Critique of pure reason*) are useful as are those of Hegel. Hegel sought to reveal internal contradictions within an argument which would lead it, by its own logic, to an opposite position. Marx's actual writings (e.g. *Capital;* and his *Critique of Hegel's philosophy of right)* and Lenin's writings on the 'Friends of the people' (ideologists of small producers) as well as his philosophical writings are excellent examples of critique. Boer and Sonderegegr (2012) discuss ideas about the critique from the standpoint of several individual scholars (e.g. Kant, Marx, Spinoza, Derrida, and Frankfurt school scholars). This chapter forms the basis of a future paper which will deal with many of these individual writers in order to further develop some of the ideas introduced here.

[13] http://www.marxists.org/archive/marx/works/1845/09/fourier.htm

[14] http://www.marxists.org/archive/marx/works/1843/letters/43_09.htm

[15] In critiquing the so-called critical work in this chapter, I generally avoid naming names. I make criticisms of specific ideas rather than of specific writers. What kind of ideas I am critiquing will be recognized by the reader

projects which are generally long on facts and on how these facts are arrived at, and which contain elaborate discussions on how one's positionality (e.g., whether one is a white male) influences one's ways of thinking. There is also much discussion on how these ideas can be used: so-called knowledge mobilization idea[16] is popular today and attracts much grant-money. Much of this research is short on rigorous theory, which presupposes critique of existing ideas and which itself is a form of critique. That is, it is short on both explanations and critique.[17] Some of this work is of course critical but only in a limited way. It is critical in the same sense that my living room fireplace is a place of fire that can burn things or that a person with hundred counts of hair is hairy-headed rather than bald.

One important reason why the critical edge of much so-called critical work is blunted – or why what is considered critical is inadequately critical -- is the belief that there is no distinction between reality and representation (Baudrillard style), and there is no distinction between true and false ideas. Given this kind of belief, the main kind of critique that is possible becomes the one that seeks to merely see hidden binaries and silences inside texts (as in Derrida) in isolation from the real world processes the text refers to (Rosenau, 1991; Foley, 1985). Much of the critique that is being produced is really more one of beliefs and linguistic constructions people have and less of contradictory material-social practices underlying these. When scholars confuse knowledge of an object with the object of knowledge itself, they mistakenly think that differences in beliefs about a given object indicate multiple realities, and they blur the boundary between words and worlds. 'This view is also dangerous in that it evades critical evaluation—'my critics [whose views are different from mine] are in fact talking about *different realities*' (Sayer, 1992:53; italics added). Such a view which drives much critical work is considered Leftist (by the holders of this view themselves and others), and it merges with the more openly conservative view which is against social critique as such, because social critique becomes a critique against the powers that be (e.g., privatizers, oppressive governments, religious fundamentalists).[18] Through two 'different' routes, the conditions for critique are undermined.

Besides, many tend to mistakenly think that if ordinary people or the subaltern, speak something, believe something, it must be true and cannot be critiqued, and therefore our knowledge based on their views is secure. It also implies that spontaneous actions informed by relatively-unexamined ideas can be justified: if, for example, some workers fighting to get their wages increased kill a manager or break a machine, one may mistakenly accept that that is the way to fight.

---

through my critiques and through what I say about what adequate critique should look like. Similarly, chapter 2 on the Marxist form of critique will indicate to the reader the ideas of which the Marxist critique is critical.

[16] See this document about knowledge mobilization in the Canadian context: http://www.sshrc-crsh.gc.ca/about-au_sujet/publications/KMbPI_FinalE.pdf

[17] It talks more about, for example, how a few individuals feel about their sexual experiences and indeed sexual oppression perhaps, or whatever, and less about the international debt problem. I should add that I would not want to downplay the importance of sexual matters. But the sexuality concerns of middle class people are different from those poor women who have no control over their sexuality at all and who must indeed sell their sexual labor power and fake emotional labor power for a wage in unsafe and brutal conditions.

[18] While the critical project is insufficiently conducted by those who claim to be critical (and in part two of the book, this will be illustrated), there is also an attempt from conservative forces to reduce societal/governmental support for humanities and social sciences, on whose shoulders the burden of social critique generally falls. Against the more conservative forces, this must be said: as long as society exists, the need to explain what happens in society and to do so critically will exist, irrespective of whether such knowledge and critique produce *immediate* tangible results.

To the extent that one encounters critique of social reality, and not just of ideas and beliefs, much of it is a critique of this or that aspect of human practice, of society, and not of the system as a whole. Criticism is often criticism of what a segment of the population does or what happens to it, and all this mainly in terms of politics and culture, abstracted from large-scale social-material processes. With 'capitalism' as a totality 'largely left out of critical public political discourse, tensions, strife, and struggles [and criticisms] often become directed toward one or another political party, nationality, ethnicity, gender, and/or religious group' (Paolucci, 2007:279). Also, much criticism is one in which only the actions ('policies') of a somewhat arbitrarily limited group ('decision-makers') are considered open to evaluation (Sayer, 1992). Critique from the standpoint of the governed, of those who receive outcomes of policies framed by the powerful, is legitimate. However, a critique of 'power' undermines the power of critique. This happens because critique of power, which is said to be everywhere, is abstracted from historically specific material conditions for power. The resultant narrow base of critique, based on an 'over-politicized' view of society (everything is about power) would seem to derive from several mutually-reinforcing, unaware assumptions, which need to be critiqued.[19]

Apart from 'critical' and 'critique', another term one often hears is 'social relations'. The problem is that: the meaning of the social is uncritical and under-theorized in much so-called critical work. The social, like the political (as mentioned above), is often reduced to the ideational and to what *individuals* do/think. For example, the state as an aspect of the social is seen as something that people make every day. The 'making of Asia' means how is Asia thought about, as if Asia is merely or even mainly about ideas about it. Indeed, many so-called criticals are obsessed with the business of writing about 'making' and 'producing', completely trivializing the material and social nature of the process of making/producing: for these people, making/producing more or less means thinking and/or small-scale group/individual action. If an individual or a bunch of individuals could, for example, *make* the state, the waiting time for a surgery or to change one's status to citizenship from an uncertain refugee status could be easily made to approach zero. The social as an emergent effect of relations between individuals and groups, the social-material relations, which are a condition for individuals' thinking, action and interaction, is heavily under-stressed or ignored. So, the social is taken to be what is immediately seen, observed and felt – every day life, and it is seen as the discursive. If one combines these two views, one gets this: the social is what individuals and small collections of individuals (who are mutually connected by some of kind of thinking process, i.e., discursively) think (and engage in small everyday activities, or small-scale 'resistance'),[20] in abstraction from the social-whole.

[19] In the context of the critique of policies and government, these include the idea: 'that practices and relationships *not* deriving from such 'policies' are not concept-dependent and hence are not open to evaluation—as if only those parts of the social world produced by 'policies' are socially-constructed; that meaning is external to social practice, with the exception of policy, which anyway is seen as impinging on society from above; and that given this separation of meaning from practice, and policy from other actions, judgments of the former can be made without passing over into judgments of the latter. According to this incoherent view, evaluative statements about forms of social organization under [the capitalist system] are excluded as having nothing to do with 'science', but evaluations of this or that government policy are quite acceptable!' (Sayer, 1992: 28).

[20] This could include selling small items on the street. Many people – often women -- do this because they cannot do anything else for a living: there is no decent employment opportunity. So what people do *because of constraint* becomes discursively articulated as an act of *choice* and even *of resistance*. If one raises the issue of constraints, the counter-argument from critical intellectuals is: 'do not underestimate the power of the subaltern to speak and do things; do not see them as victims'.

The fact that social scientists are paying relatively less attention to explanation and critique of the system – explanatory critique of the contemporary society with its enormous systemic crisis conditions and inequalities -- is not at all encouraging. So, there is indeed a scarcity of genuinely critical critique. And, this situation is partly created by: the (perceived) near-triumphalism of capitalism (in spite of the 2008 crisis and its continuing impacts), the failure of Soviet style communism (which was perfectly anticipated by many), the degeneration of social democracy, and the failure of the new Left to pose a strong challenge to the system. What Markovic (1983) said in the 1980s still, more or less, holds true: '[T]he fundamental problem of social science today is *not* that it suffers from too much unfounded, unscientific, utopian critique of reality. Its true problem is that it is not sufficiently critical'. Its true problem further is that, 'under the mask of neutrality and freedom from any values [or indeed under the mask of critiques of relatively less significant aspects of our world, i.e., those that can be subjected to micro-political management], it [i.e., social science] simply serves well-established practical interests and invisible traditional ideological values'.

WHY IS IT POSSIBLE AND NECESSARY TO BE CRITICAL?

What must be the case for critique to be possible? Critique is possible for the same reason that knowledge itself is possible. For critique is a form of knowledge, and indeed a very important form. To be human is to be able to know, (and to be able to know both that one knows and when one does not adequately know). Critique is possible because: lay people and experts can reflect on (be conscious of) what they (and others) do, and know, and they can change their interpretations of what they (others) do and know. Humans *are* not just tool-making animals seeking to transform, through their labor, the environment in which they live. They are not just rational animals or political beings. They are also 'homo-criticus': they have an inherent ability to be critical. This ability partly reflects the contradiction between their current material (and discursive) surroundings and their social-physical and mental/cultural needs. If the world satisfied people's needs, or if a tiny minority did not frustrate the satisfaction of the needs of the majority, critique would be superfluous. In other words: there must be something wrong in the world for critique to be possible. Why is critique necessary?[21] There are many reasons.

The World is Always Changing and the Future is Conditionally Open

Changeability is a fundamental attribute of the world (both physical and human). People's ideas and their mode of interaction with one another and with society/nature are changing. Changes happen for many reasons. Changes happen not only through the transformation of quantitative changes becoming qualitative changes but also through contradictions between things and relations. There are several implications of this fact. One is that we have to constantly make sure that at least some of our ideas register that change. Otherwise these ideas are invalid and need to be critiqued. Also, if the world was *un*changing, or if the direction of change was entirely given, there would be little point in wanting to know

[21] It is difficult to strictly separate the reasons for why critique is possible and why it is necessary.

and to know critically, in order to change what is happening in the world. Because the world, including its structures, always changes, our study of the world must be critical: 'All social inquiry is *incomplete* that is reduced to …to structural analysis without examination of the change of those structures' [Markovic, 1983] and therefore is a target of critique.

Not only does the world change. There are also various possibilities, within limits, into which the world can change. The world is conditionally open. So, social enquiry remains incomplete if it 'seeks merely to explain and understand actually given phenomena without exploring the *alternative* possibilities' (Markovic, 1983: italics added) that may emerge from the current conjuncture. These possibilities are revealed by 'Objective determinants established by causal analysis and subjective determinants revealed by interpretation of phenomena'. Therefore, 'Critique is not something external to social science knowledge, it is not something that may (but need not) coexist with description, analysis, explanation and understanding' (ibid.). Once again, the future is in – emerges out of -- the present, but the present does not entirely determine how exactly the present will change and what the future will look like. Within limits, different possibilities can emerge out of the present. There is the permanent possibility of an emergent novelty.

Change includes the fact that 'things' or 'objects', including people develop new powers. An object becomes different from what it is because of a contradiction within it, between what it is and what it can be (or contradiction between itself and its surrounding context). Also, when things combine in a system (e.g., a place-based protest movement), new powers emerge, which do not exist separately in the components of the system. Much research fails to acknowledge that we have powers which may remain un-activated at a given point in time but these powers *could* become activated (Sayer, 1992). When an object, a structure, O changes, it can change into a set of many possible objects/structures (O_1, O_2, etc.), some of which are more adequate than others, from the standpoint of needs and essence of the humans, of what humans can and must do. So, critical-evaluative judgments become necessary. Ideas which reflect the status of the object before its transformation (e.g., O) will inadequately reflect its transformation process and its new status as a transformed object (e.g., O_2). Often lay people and scientists mistakenly assume that *what happens to exist now = what can exist now or in future*. This mistake makes critique necessary. Research becomes uncritical when it fails to recognize the possibility of objects developing new powers, i.e., the possibility of X being not X but Y. For example, seeing that workers are passive now and here, many people draw the conclusion that workers are not the kind of revolutionary agent that is imputed to them by Marx, a kind of agent which has the *potential* to overthrow the system irrespective of what it does/think at a given moment and in a place. It is necessary to critique this sort of inference, which characterizes much so-called critical work; it eschews any discussion of essential properties of a thing, without which that thing will not be what it (usually) is. Similarly, people voting democrats now can vote more radical parties tomorrow or indeed may lose illusions in the power of elections to bring about genuine changes and therefore start getting organized outside of the electoral system.[22] Or, anyone who says that because many women have been spending much time in the kitchen and therefore their true place is in the kitchen is simply wrong. Anyone saying that people have a natural tendency to be only selfish or to buy and sell things for a profit is equally wrong. People – whose properties are a product of more

[22] Even in studies of nature, ideas produced today are critiqued when new evidence and/or new ideas contradict existing ideas.

universal conditions and more historically-specific ones -- can be a lot different from what they are, when social conditions/relations significantly change and/or when the effects of universal conditions are mediated by those that change. A critic needs to evaluate all the different possible things that can happen. 'Social science must *mediate* between existing reality and its optimal future possibilities by examining specific phases of the process and possible practical steps which lead from the one to the other'.[23]

Once again, (much of) what is need not be. The world can be a lot different from – and in many cases, and in most fundamental ways, opposite to - what it is now. And what the world can be[24] but is not (which is why it is inadequate) is partly rooted in what it already is. So the world in its current form must be critiqued from the standpoint of what it can be and what is not. As indicated earlier, 'while we observe an object as an actually existing phenomenon, we are also aware of those of its structural and dispositional properties that constitute its potential [to be what it is not]. Our consciousness of the object is thus polarized into consciousness of what the object *is* and what it *could be* but is *not yet'* (Markovic, 1983). A research which fails to take into account the contingent status of objects of study and 'their ability to change' that status 'would be deficient as an account of what is' (Sayer, 1992). The more general point is that: 'to deny the people we study the status of subjects, however circumscribed their field of self-determination, is to fail to represent them 'objectively' (ibid.). This means that being critical is a part of paying attention to what objectively exists.[25] Uncritical work equates what can exist with what does exist, and thus becomes status quo-ist (Callinicos, 2006). We can think differently from how we think. We can live differently and in different places from how and where we live now. To the extent that critical research imagines that things can be different from what they are, the limits of possibility of change are defined as extremely narrow: mere small and localized changes are all that is possible. Therefore, strategies of change are also imagined as local.

Ideas, whether they are true or false, have effects, including effects of reproduction of power relations, and are therefore important.[26] No social critique can under-value ideas: if ideas were un-important, critique would be redundant. The 'effects of actions which are informed by false ideas will often differ from those which actors expect them to have. If we are to represent such situations adequately, we must attempt both to report those ideas, as they are held, authentically, and show in what respects they are false.[27] Therefore, in order to understand and explain social phenomena, we cannot avoid evaluating and criticizing societies' own self-understanding' (Sayer, 1992:27). For example, 'an account of South African society would not be explanatorily adequate if the constitutive meanings concerning racial superiority and inferiority that inform and are objectified by *apartheid* were not criticized as false, although, of course, it would have to be acknowledged (it is true that) they are held' (ibid.). We must be mindful of the possibility that the reasons given by actors for

[23] Obviously critique plays the central role in all phases of social research: 'from building the theoretical standpoint to a rational selection of the research program, to interpretation and explanation, to discovery of the negative features of reality and finding ways to overcome them' (Markovic, 1983).

[24] There are two possibilities here: better things or worse things, than what is happening. In other words, barbarism and a more humane society with social and economic democracy in every corner of society, both can happen. Critique of the current form of society is from the standpoint of 'the more desirable' of the two possibilities.

[25] Abstract, concrete and critical approaches to the study of society therefore have overlapping rather than separate domains.

[26] One should not conclude that because false ideas have a certain effect, therefore these ideas cannot be false.

[27] Note that to criticize an idea as false is not to deny that it is held or that it has consequences.

what they do and think may not always be the real reasons, for they may not be aware of structural conditions or indeed, in some cases, their own hidden subconscious motivations.[28]

It is possible to argue that there is a difference between lay people's knowledge – common sense – and social science knowledge (relatively examined knowledge on the part of those who specialize in its production). We cannot assume that what lay-people think, the people we study, is necessarily correct. When a wage-worker thinks she belongs to the comfortable middle class, -- and indeed in societies such as that of the US all but the richest and the poorest think of themselves as the middle class -- are we going to uncritically accept this? Or, alternatively, are we going to register this fact and find out *why* – by virtue of what material and discursive relations and processes at the societal level and by virtue of what processes that are specific to the person – she/he thinks the way she/he does? As social scientists we cannot merely report what our respondents, the people we study, say. Common sense takes its knowledge to be self-evident and beyond challenge, so the knowledge produced by genuinely critical theories (e.g., Marxism) will appear to be false (an affront to common sense!') (Sayer, 1992). Those who study society also study lay people's view -- common sense -- as one of their objects of knowledge, so they cannot avoid a critical relationship with common sense as relatively unexamined knowledge, for in seeking to understand popular consciousness, as it is, we cannot help but become aware of its illusions (Sayer, 1992). Hence the point of critical social science's attempt to reduce illusion in society is to change its effects, not merely to provide an 'academic' critique of an external description of society' (Sayer, 1992:75). Non-illusion (true ideas) is better than illusion (false ideas). 'In principle, true ideas always serve the people; false ideas always serve the enemies of the people' (Althusser, 2001:8).

The world is constituted by the 'positive' and the 'negative'. An idea is wrong if it does not take into account the negative. 'A fully developed social science does not exhaust its task by providing answers to questions about what exists, what is its meaning, why is it the way it is, what is its potential, and how it could change in the future. It also tries to answer questions about what is *negative* (inadequate, irrational, unjust, inhuman) in the existing social reality, what are its basic limitations with respect to its own potential.' (Markovic, 1983) 'Discovery of the basic limitations of existing reality is the *negative* dimension of critique. The positive dimension of critique is the discovery of the *optimal* possibility of its future change' (ibid.). This explains Marx's admiration for achievements of capitalism, which undermines certain kinds of social unfreedom and nature-imposed scarcity that are characteristic of pre-capitalist societies.

The Real and its 'Opposite'/Other

What makes critique possible and necessary is also the nature of reality itself: that the real is different from what appears to be real. We must be critical because, as Marx says, 'all science would be superfluous if the outward appearance and the essence of things directly coincided'.[29] Because the world's appearance (e.g., the fact that the state appears to be

[28] As Sayer (1992) says, 'men who cultivate a macho image may not be aware of it let alone know the reasons for their actions. Indeed, if they were made aware of the real reasons it might (!) prompt them to act differently'.

[29] http://www.marxists.org/archive/marx/works/1894-c3/ch48.htm

neutral) is contradicted by what it often really is, there is a need, not only for abstractions and theorization to help us get to the deeper level structures, but also for critique of the ideas that reflect the appearances. As well, the reality is often different from how it is represented/seen/experienced as. For some, as indicated earlier, there is no difference between what is real and what is represented as real (or what is said in theory); this idea needs to be critiqued. Society or individuals cannot be truly studied merely in terms of how people feel/think about themselves and others, although such thinking is important to recognize. The idea that there is no false consciousness needs to be critiqued. [30] If facts are what are merely what they are perceived to be, then 'one can never be wrong' (Sokal and Bricmont, 1998: 103), and the assumption that one can never be wrong completely undermines the possibility for critiquing and necessity to critique. Any thought that aspires to be critical but extinguishes the distinction between facts on the one hand and ideas about facts on the other ends up becoming most uncritical. Such a thought must be critiqued on this simple ground, i.e., there are facts independent of what is claimed about the facts and that it is with respect to these facts that ideas are assessed, although ideas cannot be assessed entirely on the basis of facts.

Self-Clarification

Critique is also necessary for self-clarification.[31] The objects of social science include social scientists themselves – we reflect on what others write as well as what we write. The process of producing social science knowledge, this intellectual labor process, changes the laborer, social scientists themselves, in terms of how they think. Critique – broader engagement with existing literature – is necessary for self-clarification in the minds of the researcher. Critique is necessary to settle accounts with one's previous theoretical consciousness. Critique must be self-critical. It is true that 'specifically human consciousness involves a negative attitude toward itself', and this [is] 'critical *self-consciousness*' (Markovic, 1983). This is a part of being homo-criticus. Commenting on the thorough critical engagement with German philosophy of their time which Marx and Engels conducted in *German ideology*, which in turn produced their own conception, Marx said: 'we decided to set forth together our conception as opposed to the ideological one of German philosophy, in fact to *settle accounts with our former philosophical conscience.* The intention was carried out in the form of a critique of post-Hegelian philosophy. The manuscript [The German Ideology]... had long ago reached the publishers [but could not be printed at the time].... We abandoned the manuscript to the gnawing criticism of the mice all the more willingly since we had achieved our main purpose – *self-clarification (italics added).*[32]That is why it is always necessary to define one's point of view through a critique of other people's ideas and through a critique of one's own past ideas, where necessary. For this to happen, one must accept that some ideas are wrong and of more ideological character relative to other ideas; an ideology is a set of partly true and partly false ideas which reproduce unequal social relations by naturalizing or universalizing these relations and by treating what are merely the appearances of the reality as the true real). So people (lay-people, experts) have the ability to

[30] This idea undermines grounds for critique and can cause social indifference.
[31] This is a process situated between enquiry and presentation (Ollman, 2003).
[32] http://www.marxists.org/archive/marx/works/1859/critique-pol-economy/preface.htm

be critical which makes critique possible, but they are also vulnerable to ideological illusions (which makes critique necessary). It is true that false ideas do exist. It is false – it is false consciousness -- to say that false consciousness does not exist. Because there is false consciousness, there is a need for critique.

Typology of Critique

Criticisms of ideas are, at least, of four different types. One is philosophical. This is based on ontological and epistemological principles.[33] Philosophy 'helps the people to distinguish in *theory* and in all *ideas* (political, ethical, aesthetic, etc.) between true ideas and false ideas' (Althusser, 2001: 8). In making philosophical criticisms, and as indicated already, one seeks to unearth and critically examine the philosophical assumptions underlying the specific substantive assertions made by lay-people and experts. One may ask a philosophical series of questions, a few of which are mentioned below for illustrative purposes. Each question advisedly contains or represents a necessary binary-*system*, with two parts. Within this differentiated system or unity, both parts/terms are generally important (meaning that knowledge claims must not usually ignore what is indicated in the first term/part). But the second part (italicized) must be generally seen as having some primacy within the system, and especially in the context of questions numbered 1-3, 6-10 and 1-14.[34]

Does a piece of work or a statement:

1. stress the individual (and society's) thinking/discourses and actions as being more important than *material conditions of living and structural relations among people*?
2. see the material aspects of the world as purely material/natural things and processes, ignoring the historical aspect of the material as *a social practice, i.e., as a process of conscious interaction among humans and between them and nature with the intention to (re)produce conditions of life?*
3. treat humans as an element of nature obeying natural laws or as being opposed to nature, rather than *treat the relation between nature and humans as one that is, to a large extent, mediated by human labor*?[35]
4. reduce the more complex, higher level mechanisms (e.g., biological changes; consciousness) to *relatively lower level and more simple mechanisms (e.g., physical objects and processes; physiology)*[36]
5. emphasize quantitative changes ignoring *qualitative changes and leaps*?
6. focus on what is measureable, classifiable and or easily observable at the expense of *more qualitative and more or less non-observable aspects of the reality*?

---

[33] I am abstracting from methodological critique (concerning, for example, the method of collection of information).

[34] It will be beyond the scope of this chapter to elaborate why primacy is assigned to part two.

[35] Arthur, C. 1986. *Dialectics of labor, Marx, and his relation to Hegel*, Blackwell, Oxford, quoted in Rees, 1998. *Algebra of revolution*.

[36] The underlying idea here is that: having the right physiology (hearing, vocal organs) may explain why humans have the power of speech but it does not explain when and how any particular human will learn to speak, which language she will learn, what she will say, and higher level mechanisms such as trauma can affect lower level mechanisms physiology). It is a mistake to contradict this and must be critiqued.

7. conceptualize an object as unitary which happens to coexist with and to connect to other objects atomistically or conceptualizes *an object as made up of internally contradictory relations (as a unity of opposites), and as existing as a part of a wider network of relations among objects/processes, one from which powers and vulnerabilities of the object in question arise*?
8. underline harmony and stability in the society at the expense of *changeability, uneven and combined development, and contradictions within objects/relations and between them and their social-spatial surroundings, and future trajectories*?
9. highlight the difference and disconnection between things and places at the expense of *substantive connections and similarities between things and places, and how their connections form a system which influences, and is influenced by, its components*?
10. focus on what an object does or be at a given point in time and place ignoring *what it can do or be in another time and in another place*?
11. regard social and ecological relations and practices as a-spatial, ignoring *how, while certain mechanisms are spatially universal, other mechanisms and their specific effects are spatially variant*[37]*, and how individuals and groups make use of spatial strategies*[38] *to satisfy their interests*?
12. describe what an event/process merely is ignoring to *explain it as necessarily caused by specific processes, with specific effects*?
13. focus on statements about natural processes and/or the entire human species (human nature) and/or unique individuals/places at the expense of *knowledge about the historically- and geographically-specific ways in which people produce/reproduce their lives through interaction with nature and with one another.*
14. see an event/process/experience as a product of accidental factors rather than as *products of mechanisms which exist by virtue of, and which express, certain general social relations, and among which some mechanisms have greater causal significance?*
15. conflate empirical association with *causal linkages*?
16. make statements about the world which are justified on the basis of other statements without paying adequate *attention to empirical evidence for the statements* [39] *and necessity for reasoned and coherent argument*?

Other than philosophical critiques, there are theoretical, empirical, and political critiques, which are informed by philosophical assumptions. In general, abstract theory (explanation) of a fact or a process is developed through a productive relation between empirical experience and reasoned conceptual argument, so the quality of reason and its empirical content can be critiqued, leading to theoretical critique and empirical critique respectively. Theoretical critiques, above all else, raise the issue of causality. A person says that K causes T. A critic would say: ‘does K necessarily cause T?’; ‘what is the logic of the assertion that K causes

[37] Human beings have a need for food everywhere but the ways in which they satisfy that need (whether they eat rice or pasta) and indeed whether they are able to satisfy that need at all can be spatially variant, and this spatial variation can shed light on important mechanisms in society.

[38] These can be strategies to locate activities in certain locations/places (locate a factory here and not there) and at certain scales (e.g. local but not national or vice versa). The power of an agent/relation to determine the location of things in response to a social problem is an important one, which in turn feeds into power. The question of spatial and scalar fix, as geographers such as Harvey have underlined, is an important one.

[39] The role of evidence is to corroborate/prove or to illustrate.

T'?; and the critic would challenge the logic implied or provided. If one says that poverty is caused primarily by laziness or racial identity or the fact that a family has too many kids, this idea can be challenged by pointing to other more powerful mechanisms at work (e.g., a regime of low wages put in place by the market and reinforced through government interventions; unemployment caused by market forces) and by saying why the purported explanations (e.g., laziness) logically fail. The content of theoretical critique from a historical materialist standpoint, which is already being broached here, will receive explicit attention in Chapter 2. It will suffice here to say that the most consistent and rigorous theoretical critique of most of what is written and said in the world today, including in the work that appears to be critical of the world, is that it completely ignores or heavily underemphasizes or thoroughly misconceptualizes the objective class character of society and of the state and indeed of everything it deals with. Much intellectual work simply runs away from the fact of the class divisions and class struggles in society and from the implications of this fact.

Critiques are also empirical. A person says that y happens in place z, but a critic says that y happens in place p instead, and provides evidence to this effect. Empirical criticisms are usually 'weaker', relative to philosophical and theoretical criticisms. One may say that the state acts in the ruling class interests because ruling class people directly control the state, sitting in the parliaments and controlling the commissions of enquiry. In response, a critic may say that in such and such a country, the parliament is not dominated by people belonging to the ruling class and yet the state, more or less, serves the interest of the ruling class. This is exactly the kind of criticisms of Miliband that Poulantzas made in the context of state theory.

One must be careful in pursuing merely empirical critique of theoretical statements, however. One may say: abstract theory of a certain type cannot explain exactly how, for example, people in a given country are dispossessed or cannot explain when dispossessed what their living standards become, and therefore this theory of displacement must be wrong. This mistaken anti-theory, empiricist, critique must be critiqued. A theory about something cannot explain all the concrete details about it. To say that a theory of class cannot (satisfactorily) explain income or educational inequality or what newspapers specific members of a class read and therefore must be wrong is itself wrong because it conflates one level of abstraction with another.

A knowledge claim that expects a theory about an object to explain every empirical/concrete details about that object must be empirically critiqued. If a large group of people is dispossessed of its means of production, other things constant, it is going to have to depend on the sale of its ability to work, as wage-laborers. This theory, although it happened to have been developed in the context of Europe, is applicable elsewhere. If someone says that this theory is Euro-centric because it is developed in Europe, and is therefore inapplicable needs to be critiqued (see Chibber, 2013). It is however the case that the ways in which people lose their property and what else they do apart from working for a wage and how exactly they think about their lives may vary from place to place. So, an idea, which says that the abstract theory developed in the European context, will explain the specific concrete details about dispossession must be empirically critiqued as reductionist.[40] The essence of a

[40] Another example can be given. A large company may contract out the production of its raw material to peasants, so peasants may produce potatoes of a certain quality at a certain price for the company. These peasants may be small-scale operators in, say, Africa. But there is no reason why this has to be the case. Ritika Shrimali, a graduate student at York University, Toronto shows, against much received wisdom, that contract companies

mechanism (e.g., class exploitation) is one thing, and its concrete context or its effects (e.g., actual level of income of workers) are another, and ideas concerning the former are more general than the ideas concerning the latter.

Finally, critiques are practical/political. Let us consider this definition of knowledge: to know is to a) explain *why* things happen and how, b) so we can foresee, with a certain degree of certitude, what may happen under specific conditions that is not happening now, c) so that we can in turn potentially act on these conditions in order to obtain a more desirable state of social-ecological affairs in the world.[41] This clearly shows that knowledge and practice/interests are connected. Knowledge reflects what there is and has been. It also seeks to change what there is.[42] So, one can be critical of conservative as well as reformist political implications of a given assertion. Science is not to be merely for pleasure. However, academic research appears to be increasingly *for* 'pleasure' (and not just *about* pleasure). It is often incredibly flippant and frivolous. Lamenting the mainstream research, Bertell Ollman (2003:12) says: 'the age-old link between knowledge and action has been severed, so that scholars can deny all responsibility for their wares while taking pride in knowing more and more about less and less'. These scholars must be critiqued.[43] So, people are mistaken if they do not see the foundation of new society already being laid now, if they do not see certain elements of the current society as progressive in relation to previous forms of society (e.g., large-scale production improving labor productivity through the use of technology and global network of production-units), so these scholars—obsessed with an idyllic small-scale-ish past and with localism (e.g., Shiva) -- must be critiqued. [44] And if people are bearers of the barriers to the new world coming (e.g., people who think that scale of production is a problem and therefore we should go back to the idyllic small-scale or to nationally-based and regulated production in place of a production system coordinated at *multiple* scales, including the international scale), there is a ground for critique of their implied localist political practice.

If ideas (should) reflect what is happening in the world, more or less adequately, a critique of ideas will be associated with a critique of that world. The world is class divided, so the ideas about the world will be class-colored, class-divided. This applies not only to social science (ideas about the world) but also philosophy (how these ideas are constructed and validated). There are ideas that represent/support the interests of big business and landlords, of bureaucrats of unions and other similar organizations,[45] and of all those middle class people who are deeply connected to, and materially close to, the ruling classes and their fractions. There are ideas on the other hand which reflect the interests of people as objectively existing classes, that is, of proletarians and semi-proletarians, which are in conflict with the

---

such as Pepsi which require agri-products (e.g. potatoes for chips) prefer to do business with a small number of large-scale farmers than a large number of small holders in India.

[41] See Trotsky (1973/2011: 20).

[42]That is why as Marx says in *German Ideology*, it is not enough 'merely to produce a correct consciousness about an existing fact; whereas [the question is one of] overthrowing the existing state of things. http://www.marxists.org/archive/marx/works/1845/german-ideology/ch01b.htm

[43] Many of them tend to conduct intellectual work without any intention to radically change the world and in isolation from the activity of the masses aimed at changing the world, and this partly explains why many of they produce uncritical or inadequately critical work.

[44] Shiva (2014) writes: 'We tend to believe that we need big farms, big dams, big corporations to meet our needs for food and water....But the reality is that "small is big" — ecologically, economically and politically. The future of food security in India and worldwide lies in protecting and promoting small farmers'.

[45] One might include in this list powerful groups within these classes such as those who are considered racially superior, rich women, etc.

interests of the classes mentioned above.[46] This is why passion arises in the realm of fundamental critique, critique of ideas as critique of fundamental interests underlying those ideas. Indeed, 'if geometrical axioms affected human interests attempts would certainly be made to refute them'. [47] In other words, and to paraphrase Lenin, theories of society which conflict with the prejudices of the ruling classes provoke 'the most rabid opposition'. This means, a critique must not only say that a given idea is wrong/inadequate, but it must also say, for example, how an idea represents itself as universal/neutral when in fact it reflects the interests of certain dominant groups and is relevant only for a time period.

One has to be a little careful in making political criticisms though. On the one hand, given an intellectual assertion about what is done (e.g., x does to y), more than one political conclusion (i.e., a claim about what is to be done) is possible to make, within limits.. The reality (what is happening now or what will happen in future) cannot be reduced to our ideas including critical ideas, and ideas about what is desirable. Ideas and the material world are mutually connected, but the ideas have a certain degree of autonomy, within limits set by the material world. Just because an idea is in the interest of the proletarian class, it may not be necessarily true, that it may not be immune from critique. If Aristotle said that socialism could be built in his society, that idea would be critiqued even if it were in the interest of workers. One cannot have any idea about the reality and hold it to be true just because it serves certain practical interest. That would be philosophical idealism. The relation between class interests and epistemological status of knowledge claims as true or false is not an unproblematic issue. I wish to assert without elaborating here that the ruling class people and their political managers distort truth to legitimize their rule, and this is indeed where ideology partly comes from. That is, they treat a claim as true because it serves their interests. The masses must not do this. They must pursue what is, more or less, true. It is problematic to defend the truth status of a body of work based merely on its practical implications. This sort of assumption underlies much avoidable sectarianism.

On the other hand, one has often seen that reformist political conclusions can be traced to certain kinds of faulty theoretical assertions. For example, many of those who reject or treat as irrelevant labor theory of value or who think about class as merely income inequality or as a matter of attitude or those who reject materialism and dialectics or those who emphasize that labor has agency to get significant concessions or have a view of a future which is not rooted in objective conditions and contradictions but in mere political-intellectual articulation of the world, these people tend to be reformists. In practice, also, it is very difficult to separate intellectual criticisms from political criticisms, whether or not the latter are made. Usually, scholars, including positivists, hide their political/normative views, and falsely claim that their knowledge-claims are politically neutral. Even when they claim that their views are not neutral and are critical, they hide the fact that their critique is extremely limited, in the sense that, for example, it is a critique of a small part of the system and not the total system.

I will now argue that these four types – forms – of critique (philosophical, scientific/theoretical, empirical, and political/practical) must be ruthless, systemic, and

[46] Truth is on the side of the masses, the majority of the global population, and their interest is in overthrowing the system and establishing a more humane and more democratic world.

[47] Lenin continues: 'No wonder, therefore, that the Marxian doctrine, which directly serves to enlighten and organise the advanced class in modern society, indicates the tasks facing this class and demonstrates the inevitable replacement (by virtue of economic development) of the present system by a new order—no wonder that this doctrine has had to fight for every step forward in the course of its life.' http://www.marxists.org/archive/lenin/works/1908/apr/03.htm

sublative. Given that ideas – critical ideas – are deeply associated with interests, including antagonistic interests, it is not surprising that Marx argued, 'Ruthlessness [is] the first condition of all criticism'[48]. He clarified what this means: criticism has to be 'ruthless criticism of all that exists, ruthless both in the sense of not being afraid of the results it arrives at and in the sense of being just as little afraid of conflict with the powers that be.'[49] He went on to emphasize that: 'Our task is that of ruthless criticism, and much more against ostensible friends than against open enemies; and in maintaining this ... position we gladly forego cheap democratic popularity'.[50] This point is very relevant partly because many academics mute their criticisms on the ground of so-called collegiality.

Arguably, a method of ruthless criticism can be what Zizek (2009: ix) calls 'the shock of short-circuiting'. This refers to a procedure of critiquing, which is to 'cross wires that do not usually touch'. That is, to take a major piece of work, and read it in a short-circuiting way, through the lense of an author or a theory which is of non-hegemonic status, one of ideological marginality. If the latter lense is well chosen, then 'such a procedure can lead to insights which *completely* shatter and undermine our common perceptions. This is what Marx, among others, did with philosophy and religion (short-circuiting philosophical speculation through the lense of political economy' (ibid.).

One should note that ruthless criticism, including that achieved through Zizekian short-circuiting, is also *systemic* criticism: criticism of everything – of *all* things -- existing. '[One should present] the critique of law, ethics, politics, etc., [separately and then] ... present them again as a connected whole showing the interrelationship of the separate parts. [51] This idea also connects to his idea that changing a part of society requires changing the whole, that 'no form of bondage can be broken without breaking all forms of bondage',[52] and this is something that resonates with the concrete condition now. And this is something that does not inform most of the so-called critical work. Marx's call for ruthless criticism must be made again, especially in this age of extreme inequality and crisis, and that is an aim of the book. Updating Marx's call for ruthless criticism, Leo Panitch (1997: 2) correctly and forcefully says this:

> 'We need, more than ever, to ... to undertake a ruthless criticism of what exists today.... Ruthless criticism is, therefore, not a matter of striking a pose as mere 'critics'. On the contrary, it is to insist on the need for the most searching analysis, groping for understanding - critique in the proper sense - without fear of being thrown off by the charge that such analysis is invalid without an immediate answer to 'there is no alternative'.

Critique is not just to be ruthless. Criticism as fault-finding, and even when it is ruthless, is also sublative. Critiquing is not ex-communicating (Bensaid, 2002). When one critiques a body of work, it is not necessary that one disagree with everything it says. But the 'amount' of difference between the critic's view and the view she/he critiques is beyond a level of tolerance, making the difference significant, so that the critic cannot identify the view critiqued as hers/his. Often, the best form of critique is sublative. For example, and as Engels

48 http://www.marxists.org/archive/marx/works/1877/letters/77_07_18.htm
49 http://www.marxists.org/archive/marx/works/1843/letters/43_09.htm
50 http://www.marxists.org/archive/marx/works/1850/04/kinkel.htm
51 http://www.marxists.org/archive/marx/works/1844/manuscripts/preface.htm
52 http://www.marxists.org/archive/marx/works/1843/critique-hpr/intro.htm

said, 'a philosophy is not disposed of by the mere assertion that it is false. And so powerful a work as Hegelian philosophy…could not be disposed of by simply being ignored. It had to be "sublated" … in the sense that while its form had to be annihilated through criticism, the new content which had been won through it had to be saved. [53] Critique is the act of sublation, of dialectical negation partly in the sense of a seed becoming a plant and negating itself in the process.[54]

TARGETS OF CRITIQUE

Scholars have critiqued the world but the point is to change it. Indeed, what is the *point* of being critical? Marx stresses the need for 'criticisms or counter-criticisms in which we could discuss theoretical points, expose the utter ignorance of professors and lecturers and at the same time enlighten the minds of the general public--working class or bourgeois'.[55]Marx *here* unfortunately makes no distinction between professors and general public.[56] But a distinction must be made.

What happens if a professorial colleague makes criticisms of another colleague? One could say that by making (polite) criticisms of the existing ideas of scholars, we can change their viewpoints. Many academics (e.g., Gibson-Graham, 2006) hold that there are interstices in society where there are already alternatives to capitalism (e.g., farmers markets, family production, etc.). In fact, it is said, these alternatives represent resistance against the system as well as products of such resistance. Many critics of capitalism say: labor unions managed by bureaucrats, NGOs reliant on state and business funding, single-issue identity politics of the middle class, and social-democratic type parties promising reforms (including expansion of a state sector) can be used to significantly mitigate or eradicate humanity's problems in a long-term manner. This is the belief. Now: one can critique this idea hoping that the academics holding these views will change them into more critical ideas, and that this will have an impact on radical social change in the world itself.

But this hope is generally, if not entirely, misplaced. Its underlying assumption is that the change of ideas of the professoriate/academics is crucial to radical social change (=transcendence of global capitalism and private property and installment of global economic and political democracy). My experience in academia as a University teacher since the mid-1990s now tells me that it is in any case very difficult to radically change the ideas of most colleagues (and most students) – who are usually from middle-class backgrounds.. This is for two reasons. One is the structural role of academics in a bourgeois society. This or that capitalist can support the cause of radical social change by changing her/his side. Engels did.

[53] http://www.marxists.org/archive/marx/works/1886/ludwig-feuerbach/ch01.htm

[54] The sublative critique must avoid being eclectic, internally contradictory, and politically opportunistic. A critique of a body of work must incorporate within itself all that is positive in that body of work in a way in which what is incorporated does not contradict the main standpoint of the critic, and the critic must pay full attention to the fact that certain facts (e.g. those contained in the body of the work under critique) can be relevant at a certain level of abstraction/generality.

[55] http://www.marxists.org/archive/marx/works/1877/letters/77_07_18.htm

[56] This is slightly inconsistent with Marx's overall view: "material force must be overthrown by material force; but theory also becomes a material force as soon as it has gripped the masses.' Professors and the like are not the masses, neither critique of ideas – especially if this act of critique is confined to the academic domain -- is enough by itself to bring about massive radical social change.

But the capitalist class *as a whole* cannot commit mass suicide. This applies to the academics as well.. A few of these individuals may take the side of radical change, of the working masses. However, the academic stratum as such, which, more or less, represents, consciously or not, ideas and interests of a property-owning class will not. As the ideological representative of the petty bourgeois and bourgeois forces, this stratum cannot relinquish in any significant way its job of defending and protecting the sanctity of private property and capitalist private property. In that role and as a *petty* bourgeois class-stratum, they generally cannot imagine prospects of *large*-scale organized social change. The petty bourgeoisie (including the academia) has some hatred for capitalism because large producers crush them and of whose life of comforts and luxuries the petty bourgeois people are envious. But they also do not like – they are indeed fearful of -- the property-less workers. Since the academia have a class-role to play – defend capitalist property with or without some reforms—their ideas, more or less, reflect that function and the interests of the class which they defend. The academia – and ideologists of the ruling class in general -- even when it espouses some nominally critical thought, is, at best, speaking the language of the petty bourgeoisie and left factions of the bourgeoisie.[57] Its critique of society stops at the door of capitalism. At best, it may be critical of the time- and place-specific *excesses* of the system (e.g., excessive degree of commodification here; above-average poverty there; over or under-representation of certain ethnic groups in certain labor or credit markets in this or that place), of the state's anti-democratic nature, and so on, but not the system as such. The academia is critical of E-M-C (everything minus capitalism), not M-C-M'. When one critiques the ideas of the academia, one often critiques the class interests they defend.

Apart from being a representative of property owners, another reason why academics cannot really be receptive to, and act on, genuine criticisms of the system is that they pursue knowledge increasingly *in their own interest*. A large number of them pursue the kind of knowledge which is relatively easy to achieve (because it does not usually go to the root of the matter and is largely descriptive and even fashionable). They pursue knowledge about what are the appearances of the system, while often denying the distinction between appearances and the underlying mechanisms. Further, they think that these appearances can be changed here and there a little and therefore are objects of governmental or NGO policy or some grassroots action (i.e., some sort of micro-political management/regulation). And, the fact that 'problems' identified can be fixed this way often justifies (asking for) funding of their research on which their career and life depend. The choice of issues to study and 'critique' and of the choice of 'theoretical' framework in which to study these is directly/indirectly based on the 'fixability' of the problems/issues. Knowledge – including any critical component in it as in critical studies of this or that theme, where the critique is merely one of the processes which can be managed without large-scale transformation of society -- has indeed become a source of *self*-empowerment. For a large part of the professoriate, many of whom are also often the gatekeepers of knowledge and who act, through owners of grant-money, as 'financial capitalists' in the academic world, the ideas are material because ideas have material value for them.[58] They have invested in their ideas and

[57] For example, the enlightened elite who can sometimes think about the long-term interests of the class as a whole and are willing to make short-term or localized sacrifices that are perfectly reversible when the power equilibrium changes.

[58] Universities are being starved of money needed for research and are competing fo shrinking resources from the public and private sectors. This is especially true about the departments specializing in the study of society (but

have made a career out of their existing ideas, so why will they so easily change their ideas? It is very difficult to make them understand that, for example, the profit-driven production and exchange system is at the root of major social-ecological problems in different localities and in the world at large, that the question of private property is to be always asked and placed at the forefront. Many of the so-called criticals will respond to a statement of a critic by saying: 'Oh, that is just your view'. Difference rules. Views are social constructions, and one construction is as good as another. Underlying such acts of evasion is a 'defensive' act of protection: of the relations of property.

Thus, the place the academia occupies within the bourgeois ideological system defines its social role. Material and non-material benefits the academics derive or hope to derive by virtue of that place, that is, by virtue of their role as organic intellectuals of the propertied, contribute to what they do and how they think. Since their role is to defend propertied class interests and their own interests, whether by choice or not (and usually a combination of choice and coercion), the intellectual content of their critique is limited, and any amount of criticism of that limited critique will not bear much fruit either. Therefore, the fundamental aim of criticism is not to change *these* people. What needs to change is this: conditions under which these people think what they do.

And, even if one is able to change their views, the fate of radical social change does not critically depend on what views are held by academics *qua* knowledge producers, although their views are not entirely immaterial (they do have an impact on the masses in a mediated manner, including through their connection with state and media, unions, etc. and therefore their ideological role must be always countered).[59] The reason why radical change does not depend on their change of views is a simple one: they are *not* the revolutionary class. Only the working class (including its male and female members of different races and nationalities) is that class, *given* proper ideological education and political preparation. This is the class, which must sell its ability to work for some compensation and which has very little power to decide the conditions of work and how regularly it will be employed. This class produces the source of profit, rent and interest and this class can stop its production. One must critique the

this is also true about basic sciences to some extent). In this situation, there is increasing pressure (from the administration, etc.) on academics to earn research grants. So earning research grants is seen as a big indicator of scholarship itself. After all, an objective action requires a justifying and consent-creating discourse. Once getting a grant is seen as a marker of scholarship, it is not difficult to see why there is a significant danger that: research topics might be formulated by many in such a way that one would require funding and that such research would be fundable. That is: the funding agencies – governmental or not -- would see some value in the research, and this means that some social-economic policies can be potentially formed on the basis of the research conducted. In effect, the research would be about the things that are fixable, i.e., about the appearances of the underlying mechanisms. To the extent that research is about this, one can see how inadequately critical it is generally going to be, both conceptually and empirically. By saying all this, I am not at all implying that all researchers are merely interested in accumulation of research-money, or that one cannot do grant-based research, at all which is serious (non-trivial and rigorous) and which is genuine critical. No system is entirely totalizing and no system can completely rule out practices that are not in line with its central tendency. It is just that the entire culture of research – production of knowledge -- is such that odds are against such counter-hegemonic practice. If research is critical in the way that this chapter argues it should be, it is increasingly difficult to procure institutional support for it. One can sit in a colloquium or a conference for hours without hearing a word about the system as a whole.

[59] It seems to me that 'irradicalism' of the academics partly reflects not only the views and interests of the propertied class but also the views of vast sections of the masses who are under illusion and who have not developed class-consciousness. Therefore, radicalization of masses has tended to have a positive effect on academia's collective consciousness. Dialectically put, the radicalization of masses and that of academics affect each other within a system in which masses have a greater impact on academics than the other way around.

capitalist world and ideas about this world which the academia and others hold, *from the standpoint* of the material suffering, subjectivity, and potential political power, of this class.

So, the academia is unlikely to change much, and whether they do is relatively less relevant from the standpoint of the production of radical critique and of radical social change. So, the main – rather ultimate – practical reason why one should be critical of existing ideas is to contribute to the raising of consciousness of *this* class, and not necessarily raising of consciousness of professors/academics, although it is true that theory is an arena of class struggle, and that anti-hegemonic academic ideas can and must be produced. The aim should be to clarify to the *working class* the true nature of the society, the limit to their spontaneous and inadequately organized struggles and demands, and of the class and political forces that stop the society from being changed. The working class (including the semi-proletarians) is constantly being 'deceived': its thinking is characterized by partial truths and sometimes complete falsehood. In the current system, people must buy food and clothes, so the system itself makes them think that these things *by nature* are to be produced as commodities for sale for a profit, and act accordingly. This sort of socially fetishistic and scientifically inadequate-uncritical thinking (that characterizes both lay-people and experts) is an important reason – apart from blatant coercion – why the current form of society still continues in spite of its failure to satisfy the needs of the masses. The working class takes the current society as a natural form in which life has to be lived. This class does suffer from false consciousness, and even shares bourgeois consciousness, creating a gap between its subjective/theoretical existence and its material existence. This is why the working class remains politically weak and the capitalist class, strong. And this is why there is a need for critique from a historical, dialectical and materialist standpoint.

Because false consciousness is constantly created – it is created, as mentioned above, by the operation of the system itself which naturalizes/fetishizes, commodity production, by the ways in which dominant groups produce false ideas through their control over the ideological system including the media and universities, and by the reformists creating false hopes in the possibility of significant changes in the system, it is necessary to be critical of, and to remove, false consciousness in the minds of the masses. It is important to stress that false consciousness is produced by the academia, and are disseminated through media (new and old), and through family, friends, and even by professors themselves. Consider the professors advocating for micro-credit, co-ops, ethical trade, reformist unions, democratic revolution, or even 'socialism in one country', as solutions to problems of the humanity; and some of them also win prizes and grant money for knowledge mobilization, socially engaged scholarship, and community activism. These ideas create false hope in the masses, help reproduce the system, and are therefore, more or less, ideological. A genuine critique of the ideas held by the academia will therefore be – can only be – from the standpoint of the interests of the proletarians. Capitalism is critiqued by many people. A critique from the standpoint of the majority – the working masses -- is a different critique. It is ruthless, systemic and sublative, as mentioned earlier. By critiquing the ideas of the academia, which contributes to false consciousness, one creates some of the conditions for the self-realization of the working class as a class, the realization of its own power and of what needs to be changed and how. And, if the more important target of our critique is the masses, then this has implications for practice. Firstly, critical ideas must be produced – within academia and outside -- for the working masses *and* through the process of engagement with them, through involvement in their struggles and daily lives. Second, producers of ideas must write *for* them, and not just for the academia. Like many chapters of this book, this chapter is more or less in line with this argument.

Summary and Conclusion

To be critical is to find fault with the world, a world of unequal social relations, a world that fails to satisfy people's needs. It also means being critical of the ideas about the world, which are inadequate. Critique is possible simply because we can think differently and live differently than we do. Critique is necessary because the world and people working and living in it can be different from what is the case now.

As indicated earlier, the dual forms of critique – critique of the world and of the ideas about it -- are connected. Critique must be a critique of ideas, of ideological consciousness and its origins in objective social structures and in status-quoist political actions of those who seek to preserve the current form of society, including in a slightly modified manner, and in their own interest. In other words, ideas are to be critiqued partly on the ground that they appear to be – are represented as – hanging in the air. Ideas are to be critiqued when they appear to be not connected to historically-specific social relations and to the interests of powerful groups, and more specifically of the propertied classes, and instead appear to be neutral. Critique of ideas, of ideology, cannot be separated from the *critique of material reality* that produces ideological consciousness. The critical status of a knowledge claim, howsoever critical it may fashionably claim to be, is thoroughly undermined if it mutes/ignores the distinction between ideas and that which the ideas refer to outside of the realm of ideas. And the critical status of a knowledge claim is undermined if it ignores/under-emphasizes the material character of the world that frustrates the satisfaction of human needs. Inadequacy of the world is behind the inadequacy of ideas, which is why critique is necessary. Because there is something wrong with the way people think and behave, and because there is something wrong with the way the world is, social scientists seek to critically know their objects which they also seek to change. This means that knowing something is not *just* to represent something as in a mirror. Criticism cannot reasonably be limited to false ideas, abstracted from the practical contexts in which they are constitutive, but must extend to critical evaluation of their associated practices and the material structures which they produce and which in turn help to sustain those practices. As Sayer (1992) says, when we say hoarding money is irrational or wrong we do not mean that only the idea of it is wrong: we mean the practice is wrong. Likewise, it is not just the *ideas* (of racial differences, etc.) behind *apartheid* in the abstract that are wrong. What are wrong are also the actual practices (enforcement of pass laws, etc.) and material structures (segregated and materially deprived townships, etc.) which legitimate, and are legitimated by, those ideas.

Those (e.g., positivists) who advocate for a value-free, 'disinterested' stance in social science fear that permitting such evaluations will produce a distorted picture of the facts. Yet it would be factually incorrect to say, as Sayer argues, that the architects of *apartheid* were factually correct in their beliefs about race. We can't simply refuse to make *any* evaluation, negative or positive, because unless we decide whether the actors' own explanations of their actions are right, we cannot decide what explanation to choose ourselves (Sayer, 1992).

There are various types of critique: philosophical, theoretical, empirical and practical. [60] In terms of the philosophical criticisms, one can make a few general points. 1. A statement is uncritical if it underestimates/ignores the fact that the reality exists more or less independently of the thinking mind/s at a point in time and that reality produces certain effects. Similarly, a statement is uncritical if it underestimates/ignores *material aspects* of human life – the fact that we need to produce and reproduce the means of our subsistence and of production.[61] Humanity's 'mode of dealing with Nature, the process of production by which it sustains its life ...and [the associated] mode of formation of its... social relations' forms the material basis of society. 'Every history of religion', or indeed of ideas in general, 'that fails to take account of this material basis, is *uncritical*' (Marx, 1977). 2. Any theory that sees society merely in terms of its parts in abstraction from the whole and eschews totality is uncritical. Any theory that thinks about society merely in terms of individual actions and thoughts in abstraction from the totality of social relations is uncritical. Indeed, 'the human essence is no abstraction inherent in each single individual. In its reality it is the ensemble of the social relations', which exist independently of, and outlive, given individuals. 3. And, any knowledge claim is uncritical if it abstracts from the fact that reality is always changing because of the contradictory nature of it, of social relations – especially, of antagonistic social relations around the material basis of society. 4. Ideas are also inadequate if they do not conform to empirical evidence and/or are not based on reasoned argument represented in a coherent manner.

'A democracy of ideas' is a false proposition: this is the belief that because certain ideas exist, they must be of value and are valued. This mimics the myth of the market-place of commodities: because a commodity is in the market, it must be useful for an individual and for society. False consciousness, false ideas – like useless and unhealthy commodities which are nonetheless bought and sold -- are a real possibility. Ideas are fallible. But at a given point, some ideas are better and are more adequate than other ideas, from philosophical, theoretical-scientific, empirical and practical standpoints. Inadequate ideas have to face criticism from more adequate ones. When one says that a given body of ideas has no monopoly over truth, is partial, and *therefore* inadequate is thus likely to be a way of protecting less adequate ideas. To say to an opponent that 'your idea is not privileged and therefore my idea is as relevant as yours', is just a way of hiding inadequate and uncritical ideas behind an idealistic wall. Such a relativist epistemological strategy often deployed in so-called critical work makes the practice of critique impossible. Critique is the fountain of intellectual and social life.

If critique 'means discovery of the limitations and realization of the possibilities of their transcendence', it is also true that there are different kinds of limitations: limitation in the world and limitation in our views about it. In terms of the latter, there are: 'limitations in the description and explanation of reality', 'limitations in the interpretation of the meaning of that reality' (i.e., what meanings people attach the world), 'limitations in reality itself' (Markovic, 1983). Social critique depends on – potentially furthers -- the possibility of transcending the

[60] One does not criticize everything one reads/hears. In developing a critique, one presents a selected number of major criticisms, which may include sub-criticisms (part of a major criticism). One must also try to avoid the mistakes which one accuses one's opponents of.

[61] These include food, shelter, technology, and indeed people themselves. The latter point (production of people) means that social reproduction and its gendered character are absolutely important to social critique (see Vogel, 2013).

present; social critique helps us redefine the limits of what is normally considered to be possible. It is necessary to offer a reasonably precise and empirically corroborated account of what the limits of the possible are (for example, is it possible to feed everyone now?), and that means paying attention to the present, its potential (and to the fetters on its potential being realized). As Marx says: ‘we do not dogmatically anticipate the world, but only want to find the new world through criticism of the old one’.[62] So the art of critiquing is opposed to constructing the future and settling everything for all times’. It is opposed, to, say, utopian thinking produced at our writing desks. Criticism is oriented towards the present, without losing sight of the future, because critiquing is ‘what we have to accomplish at present’.

[62] http://www.marxists.org/archive/marx/works/1843/letters/43_09.htm

Chapter 2

MAPPING THE MARXIST CRITIQUE OF SOCIETY: OR, WHAT REALLY IS MARXISM?

What a body of ideas *is* can be seen in relation to what it *is not*, and what it is critical of. So a body of ideas seeking to describe/explain its objects of analysis can be seen *as a critique*. In the light of the previous chapter on critique, this chapter elaborates the idea of a specific form of critique -- Marxist critique -- as the Marxist theory of society. It does so by *reasserting and re-articulating* the central categories of this theory, which are relevant to the understanding of contemporary problems facing the humanity and which can produce powerful critiques of existing ideas. An *implicit* aim of the chapter is to distinguish Marxism from not only non-Marxism but also so-called 'post-Marxism'.[63] In the process, it indirectly speaks to some of the criticisms against Marxist critique/analysis that are unfortunately driven by a misunderstanding of it as intellectually rigid, reductionist, economistic, and race- and gender-blind and as a politically undemocratic project.[64]

Marxism – Marxist critique – was begun by Marx and Engels and has been continued by Lenin, Luxemburg, Trotsky, Gramsci, etc. and those who, more or less, agree with their central conceptual ideas. The totality of Marxism has, arguably, four main components. In terms of theory, these are philosophy (materialist dialectics or dialectical materialism), social theory (historical materialism), and political economy (the most important of the three theoretical parts). And then there is political practice aimed at radically changing the world which is in line with the theory. Marxist philosophy is materialist and dialectical. This

---

[63] Laclau and Mouffe (2014). They say: 'To reread Marxist theory in the light of contemporary problems necessarily involves deconstructing the central categories of that theory. This is what has been called our 'post-Marxism''. [The latter stands for] 'the process of appropriation of an intellectual tradition [Marxist theory], as well as the process of *going beyond it*' (ix; stress added.). To put it simply, post-Marxism, is, more or less, a variety of non-Marxism, a form of which as applied to state theory will be discussed in chapter 3. Post-Marxism is non-Marxism in many ways, one of which is that: class relations are seen in terms of how they are perceived and articulated as, and not in terms of what they are (i.e., as a structure of relations that exist objectively) (see Geras, 1987; Wood, 1990; Brass, 1995a; Das, 2012c for critical discussion on this sort of intellectual tendency, which is widespread). It is also anti-Marxism because of: its distrust of metanarratives; its view of the political which is autonomous of the economic; its view of the economic which is devoid of its social relations of production aspect;, its rejection of the distinction between essence and appearance; and so on. Post-Marxism applied to the study of the imperialized periphery is post-colonialism, which is critically discussed in Chibber (2013). See also Therborn (2008) on the non-Marxist Left in relation to the Marxist Left.

[64] The discussion is pitched at the level of a beginning graduate and advanced undergraduate scholar and is also aimed at any educated person who seeks to at least explore what Marxism is in an open-minded way.

influences Marxist social theory or historical materialism, which outlines the broad ways in which major historical changes regularly happen at the societal level. What is Marxist social theory can be more or less seen as the discourse on common elements of all class societies (e.g., slave society, feudalism, capitalism) and what differentiates them. Marxist political economy – informed as it is by materialist dialectics and historical materialism – is the study of concrete time- and place-specific societies in terms of how wealth is produced, exchanged, distributed, and consumed. Standing for concrete application of historical materialism, much of political economy has focused on the study of capitalist societies.[65] Marxist political practice, the last component of Marxist critique/theory, seeks to remove the obstacles to human flourishing, the obstacles to the satisfaction of people's needs, the obstacles to them becoming what they truly *can* become under a condition of genuine freedom from economic and extra-economic coercion and from natural scarcity; these obstacles are identified in Marxist intellectual practice. It is through political practice,[66] informed by theory or theoretical practice (as elaborated in the first three components of Marxism) that theory is tested and enriched, which, in turn, contributes to political practice.

THE MARXIST WAY OF KNOWING

For Marxist philosophy,[67] and as indicated in the last chapter, these elements are crucial: 'materiality' + 'sociality' (social relationships) + system/totality (including relationships between parts) + change-via-contradiction. This philosophy is materialist because it says that there is a reality which more or less exists independently of how it is thought to be: independent existence of reality (including that part of it which is more humanly created) vis a vis consciousness. Consciousness emerges from and reflects material conditions, although it cannot be reduced to material conditions. The reality cannot be perceived except through ideas, but there has to be reality in the first place for it to be perceived. In its more concrete aspects, the material refers to nature and to production and reproduction of conditions of life, including through relations with nature and through the deployment of bodily powers.[68] The

[65] On Marxist political economy, my personal favorite is Marx's *Capital volume one* itself. Other works include: Harvey (2007); Kliman (2007); Laibman (1992); Lebowitz (2003) and Wolff and Resnick (2012: chs 4&7).

[66] Political practice is a subset of practice. 'Man's social practice is not confined to activity in production, but takes many other forms--class struggle, political life, scientific and artistic pursuits; in short, as a social being, man participates in all spheres of the practical life of society. Thus man, in varying degrees, comes to know the different relations between man and man, not only through his material life but also through his political and cultural life (both of which are intimately bound up with material life). Of these other types of social practice, class struggle in particular, in all its various forms, exerts a profound influence on the development of man's knowledge.' (Mao, 1937).

[67] On this topic see: Arthur (2002); Callinicos (1985); Collier (1994); Harvey (1996: chs 2 and 4); Ollman (2003), Paolucci (2007); Rees (1998); and Timpanaro (1980).

[68] The material in Marxist critique/theory refers to things – natural objects such as land and rivers, and the human body and its tendency to be sick and die and to be happy and unhappy, because of certain physiological-neurological mechanisms – that are a condition for consciousness and action. The material also refers to a *social process* of the production of things through two kinds of relations mentioned here (relations with natural objects and mechanisms and relations among people which mediate the former relation). There was a time when some people reacted against the structuralist Marxism and thus emphasized human subjects/agency. The obsession with the human is waning a bit. The fad is now the non-human (non-human objects having agency). This fad trivializes the concept of agency by divorcing agency from consciousness and intentionality and the ability to shape the material environment through conscious and organized action. Also, because natural objects

material conditions influence, and are influenced by, social consciousness (including false consciousness), within a whole in which material conditions have an ultimate primacy.[69] This worldview emphasizes the social character of human beings and of the reality, treating the human as an ensemble of social (and social-ecological) relationships, some of which are more global and others more local. And the social is a space of material as well as political and ideational/discursive relations and processes. And the Marxist philosophy emphasizes the systemic nature – totalizing – nature of the reality in which what one thing is depends on its relations to other things, although some of these relations are more 'significant' and 'more fundamental' than others. The totality, which must be the starting point of any analysis, is seen as more than sum of the parts inside it. And the worldview sees change in everything and everything as changing, through contradictions inside it, and between it and its social (social-ecological) environment, the contradictions that are, more or less, registered in consciousness which, in turn, responds to these contradictions.

A way of thinking that is permeated by these four philosophical elements will compel an analyst/critic to ask the question of all questions, the class question:[70] who owns and who does not own/control society's resources, and how this cleavage – how this contradictory relation between those who own/control society's productive resources and those who do not -- shapes other cleavages. It will compel people to ask: 'Where do you stand – where do I stand -- on the question of property?'. *Arguably, and this is the main theme in the chapter, it is the class question that touches and connects all the four components of Marxist critique/theory as such, in one way or another.* So, a most brief and basic definition of what is called Marxism – Marxist critique -- would be that: Marxism is about class. It is about the analysis of class relations and their impacts on other relations, within the totality of social relations, and it is about the necessity for the ultimate abolition of class relations through a struggle by the masses against these relations, which are to be replaced by a feasible democracy-from-below in all spheres of life, a democracy that is qualitatively far superior to liberal democracy, in form and content.

Marxism explains the world in terms of the operation of class relations at multiple geographical scales and in multiple spheres of life (economic, political, cultural/discursive, ecological). It says that class relations, and most importantly capitalist class relations, are the most fundamental cause (if not the only cause) of the most fundamental material, cultural and political problems of the humanity.[71] Therefore, Marxism calls for the abolition of the class

(e.g. plants) guided by natural processes are being interfered with (in pursuit of profit), the fact that there is something called natural is being increasingly under-emphasized, so much so that nature is equated to what is thought about nature or what is done to nature; and to the extent that the existence of nature is noted, its relevant material effects on humans are often abstracted from (see Castree and Braun, 2001). Transformation *of* nature is mistakenly seen as denying that there is something irreducibly natural in the world. Underlying these ideas about so-called social nature(s) is a fundamental anti-materialism. On an excellent discussion on materialism, see Timpanaro (1980: chapters 1-2). Lenin's *Materialism and Empirio criticism* is also useful.

69 This idea is true even at the level of the body (or body-brain complex): modern neuro-science (see Davidson, 2012) says that consciousness can affect physical-chemical changes in the body including in the brain, but no thought can be thought or can exist without it emerging from – being rooted in – a certain part of the physical brain. The material is a condition for consciousness but the latter cannot be reduced to – and can indeed impact -- the material. This principle, more or less, applies to an individual and to wider society.

70 There is a large amount of literature on class. See Wright (2005); Das (2012c).

71 These include the following, many of which have been alluded to earlier: lack of nutritious food, decent housing, clothes, education and health care; environmental degradation; access to transportation; social oppression; increasing relative impoverishment; repression by state authorities and threat to democratic rights; economic insecurity caused by recurrent economic crises; and new imperialism and constant threat of war from which

system and its political cultural support-systems, through independent political mobilization of those who are exploited and oppressed by class relations, in order to establish a society that is democratic in economic, political and cultural spheres and that is more ecologically harmonious.

A dialectical, historical and materialist way of knowing, Marxism is a form of explanatory critique of society with a practical intent. It is a class-based interpretation of society, including its interaction with nature and how it organizes its spatial relations, from the standpoint of radically changing that society.[72] The '1% vs 99%' debate, to some extent, speaks to that. The definition of Marxism as class-based critical explanation/analysis, and class-based practice is not as simple as it appears to be. This idea will be elaborated in the remainder of the chapter. Given the all-encompassing nature of the topic, the presentation will be conducted, in the interest of brevity, in a schematic form.

The Economic, the Political and the Cultural in Class Societies

1. Human beings must produce and reproduce their means of subsistence and production. They do this through their relations with nature, and with one another (social relations of production). Through such relations, they aim to develop the productive forces, producing more in less time, to satisfy their (changing) material and cultural needs.[73] Thus, productive forces gradually develop (although unevenly over time and in space), within the framework of social relations.
2. At a given point in time, the gradual development of productive forces reaches a critical level: society produces more than what is (minimally) required for sustaining life. In other words, a quantitative increase in the level of productive forces leads to a qualitative change. A system of class relations develops, one in which some people do not have to directly produce means of subsistence. They form the ruling class: they control the surplus product, which is produced by others (direct producers such as slaves and serfs). The ruling class in a territory not only appropriates the surplus product of direct producers in that territory; it also sometimes appropriates the surplus product – and even direct producers themselves (e.g., slaves) -- from another area, through plunder and trade.
3. The most fundamental cleavage in society is class: class in the sense of class relations of exploitation or the appropriation of fruits of labor of the direct producers who do not own/control property in the means of production and exchange by those who do. Associated with this is unequal distribution of property *among* property owners and competition among them. The relations of property and exploitation

masses suffer in both imperialist and imperialized nations; and absence of opportunities to pursue spiritual goals, including universal compassionate love for humans and love for activities not immediately directed at earning a livelihood.

[72] It combines explanation of current conditions with critique of these conditions. Critique is necessary because what appears to be the case is often not the case. And 'explanation … [is to be] adapted to the practical needs of the masses' (Lenin, 1964:23).

[73] The satisfaction of these needs leads to happiness. It is assumed here that generally speaking, humans prefer material comfort to the lack of it, and that they prefer happiness to unhappiness.

between classes along with the relations of competition within classes -- in other words, social relations of production, broadly construed -- provide the framework which promotes or blocks[74] society's productive powers (e.g., powers of people to work; technological change; altered soil fertility; spatial framework of cities and villages).[75] The social relations and the productive powers, which bear the influence of these relations, are intertwined and form the economic system, within which the social relations of production assume a certain degree of primacy.[76]

4. The economic system influences – sets limit on – and is influenced by, the political management of society's common and conflictual affairs, and forms of relation between political managers and ordinary people (state-people relations).[77] In a class society, institutions of the state, more or less and seen from the vantage point of a long period of time, manage the common affairs of those who control production and exchange. These common affairs of the ruling class include the need to suppress intellectual and political dissent of direct producers to the class that controls the lives of the majority. Indeed, the most fundamental aspect of the state is that it is coercive *and* that its coercive power – body of armed people – is separated from the society at large, from the democratic control of ordinary people. The state also negotiates relations of competition and conflict between ruling class groups, including between geographically circumscribed (e.g., nationally based) ruling classes, in order to help reproduce the *overall* dominance of the class over society.[78]The class system and the political system are internally related: the political system is an arm of the class system, with its appropriate degree of relative freedom vis a vis the latter, a freedom which is necessary to perform its assigned task. The extent to which the class which controls society's resources is also the politically governing class has varied from one form of society to another. In pre-capitalist societies, because direct producers have direct access to (at least some) means of production, extra-economic power is

[74] The relations can fetter development here and promote development there. But the relation between the two must be seen at the international scale, rather than merely in the context of specific places or countries.

[75] Much of humanity's knowledge (or what sometimes known is as indigenous knowledge) – in medicine, farming, spatial organization, etc. – has been accumulated on the basis of the logic, not of profit-making, but of the satisfaction of needs of ordinary people (plus luxury needs of the ruling classes as well as needs of warfare).

[76] Which of the two – forces of production (including technology) or relations of production – is primary has been at the center of much discussion (see the special issue in *Science & Society*, 2006). Cohen (1978) believes that forces have primacy and that Marx believes so. If Marx believed so, he should be wrong. The best way is to see the relation in a dialectical way, which is how it is pursued here. And this dialectical way, Marx, I believe, would endorse.

[77] So in the Marxist critique, the economic, which itself is constituted by the combination of productive forces and *social* relations of production with their associated accumulation processes, and which is influenced by political relations/processes (and by the discursive realm, as mentioned below) is immediately a *social* process. Mainstream economics abstracts the non-economic from the economic and never combines them. So its economic is often the imagined economic, not the real economic. And the post-modernist economic analysis often treats the imaginative/discursive aspects of the economic – how the economic is discursively constructed or seen (as in cultural economy type studies, which are fashionalble now-a-days) -- so its view of the economic, as its view of everything else, is also idealistic. Thus, while mainstream and postmodernist economic analyses appear to be different, they seem to be occupying a common space. Besides, both of these traditions emphasize the individual (or a mere collection of individuals) and under-emphasizes social relations of production and their dialectical connection to productive forces.

[78] The state also performs common affairs of a society as a whole. This is an issue, which will be taken up in the next chapter, under the idea of government (Hoffman, 1995). These common affairs may include society's interaction with nature (e.g. dealing with a drought), fighting a disease that may affect both the rich and the poor, and so on. However, the state treats these common issues in a way, which is, generally, affected by class relations and class struggles.

generally used to make them deliver the surplus product to the ruling class (e.g., slave owners, landlords).

5. The economic/material and political systems/processes, in turn, influence the realm of ideas/discourses. The latter is to be seen both in the sense of consciousness of ordinary people (common sense) as well as ideologies/theories (and even many religious and spiritual ideas), which are more systematically produced through specialized intellectual labor.[79] Ideas about ourselves (including about who we are, our identities), about society, and nature (slowly and unevenly) change as conditions under which we live and work change.[80]
6. A specific form of social consciousness is class-consciousness, i.e., consciousness of class-interests. Although direct producers are a class by virtue of the fact that they lack control over means of production and are exploited, they are not necessarily or automatically (fully) conscious of the mechanisms of exploitation, of their class position, and of what is to be done about this. Slaves or serfs or workers do not automatically become class conscious merely based on their objective interests; such consciousness develops in a gradual and non-linear way, through the active mediation of political actions and conscious ideas (which are influenced, for example, by spontaneous thinking). Class is *not* class identity (any more than gender is merely about gender identity): class, which is a relation, or a structure of relations between classes, exists irrespective of how people of a class see it at a given point in time and in a place. A class can be more or less conscious of itself as a class. Indeed it is class-system – 'class-being' -- which broadly influences and is influenced by class-consciousness. It explains why many working people, for example, find it difficult to see that they are working class.[81] This consciousness has to be worked for, based on the consciousness of the effects of underlying mechanisms of exploitation and inequalities, the effects which are experienced in their daily lives (e.g., cultural oppression; poverty; homelessness; violence). Ideas ultimately reflect interests of classes and class-fractions. The class-system creates many ideas – both commonsensical and more theoretical ideas – which justify class relations and the interests of political managers and the ruling classes and their allies (small-scale producers).[82] Ideas, which dominate the material and discursive lives of ordinary people and reproduce the system of class relations, are generally the ideas that are of, and are consciously produced by, the ruling classes.[83] This also means that not *all*

[79] That the economic and the political form a system in which both interact but the economic ultimately explains—sets limit on -- the political is the materialist approach. .

[80] That is why explaining what is happening in society merely in terms of what people think (ideas) is not adequate. Also, explaining what is happening in a society in terms of human nature – what humans are by nature – also is inadequate because much of human nature – and how it is manifested -- also changes in time-space. The fact that humans are humans because they transform the environment in which they live by using their bodies and technologies cannot itself explain the level of economic development in this or that place. But that idea is significant in countering idealistic ideas, those in which humans are seen mainly in terms of their mental activities.

[81] The issue of false consciousness is briefly discussed in the previous chapter.

[82] Many scientific ideas leading to profit-making innovations fall in this category suggesting the subordination of science to the needs of private accumulation, which is increasingly the case, whether in biotechnology or information and communication technology.

[83] 'The ideas of the ruling class are in every epoch the ruling ideas, i.e., the class which is the ruling material force of society, is at the same time its ruling intellectual force. The class which has the means of material production at its disposal, has control at the same time over the means of mental production, so that thereby, generally

ideas are ruling class ideas, because ruling classes coexist with exploited classes. [84] The conditions of the masses produce counter-hegemonic ideas, even if they have a relatively marginal status at a specific point in time and place. These ideas come both in the form of commonsense (or relatively less developed class consciousness coexisting with non-class consciousness) and in the form of more fully developed ideas and theories, reflecting masses' class conditions. Marxism – Marxist critique – is the most advanced form of counter-hegemonic thinking, because of its totalizing explanation of social issues and because it seeks to radically transform *all* aspects of the current society.

7. Just because counter-hegemonic ideas/actions are possible, it does not mean that class structure does not have the determining[85] influence on people's lives. And, just because the class structure has the determining influence, it does not mean that counter-hegemonic ideas/actions are not possible. Nor does it mean that one can completely understand ideas/actions of an *individual* or indeed a group of individuals in terms of class interests and ideas. Class structure determines in the sense of setting limits on consciousness and actions of the masses and individuals. The fact that class structure determines does not mean that nothing can happen that is against the logic of that structure. It is in fact written in the 'body' of the class structure, which is contradictory, that counter-hegemonic ideas/actions (at both individual and group/collective level) will happen, but these ideas/actions remain marginal as long as the class structure remains, until a critical point appears in the history of the development of the ideas and actions of the masses when the structure is successfully challenged and replaced. Reproduction of class structure is not at all given: it can go any day. But as long as it exists, it limits. While class interests and relations influence class conscious and actions, the latter cannot be reduced to the former. Ideas are absolutely important. But people just cannot have any idea or any notion of agency in their heads, which will work: slaves cannot think about cooperatively managing a computer-producing factory. For notions (including notions about agency) to work, political and discursive mediation/articulation is necessary, but the notions must be based on, and presuppose, definite objective conditions/interests.
8. Class interests, which emanate from relations of production and associated processes of accumulation and distribution of things necessary for life, are the dominant

speaking, the ideas of those who lack the means of mental production are subject to it. The ruling ideas are nothing more than the ideal expression of the dominant material relationships, the dominant material relationships grasped as ideas; hence of the relationships which make the one class the ruling one, therefore, the ideas of its dominance. The individuals composing the ruling class possess among other things consciousness, and therefore think. Insofar, therefore, as they rule as a class…it is self-evident that they …rule also as thinkers, as producers of ideas, and regulate the production and distribution of the ideas of their age: thus their ideas are the ruling ideas of the epoch.' [Marx's *German Ideology:* http://www.marxists.org/archive/marx/works/1845/german-ideology/ch01b.htm

[84] It also means that a given idea may not be un-problematically a ruling class idea because there are differences in interests between ruling class fractions.

[85] If A completely determines B, meaning that whatever A is, B is, or that our knowledge of A will give us our full knowledge of B, then why should we talk about B? The fact that A and B exist means that B cannot be reduced to A. 'Determine' simply means that: B emerges from A (that is without A, B will not exist), but B cannot reduced to A. A sets limit within which B can take many forms and acquire many attributes (including its temporal and spatial variation). There is something about B, which is not in A. In this chapter, A stands for the objectively-existing reality, the economic, and class (including class-fractions), while correspondingly, B stands for the discursive (ideas, consciousness), the political, and non-class relations.

interests people have, but they are not the only interests they have. There are political conflicts of other types (between groups defined in ways other than class), but these are ultimately conflicts between interests of classes and/or between fractions inside a class. Or, They are, at least, colored/influenced by class and class-fractional interests. The latter conflicts are also mediated through various non-class interests and associated ideologies such as those of specific races, genders or nationalities. Within limits set by class relations and in specific time and place contexts, non-class interests can take on a life that appears to be somewhat independent of class. But once again, over the long term, underlying these interests lurk class interests in certain ways. Often it is the case that when class struggle from below (from the masses) fails for some reason (e.g., suppression by class struggle from below; treachery committed by leaders of masses), non-class type conflicts/differences appear to be significant in discursive and political imagination. Or, when class struggle becomes intense or has the potential to do so, the ruling class stokes up passions around non-class interests. The 'non-class' interests (e.g., the right to be treated equally irrespective of race or gender) exist, but the satisfaction of such interests is frustrated by scarcity caused by the ruling class control over society's resources, and by ideologies that justify discrimination on the basis of, for example, race and gender.

9. In all class societies, there is class struggle, both the struggle of the dominant classes to reproduce the system, and the struggle from below. Working masses indeed fight against the exploitative class relations and the political mechanisms, which support these. Their class struggle happens both in the political realm and in the realm of consciousness. This fight can be overt or covert. It succeeds sometimes and in some places. It fails at other times and in other places. The struggle is both aimed at changing things inside the system and at transcending the system. Class struggle is often not informed by fully-formed class consciousness, and it is often deflected through, and mediated by, struggle over non-class interests (race-, gender-, location, or nationality-based conflicts).
10. As mentioned earlier, productive forces develop in the context of specific production relations. The development of productive forces beyond the level required for survival represents a form of qualitative break in history, when class relations based on the production of a surplus develop. Another type of qualitative break happens when a given set of relations of production block the further development of productive forces. At this point, a class which has been hitherto subordinated challenges the ruling class, and furthers the development of productive forces in its own interest. So the contradiction between productive forces and relations and associated class struggle result in the emergence of a new form of society. From the womb of a cooperative form of society, the humanity has progressed through various forms of class-society, including slavery and feudalism. Capitalism is the most modern form of class-society.

Class and Accumulation in Capitalism and in Contemporary Capitalist Societies[86]

1. The capitalist class relation is the dominant class relation in the contemporary world at large and at the national scale in nearly all the major countries.[87] Capitalism exists when conditions of life (food, clothes, etc. and machines needed to make these) are produced by wage-laborers as commodities for exchange for a profit. In this process of production, the vast majority of working people work under the control of a minority which owns/controls the productive resources (e.g., land, factories, banks) and who decide how they are used and for what purpose. The capitalist class relation operates through its law of value,[88] its associated inter-capitalist competition, socially-unplanned technical changes and production processes, which compel the producers to produce at a (globally) competitive price for greater profits.
2. In the system of exchange of things, it is possible for some property owners in some places to make a profit by buying cheap and selling dear (or indeed by lending money). But ultimately, at the level of society, profit must come from a surplus that is created above what is needed to reproduce workers and the means of production. Workers generally lack control over the production process and not just over means of production and the value of what they produce. Profit is basically created through the fact that property owners, using their *power* as property owners, pay to workers just enough (at best) for their reproduction, and not the full value of the product workers create. In other words, because of their class power, which is not matched by that of workers, property owners force workers to work longer than it takes to produce the things they ordinarily consume via the wage received. That is, workers are paid only a part of the net product they produce. And, if one accounts for the unpaid work that workers, and especially, women workers, perform at home in the reproductive sphere, workers-as-a-whole, including men and women, are actually paid a very small part of what they produce. In other words, surplus comes from a class relationship, a relationship that revolves around control over means of

[86] The previous section – that deals with class in general – deals with Marxism, more or less, in terms of its social theory component. This section deals with Marxism mainly in terms of its political economy (and especially, political economy of capitalism), the third and the main component of Marxism. It must be said that the different components overlap with one another. There is a relation of identity and difference between/among the components.

[87] This does not, however, exclude the possibility that apart from capital and labor (including their various factions such as agrarian capital and agrarian labor, and industrial capital and industrial labor, etc.), there are landlords appropriating ground rent, peasants paying rent and/or performing part-time wage labor, and so on. Even in advanced countries, millions of people are self-employed. In the Third world countries, land does remain an important means of production, and is unequally distributed. However, whether in rural areas of the Third World or a Third world country as a whole, the major part of the surplus product takes the form of surplus value, appropriated from workers, some of whom may own some land or other means of production.

[88] This means that the value of a commodity is determined by the amount of labor time that is socially necessary to produce it, and not by its usefulness (actual or perceived), although the latter – like relative scarcity in a time or a place -- can influence the price, which can rise and fall below value. To put it crudely, commodities are exchanged in the same proportion as the amount of socially necessary labor time that has been 'embedded in them'. A computer which, on an average, requires 6 hours to produce it, will exchange for 3 cameras, each of which takes, on an average, 2 hours to make. If it takes, on an average, 6 hours to produce a computer in a society, and if a firm spends 7 hours (embedded in living labor and in technology, processed raw materials, etc.), it must sell its computer *as if* it has spent 6 hours to make it. So, the firm loses an hour of value.

production and over labor at work (and the latter – control over labor -- is connected to that at home).[89]

3. Unlike in pre-capitalist systems, under capitalism, generally, a given employer cannot force a worker to work for him/her, so exploitation happens dominantly through economic coercion: the fact of economic coercion simply means that without direct access to means of subsistence and production, workers are compelled to work for some for a wage. They are not free not to work for someone for a wage but they have the freedom to choose their employer to enter into and exit from an employment contract (just as they have the freedom to choose what to buy from whom). However, certain employers or indeed a large number of employers, in order to depress wages and inhibit class struggle from below, deprive workers of their ability to freely sell their labor power.[90]
4. The capitalist class relation has promoted the development of productive forces and encouraged scientific attitude and a certain degree of political and economic freedom, *as compared to* the pre-capitalist systems. It is also responsible for a variety of adverse effects on the masses. Although workers' commodity (their ability to work) should receive its full value (i.e., the value of what is needed to make it such as food and shelter), wages of millions of workers remain inadequate to procure the things that they need for a decent life. Millions do not even know if they are going to be able to properly eat tomorrow or next month, as they may not have access to wage-work due to uncertainties in the labor market. On any given day, millions do go hungry or near-hungry. Capitalism constantly creates new needs. And, it constantly frustrates the satisfaction of these needs, and even basic needs on the part of most people.[91] This is not necessarily because society does not produce adequate resources, nor because natural scarcity exists (as it did in pre-capitalist societies in most places). Resources are being used for making profits and not to satisfy human needs. And much of the resources produced by ordinary people is being squandered away in wars, surveillance, and such socially-unproductive ventures and in luxury consumption of a tiny minority, which is necessary to discursively reproduce the class distinction between them and the rest.
5. Workers are being subjected to both absolute impoverishment (they cannot satisfy their absolutely minimal needs) and from relative impoverishment (relative to income and wealth of the bosses, and of a section of the population, which is most closely connected to the bosses as their taskmasters). Impoverishment happens due to exploitation through the regime of long hours-and-low-wages and through the use of productivity-raising technical and organizational changes. The productivity-increase, along with the fact that workers work long hours every day mean that: more of what is produced is going to the bosses relative to what working masses get in compensation. Workers are being constantly thrown into the reserve army of the unemployed, underemployed and discouraged workers, because of consolidation (mergers and acquisitions) and because bosses are using labor-saving technology to reduce costs and to discipline labor. The reserve army – sections of which have

[89] See Vogel (2014) for an analysis of class nature of gender and gendered nature of reproduction of labour power. Also, Giminez and Vogel (2005) and the *Science & Society* special issue on Marxist feminism (69:1).

[90] This issue is discussed in chapter 5 in details.

[91] On the relation between human needs and capitalism, see Lebowitz (1992); and Heller (1976).

indeed no hope of gaining decent employment – that is constantly produced and replenished pulls down wages of those employed through competition for work. So wages fall even if workers produce more and more wealth. Because workers of the world[92] are being increasingly more productive, i.e., they are producing more in less time and more per person, they are losing their jobs, as fewer people are needed at work. Also, it is partly because of their rising productivity that big business is able to economically outcompete smaller-scale owners and self-employed people and thus drive them to precarious ranks of wage-dependent workers. This process by contributing to the reserve army further puts pressure on the wages of the currently employed. So, when employed, people do not receive the value of the new wealth they create and, they do not even receive what they need to live as humans (they have no control over production and the surplus). There is also little guarantee that they will be even employed. And, when they are not employed, millions live like paupers and as lumpen elements.

6. Capitalist class relation is a threat to the physical and spiritual integrity of the body-mind complex. Workers are being crippled and turned into an appendage of the machine and alienating production process. While millions are unemployed or under-employed, those who do work are under constant pressure to perform more work every day and every hour. Not satisfied with the adults, capital even makes use of children, who work at a lower-than-average wage and are less likely to protest super-exploitation. . Workers are subjected to speed-up and high intensity of work and constant pressure to meet deadlines, in order to make more money every minute, every day, thus indicating that capital's time and body's time (the time the body needs to recuperate itself) are not in line. Workers are also subjected to: constant surveillance and control at work and physically unsuitable working conditions, including the use of chemicals. Industrial disasters – 'accidents' at work (e.g., explosions in the factory) – are common due to reduced expenditure on safety issues. Thus, capitalism puts a stamp on the body-mind complex of the worker.[93] When the profit logic is manifested in and indeed drives the potentially unsafe sectors such as nuclear energy and weapons production, it can result in the destruction of the human species itself. Also, because of the profit motive, commodities are produced and sold to the masses (e.g., GMOs) whose long-term effect on health can be negative. Whether at work-place or in the market-place, the profit motive is an attack on the human bodies.
7. Nature has been integrated into capitalist relations of production and exchange (and indeed speculation). The profit motive and incessant money-making-for-its-sake are responsible for increasing commodification and massive degradation of the natural environment. Even conservation measures are commodified and subjected to a profit motive. This happens through the policies of governments that work more or less on behalf of capital, which is behind commodification. So, so-called neoliberal conservation measures are not merely government measures, but are in fact *capitalist* measures. It is capital (and its state) that decides the exchange value (price) of elements of nature (trees, water, etc.), so an under-valuation potentially increases

[92] I am abstracting from the fact that the level of, and the rise in, productivity are geographically uneven. See the point numbers 8-10 below.

[93] See Fracchia (2008). The issue of industrial disaster is discussed in chapter 10.

profits for capital as a whole, although the process harms society, or its common natural basis. The physical environment suffers from the similar problem as the worker herself/himself: the class system takes a lot more (of useful items) out of nature than it gives back to itself, a process which ensures higher profits.[94]The fast pace of accumulation of money – the quick turnover time – outstrips the rate at which nature (e.g., trees, soil, groundwater, etc.) regenerates itself, suggesting that nature's time (like body's time) and capital's time are out of sync.

8. The capitalist class system impacts the working class and the environment through a social-spatial system, which it creates, which is internally contradictory, and which is therefore constantly changing. Like all forms of productive force, the socio-spatial system – the built environment, including the network of roads, and cities -- bears the imprint of class. The capitalist class system, as mentioned earlier, is based on the production and sale of commodities, including people's abilities to work. Commodities have to move. People – workers, managers, petty producers, everyone -- have to move. In other words, for a capitalist commodity economy to work, productive units and people living in different places in a country and in the world at large need to be connected through a geographical network of transportation and communication lines and nodes of human activities (e.g., villages, towns and cities). A part of the capital must be sunk in a place for the rest of capital to be able to move, but this is always a contradictory affair because capital that is sunk may not generate enough profit.[95] Also, a system of places which is good today for money-making may be dysfunctional tomorrow, as new transportation technologies develop or a new place of accumulation emerges, making old built environments – including of an entire region or a country -- *relatively* uneconomical. Workers suffer. If not enough profit is made, unemployment results: the burden (failure of realization of profit from capital invested) is shifted to the working class. It is a class fix. Having arrived at a place for work, people may find jobs vanish in a few years' time, forcing them to return to where they came from or to move to new places.[96] Besides, the geographical space itself is deeply a class-object. Often the state invests money on behalf of capital in creating an appropriate geographical framework for capital (e.g., super-highways) to increase the efficiency of commodity movement. But the money invested in spaces can also be used and -- often comes at the expense of – providing healthcare or schools for the lower classes. And, often the modes of transportation (e.g., affordable public transit) that ordinary people need remain under-funded while society's resources are used in areas which directly cater to money-making in the hands of powerful property-owners.

9. While capitalist class relations and development of productive forces under it must take a spatial form, exactly what form that will be at a given point in time (e.g., concentration or dispersion and at what scale, urban or not) is a different matter, and this has important implications for practice.[97] It is generally the case that to minimize

[94] See Foster (2000); Burkett (1999).

[95] See Harvey (1985).

[96] During economic crises, return migration of workers from cities to villages has been noticed in several parts of the world, including in India.

[97] While ruralization of capital does not license the near-exclusive focus on rural struggles (an idea that is popular in a certain kind of Marxism, as discussed in Chapter 11), an exclusive focus on city-based workers may not be

costs of movement and to increase profits, concentration of people and things is necessary. This leads to *urbanization of capital* [98] in the sense of the concentration of productive forces, workers and certain cultural attitudes in the cities. But there is also its opposite: *ruralization* of capital. Urbanization of capital, beyond a certain point, and in specific contexts, can have significant negative impacts (rising land values, possibility of organization among geographically concentrated workers). In contrast, rural areas offer cheap land, including land obtained through extra-economic and semi-legal means. The geographically dispersed workers in rural areas may be less organized than urban workers, and may offer good locations for branch-plants. Given new technologies of communication and transportation, ruralization of capital, especially in locations not too far off from major cities, offers a distinctive spatial opportunity for making money, including in businesses, which specialize in, for example, extractive industries, nature-dependent production processes, and storage facilities requiring a large amount of space. If these rural areas are places where socially marginalized people live (e.g., aboriginal people; those who are displaced by so-called development projects), then capital's job of exploitation of labor and extraction from nature becomes easier.

10. Because of its constant search for profits across the globe, capital always plays a see-saw game (it is here today and there tomorrow). When the crisis of over-accumulation happens here, capital seeks to transfer its effects elsewhere, and the crisis itself does not happen everywhere at the same time and with the same effects. The see-saw game of capital and the geography of crisis and the like contribute to historically dynamic uneven economic development at multiple scales.
11. The see-saw game at the international scale is fuelled by, and feeds into, the fact that competition between companies has resulted in the emergence of very big companies (monopolies), which are involved in international trade and global finance as well as globalized production (branches of big transnational companies produce different parts of a given commodity in different countries). Competition is between not only nationally and regionally embedded firms but also between trans-national monopolies at the national and global scales. Operation of capitalism has given rise to – and had to give rise to – capitalist imperialism understood as capitalist accumulation, competition and exploitation operating at the international/global scale. More specifically, imperialism is capitalist class relation at the international scale: between the monopolies of the imperialist countries on the one hand and workers and self-employed small-scale owners in the periphery on the other. It is a process, which makes use of, and thus reinforces, nationality/racial differences in its own interest. And it is a process that is driven by, and fuels, inter-imperialist economic and military rivalry, Subordination of economically under-developed nations with their less powerful and pliable states ensures the exploitation of direct producers living there. Low-cost access to their land/resources and to workers becomes a means of competitive advantage for capitalists of advanced nations with

useful to launch wider struggles against capital either, especially in the global periphery. Perhaps, and geographically, the focus should be city-based regional approach to struggle, one that includes cities and surrounding villages, an approach underlying which is the idea of a class-alliance between urban workers and the rural poor (low-income working small-scale producers).

[98] Ibid.

more powerful states. Just as technology is used to cheapen costs and enhance competitiveness, so is imperialism: making use of cheap land and labor, achieved ultimately through political-military domination, which is supported by a cultural construction of imperialized places as inferior (racially or otherwise), becomes a competitive strategy, and this is where inter-imperialist rivalry comes from. Imperialized countries also become dumping grounds for surplus products and over-accumulated capital (not to speak of pollutants and wastes) from imperialist countries, and are subjected to exploitation in sphere of financial capital (e.g., trade; debt; speculative capital). Imperialism – capitalism that is geographically divided at the international scale into a core and a periphery[99] -- indeed produces a distinct stamp on the periphery of the capitalist system, a system of global uneven development. Partly due to the impacts of metropolitan capital during formal colonialism and neo-colonialism on pre-capitalist and emerging capitalist class relations, a form of capitalist class system is now in place in the periphery which is in certain ways different from the kind of capitalism we have in the core (although there is capitalism in both parts of the world): it is a capitalist production system that is less based on a regime of *systemic* technological change aimed at increasing labor productivity per hour that has generally characterized advanced countries in the last 200 years or so, and it is, relative to the advanced nations, more based on a regime of exploitation through long-hours and low-wages as well as increasing dispossession of small-scale producers, the ranks of which still provide labor and products to the capitalist system (often not always in fully commodified form). The two parts of the single capitalist system – imperialized and imperialist countries -- are deeply connected. The imperialist world continues to be characterized by the transfer of resources and products of labor power as well as labor itself (indeed the imperialist system sucks up the highly skilled labor from imperialized, lower-income nations, a type of labor whose reproduction costs the imperialized nations do not bear but which by increasing the supply of labor keeps their wage bills at a competitive level; this is a process which feeds into the imperialist advantages and existing global inequalities). The imperialist system is also marked by sheer subordination of peripheral states and cultures to imperialist capital's economic and geopolitical interests, a process in which big businesses of peripheral countries are complicit and work as junior partners of imperialist capital.[100] What happens inside any country in

[99] Note that which countries will belong to the core or periphery is a different matter. A country which is in the periphery now can become a part of the core in the future, although such mobility is extremely slow. Also note that: in so far as imperialism is about the process of exploitation of labor, appropriation of natural resources, and access to the markets of poorer nations -- a process which is conducted through political-military and ideological subjugation of these nations and which is driven by the imperative of world-scale accumulation and operations of international financial capital (consider the effect of credit rating agencies of the West on Third World economies) and by competition between monopolies based in economically advanced and politically powerful nations -- in so far as this is the case, the absolute amount of capital exported to those nations relative to what is moved between imperialist nations is relatively less important to the operation of imperialism. What is important is this: *relations* of world-scale accumulation, which subjugate economically and politically weaker economies, the relations which are controlled by the big monopolies which are based in imperialist countries and make use of their state power in their own interests.

[100] The role of imperialism is not diminished by the fact that at given point, inter-imperialist rivalry is less open nor by the fact that a given country in the periphery may catch up with a given country in the core. It is not diminished either by the fact that capital is hypermobile nor indeed by the fact that a part of production is the production of so-called immaterial goods. As long as capitalist class relation exists, uneven development at

the world – whether imperialist or imperialized-- cannot be adequately understood at all except in relation to capitalism-as-imperialism, i.e., the socio-spatial totality of capitalism, called imperialism, the power of which is *concentrated* in the hands of imperialist businesses and imperialist states. Indeed, the imperialist world economy and world polity must be the starting point for any analysis (including of so-called trans-national issues), in which its impact from the standpoint of working masses is examined.

12. Capitalist class relation, in a wider sense, is not just about accumulation by exploitation, although that is its primary moment. It is also about accumulation by dispossession[101]: the creation of conditions for such exploitation to take place. Whether in the periphery or in advanced nations, semi-proletarians and small-scale producers/traders, are being constantly dispossessed by larger domestic and foreign capitalists through extra-economic coercion. Smaller owners are constantly being displaced because of big owners requiring their land for business (e.g., to lay out transportation lines and set up big factories), to speculate on their land/assets, and so on. As well, various kinds of social commons that ordinary people had fought for in the aftermath of the famous proletarian revolution in Russia – government provision of health care and education, etc. – are being privatized and converted into new means of profit-making. Society's inalienable resources (land, water and natural resources and historically developed system of indigenous knowledge about nature and culture) are being converted into commodities, real and fictitious, and turned over into big business. There is a long march of commoditization, making all aspects of human life (including knowledge about plants and animals and our own body) avenues of profit-making. In these days, when the rate of profit from actual production has fallen, buying cheap and selling dear as well as plain plunder and financial swindling in the sphere of fictitious capital have become popular with big business and its political backers (in both the North and the South). [102] The process of dispossession by extra-economic coercion feeds into, and adds to, another process of dispossession: through class-differentiation, which happens when smaller owners gradually lose their assets because they cannot compete with larger owners.[103]
13. Thus capitalism is really marked by three logics as far as relations of production and exchange are concerned. These logics include: accumulation by exploitation of wage-labor (including that of the people who may have access to some productive resources, and some of whom may be unfree labor). They also include: accumulation by dispossession by extra-economic means; and accumulation by class-differentiation. Some of the people who lose access to their land and other assets through these two logics of dispossession/differentiation may be already dependent on the sale of labour power, and will be so increasingly. On top of these, there is accumulation by financialization of various forms. The actual combination of these different logics of accumulation and their relative balance can be time- and place-specific at multiple spatial scales (regional, national, etc.), within the overall long

national and international scale will remain, and the less developed world represents the lower end of the scale of international uneven development, and monopolization of capitalist assets and imperialism will go together.

[101] Harvey (2003). For a brief critical commentary on this concept, see footnote number 166.

[102] See Smith (2010).

[103] This is the process Lenin (1899) emphasized in his *Development of capitalism*.

term dominace of accumulation by exploitation, and thus can be a powerful force behind uneven development.

14. Underlying these necessary effects of the capitalist class system and associated accumulation regimes are its fundamental contradictions: between production for human use and production for exchange; and between the fact that world's production is a socially integrated process but the means of production as well as what is produced are privately owned and controlled, and between the economic-political-cultural interests of a tiny group of property owners and those of ordinary people, who are the vast majority. There is also an immense geographical contradiction: between a production system that is fast globalizing and in many respects already more or less fully globalized, and a political system of regulation which is, more or less, based in the nation-state system. Further, as businesses produce products (e.g., cars) and services (e.g., bank mortgages) without regard to the market, there is a constant tendency towards the overproduction crisis, which leads to commodities, workers and capital sitting idle. This process is reinforced by the fact that capitalists also economize on wage-payment, which means workers cannot buy what they produce; their consumption accounts for most of what is sold. Besides, as machines are used to replace labor, which is the only source of new value (new wealth), the rate of profit over time tends to fall, leading to a crisis: investors do not invest in producing things/services. And this leads to a process where property owners in both the North and the South increasingly switch to speculation to make money: invest money (and often government money and not 'own' money) to make more money without producing anything that can be used by anyone at all to satisfy a need. This gives the false impression that something can come out of nothing, that money can grow out of money, without the mediation of production or even actual exchange of things.[104]
15. Thus the capitalist class system and associated accumulation regime produces immeasurable wealth for the ruling class and countless adverse effects for the working masses: alienation and exploitation; growing inequality between owners (and an upper middle class as its task-masters) and ordinary workers; recurrent economic crisis causing economic insecurity; unemployment and underemployment, low wages and poverty; imperialism; growing authoritarianism; privatization of social and natural commons; degradation of the environment and crippling of the body-mind complex; and reinforcement of politically disabling divisions within the working masses of the world based on race, gender and other practices and notions/discourses. And it creates a situation conducive to profit-making, one in which people's cognitive abilities are stunted through the promotion of various ideologies and through the corruption of culture (including media as well as universities which are increasingly under pressure to serve, and be run like, businesses).
16. Given these and many other adverse impacts on the masses, and given the exploitative nature of class societies, class struggle is always a potential. Class

[104] That one can entirely understand an idea in relation to another idea and the latter in relation to still another idea, and so on, all within the system of ideas, and without any access to things outside of the system of ideas, all this is very much in line with the idea that money can grow out of itself without any objective act of production.

struggle happens over a greater share of the social product and for making daily living and working conditions tolerable. The struggle is aimed initially at one or two employers, and then a group of employers, against all employers, and against the state itself. Class struggle becomes more acute when the contradictions such as those shown above become more severe. This happens when contradictions deepen between social/class relations and productive forces, resulting in the development of the latter being blocked, and when the ruling class, resorting to a class fix, seeks to shift the burden of the crisis on to the masses. This is achieved through heightened levels of exploitation and withdrawal of state support for reproduction of masses. Currently, Arab Springs, Occupy movements, anti-austerity protests, factory strikes, struggles in aboriginal areas against dispossession and so on testify to these processes.

17. Capitalism -- both as a class relation in general and as a class relation in the specifically capitalist form -- cannot exist for a day without the capitalist state. Capitalism, like all forms of class relation, needs a state to manage conflicts – economic, political and ideological – within the ruling class, and to protect private property relations from the property-less. The capitalist state protects property relations in many ways. Assuming the democratic form is one of these: giving formal political equality, a vote to each person. This helps in masking substantive equality, and channelizes some anger against the system to the safe route of changing the government to manage the affairs of the capitalist state and deciding which members of the ruling class are going to govern. When inequality in the system rises significantly, when a small section is numerous times better off than the vast majority, and when it is increasingly difficult for the state to provide even small concession to the masses (in 'return' for their democratic consent), maintaining the democratic mask becomes increasingly difficult, however. This is why we see increasing authoritarianism even in so-called liberal democratic regimes in North and South. Using surveillance and repressive measures, the state attacks the minimal democratic rights of the people, including the right to form independent unions (independent of companies and of union bureaucrats) and right to strike and to launch fundamental criticisms of the system.[105] Repression and sheer deception are not always effective nor are they always cheap. When there is a serious threat to property relations, or when certain dominant fractions can benefit from a market for goods and services, and to sustain a general climate of peace, the state can offer, and has offered, limited concessions to the masses (e.g., minimum wage, social housing and health-care), and this has happened especially when accumulation process is nationally embedded allowing the state to have a certain amount of 'control' over business; however, the state gives concessions in a such a way that the masses remain politically and ideologically disorganized in the long-term, and that these concessions can be withdrawn
18. But protecting class relations at the level of property relations is not enough in capitalism. The state must ensure conditions for capitalist accumulation: without accumulation of money, private property relations are of no use to property-owners.

[105] Capitalism results in and/or makes use of undemocratic practices. A fight against these by the masses, if it has to have a global and lasting success, must be against capitalism itself and not just against this or that undemocratic aspect only.

Merely holding on to private property (including money) will not deliver surplus product – profits – to the owners. Money has to be put to use. Promotion of accumulation (in production or in finance, etc.) becomes a means of protecting and sustaining private property relations, which in turn make accumulation possible. To be able to manage conflicts among property owners and to be able to ensure in particular, that general economic-political conditions of accumulation are produced/ reproduced, even if doing so may hurt some owners, the state must have some autonomy vis a vis the whole class and even its dominant fractions. However, because of competition between capitalists (even among monopolists), specific capitalists or blocs of capitalists try to influence the state (including through bribing) – its specific officials, politicians, parties and trade union bureaucrats -- to gain a competitive advantage, and the state is amenable to this, within the limits of its more general function (i.e., protection of capitalist class relation and ensuring general conditions of accumulation). When ordinary people are not able to sell their only commodity to earn a decent living, states, in which powerful positions are increasingly occupied by individuals from the world of business and their intellectual backers, make sure, and are made to make sure, that moneybags lose no opportunity to make money, not only to buy cheap and sell dear but also to ruthlessly exploit workers through both normal market mechanisms as well as by other means. Not only are social commons (state support for the masses) being privatized and the regime of social regulation (including taxation) over big business being lifted/weakened and indeed disregarded/violated producing disasters, but also the big business is being provided increasing direct financial support from the states, which ultimately comes from pockets of ordinary people.

19. If the state fails to do this or that for the masses, it is not necessarily because the ruling classes do not allow it to do so: the so-called ruling classes comprise a very small minority of the population in every country, and it would be extremely easy for the state, with all its monopoly over force, to control these people and dispossess them, and work on behalf of the majority. This would be the democratic thing to do. This would be especially expected on the part of the states which claim allegiance to the nation of democracy and in whose name indeed they kill people and destroy countries. But to say that the state can get rid of the ruling classes is to assume that the state and ruling classes are externally connected. The capitalist state is a state of, and for, the. ruling classes of different countries. It is a class institution, pure and simple, no matter what else it may be from time to time and in this or that place, no matter how democratic and rule-bound it may appear to be.
20. Controlling the masses through concessions, trickery, deception and fear and repression – is not enough. The system makes use of pre-capitalist relations of race and gender to *divide* the masses and obfuscate their real interests.[106] These ideologies allow employers to socially construct – define – large segments of the working people as less-than-human, so they can be justifiably paid below-average-wages and be denied normal democratic rights, a process which in turn allows employers to stay competitive in the national and global markets; the same ideologies make sure that

[106] Veblen (1904) talks about capital's ability to exploit irrationalities such as nationalism and racism (through its control over media) in its conflict with labor.

these segments are defined as docile and as lacking power to resist super-exploitation (=above-average exploitation). Capitalist class relation divides the majority of the humanity – all those who must sell their ability to work or who must sell the product of their own labor to eke out a living -- on grounds (e.g., gender or skin color) which are, scientifically or politically, not acceptable. Ideologies of race and gender, dominantly aimed at the economic super-exploitation and political oppression of large segments of the working population, are then generalized (which is why working people also accept these as real and even practice these same ideologies). And these ideologies, reinforced by discriminatory practices, make sure that, for example, when some women or low-caste people, or aboriginal people or Blacks are poor, poverty appears to be caused by – and poverty is sought to be explained by most elements in the academia/media mainly in terms of-- gender or caste, indigeneity, or race relations (or worse, these identities), rather than in terms of underlying property relations and associated accumulation mechanisms, which may be reinforced through the above-mentioned social relations such as gender and race. Consequently, 'appropriate' policies are fought for and sought to be implemented (e.g., various anti-discrimination policies seeking equity) in abstraction from the issue of who controls society's resources and their use. The only product of these fights and resultant policies is to further reinforce gender and race relations and their ideologies (it is true some relatively privileged sections among these groups (so-called equity-seekers including middle class professors, government servants, small-scale entrepreneurs, etc.) do get some benefits from time to time, a result which also produces another ideology, which is mistakenly-held idea that the exercise of human *agency* by putting little pressure on the system can bring significant results and that the *system* is not as rigid as it is thought out to be, and that the system's rigidity and totalizing character is merely an imaginary thing. The major objective effect of these practices is to eschew the only politics that will free women, racial and ethnic minorities and aboriginal people from poverty and many other crushing problems: putting society's resources in the hands of all working people irrespective of who they are in terms of race, caste, gender, and indigeneity.

21. Many other types of ideology are produced to mask/justify capitalism. Neoliberalism – the idea that market knows the best, and when it fails, the state supporting the market or big business knows the best.[107]Other ideologies include: possessive individualism, commodity fetishism, legal citizenship (which helps to channelize anger against class relations to safer legal channels), electoralism, 'growth-ism', reformism, localism as well as freedom, deserving poor, booms and bust as natural events, eternally competitive human nature, self-help and social capital, empowerment through micro-enterprises, free trade as a panacea, and so on. These ideologies are produced by objective conditions. For example, because people must buy food in capitalism, they think food being bought and sold – food being a commodity -- is an inherent characteristic of food itself, thus what is a social relation is naturalized.[108] The ruling class as well as middle class people who support the

[107] This is discussed in detail in Chapter 8 on the topic.

[108] It is interesting that under capitalism, what is not natural (that things do not have to be bought and sold for a profit) appears natural, and what is irreducibly natural (i.e., aspects of nature) appears to be totally socially produced, i.e., not-natural.

reproduction of the system in slightly more tolerable forms also create and disseminate certain ideas – false ideas and false hopes -- in the minds of the masses. This fact partly explains why the masses treat what are actually interests of the ruling class as their own interests. So while the system, more or less, has come to *exist* independently of the will and consciousness of the people, both property owners and the masses (indeed, capitalism preceded the theory of capitalism!), its reproduction – continued existence -- is very much dependent on, among other things, a certain form of social consciousness, including false ideas. This is not to deny that: the actual and threatened use of coercion (both economic and physical) is much more fundamental than false ideas to the reproduction of the system.

22. But the space of that social consciousness is uneven. The fact that the objective structure of class relations determines our consciousness does not mean that there exists only system-reproducing ideas. Given its contradictory character, its effects on ideas must be contradictory. Both system-supporting ideas and critiques of the system are produced. The task of Marxism as the most intransigent of explanatory critique of the system is to transform the social consciousness of a significant numbers of workers, and win the majority of them *for* the idea against the system. Ideas – both system-supporting and critiques of the system -- influence class struggle, i.e., struggle of the capitalist class,_which is conducted through the state policies and through its own economic strategies of (e.g., the strategies aimed to increasing the level of unemployment which weaken the power of the masses), as well as the struggle of the masses. The struggle of the masses happens over concessions within the system and are aimed at transcending the system.

From Class Analysis to Class Abolition, or, from Explanatory Critique to Radical Practice

1. The existence of adverse effects of the capitalist class system on the masses – economic, political, ideological and ecological -- is internally connected to the capitalist system, meaning that they are essential consequences of, and cannot be separated from, capitalist class relations and the associated accumulation logic, although the form in which they appear and their intensity can vary over time and between places. Therefore: the capitalist class relation, along with its law of value, plus the remnants of any non-capitalist relations, must be *transcended* at the urban, regional and national scales, and most importantly, the global scale. What also needs transcending is the political-intellectual/ ideological support system, and the system of race-, gender-, caste-, nationality-based ideologies and practices as well as manual-non manual labor and rural-urban distinctions, all of which capitalism makes use of. Such transcendence of the capitalist class relation and the processes and discourses that support this relation, in an integrated and uninterrupted multi-scalar process is a necessary condition for world socialism. Such a project of transcendence can only be a global affair, although it may begin at lower scales, and this is because the capitalist class relation works through the law of value (and not merely through political discourses/actions), a law, which works globally. It also recognizes that

female and ethnic-minority capitalists cannot escape the global law of value and the gaze of the mobile financial capital and they will exploit the working class as ruthlessly as any other capitalist[109], and that emancipation from class is the necessary condition for gender- and race-based discrimination. [110] Given the huge misunderstanding of Marxism, it should be re-emphasized that Marxism is fundamentally against racial and gender discrimination, wherever it exists (including within the working class).

2. Socialism includes a system of cooperative production, which is guided by the logic of human need (not profit, rent and interest). It is guided by an ethic of 'work as need', and as enjoyment, rather than work as an expenditure of abstract labor time, and by a principle of optimal care for nature and for one another. And the fight for socialism is not only a fight for substantive equality and genuine popular democracy, and democracy in all spheres of human life, but also for a world without domination and wars, the wars in which it is mainly the working masses, not property-owners, who die. The fight for socialism is a fight for food, democracy and peace. It was this a hundred years ago. It is this now.
3. The humanity's – or the global majority's – interest, objectively speaking, is in world socialism, and not in a capitalism which is less neoliberal, less corrupt, less commodified, and more democratic, more ecologically friendly, more egalitarian, more inclusive. It is not in a capitalism, which is less imperialistic or one that is less influenced by imperialism. The humanity's interest is not in a capitalism with a human face, one which cares for one gender a little better or gives concessions to an ethnic minority group here or there, which are entirely reversible and which hardly cost the ruling class as a whole anything much. In other words, what is not the immediate or long-term destination/goal is a capitalism that is slightly more regulated, whether it is regulated: by unions (which, more or less and economistically, see workers merely as sellers of commodity-labor-power in this or that place), by smaller producer's associations (seeking to protect small producers against competition from big business), by Left political parties (which see working masses mainly as Left voters who can put pressure on this or that government for reforms), by nationalistic governments (which see masses as fragments of a class-less nation and which seek a space of autonomy vis a vis mobile global capital), or by NGOs, (new) social movements, cultural politics, or charismatic leaders.
4. All of them seek to play a role in making the system a little more tolerable (and locally), and so-called critical scholars have put much faith in them. For them, the best that is possible is social democracy of some form.[111] All of them, more or less,

[109] Women CEOs (e.g. the Indian-origin Indra Nooyi) of Pepsico or Black employers/managers in South Africa or aboriginal and low-caste businesses are every bit exploitative as other kinds of capitalists.

[110] The recent episode in South Africa of the miners' strike in which black workers were killed by black police exposes the vacuity of racial politics abstracted from class. Racial and gender politics, in abstraction from the centrality of class, more or less represents ideas and interests of petty bourgeois and bourgeois interests among women and minorities.

[111] They often see the masses as those *to whom* good things can be done or as those whose spontaneous actions are enough to make big changes. They also see the masses as those whose level of radical consciousness against the system can *at most* be what *these critics* supporting the continued reproduction of capitalism in a slightly reformed state have managed to have reached and can reach. They see the reflection of their own political-discursive identity in the masses at the current level of consciousness of the latter. The issue of social democracy is taken up in chapter 7.

seek to engage in (cultural-political) recognition and/or some redistribution. [112]They seek to 'restore the centrality of politics over the tyranny of market forces'.[113] These forces seek to deal with or regulate [114] -- *the appearances of the mechanisms*[115] of the system or certain effects of the ways mechanisms are played out (e.g., excesses of capitalism or specific social-spatial forms of capitalism such more globalized/ monopolistic capitalism or financial form of capitalism or its more authoritarian political forms or its patriarchal or racist forms). These forces do not want to confront and deal with *the mechanisms as such*, with the class character and the associated drive to accumulate for the sake of it, without regard for human need or ecological sustainability. The forms through which capitalism is reproduced and the excesses it produces are the more concrete processes (advisedly called appearances here) through which capitalist class and accumulation logics are reproduced in specific times and places, and therefore the fight against these excesses and forms can only genuinely succeed, and succeed for the majority of the global working population (i.e., the working masses) and on a long-term, sustainable basis, only when that fight becomes one against these logics as such, against the very system of class relations. The appearances or the excessive effects of the operation of the mechanisms (the appearances that are not unreal though), cannot be controlled/regulated over the long term and globally unless the mechanisms themselves are controlled: here control means elimination, because class mechanisms (antagonistic class interests), because of their nature, cannot be controlled.[116] Class relations control the 'mechanisms of control'. When the appearances succeed in making people believe that they (appearances and excesses) can be effectively controlled without doing anything about that which causes them in the first place, the ideological function of the appearances – and the individual and social agents which are bearers of the appearances (e.g., bourgeois unions, reformist Left parties) -- is complete: the appearances have been able to mask the real thing that underlies the appearances. If capitalism is democratic here and makes use of gender there, a fight against the absence of democracy or against gender inequality can only genuinely succeed when it becomes a part of the fight against capitalism as such. There are many things wrong in the society. Dialectically seen, these are all inter-connected. We live in a concrete conjuncture, in which 'even partial reforms are impossible without a complete overhaul of the system (=revolution)'.[117] This is precisely the

---

[112] No one can be against recognition. Everyone needs to be treated with self-respect and dignity. But people also need to eat and find shelter. And any political project that merely emphasizes redistribution forgets that production/class relations set limits on what is possible to redistribute, because patterns of distributive inequality emerge from specific patterns of production relations.

[113] Laclau and Mouffe (2014): p. xviii-xix.

[114] Note that the problem is not regulation as such. The problem is regulation in what class condition? When workers and poor peasants take power and control state power, existing big business enterprises may not be immediately socialized, but these are under the control of, regulation of, workers and peasants and their directly elected representatives. Lenin: 'The question is not how fast to move, but where to move' (Lenin 1964:33).

[115] I am aware that many people on the Left do vehemently oppose the distinction between appearances and deeper structures. This is a completely mistaken opposition as is the opposition to determination, metanaratives, and privileging certain processes over others.

[116] Our society 'is like the sorcerer, who is no longer able to control the powers of the nether world whom he has called up by his spells'. http://www.marxists.org/archive/marx/works/1848/communist-manifesto/ch01.htm

[117]This is the kind of ideas Trotsky made use of to construct his theory of permanent revolution (a concept which was first introduced by Marx). This is a theory which forces a dagger to the heart of all kinds of Marxist

reason why Marxism is counter-posed to political proposals of, and theories underlying, the following: social democracy, identity politics (which s divorced from class politics), class collaborationism with sections of the ruling class or the whole ruling class and an attempt at some kind of socialism in one region/country. [118]

5. If capitalism is the immediate target, what is needed is political-ideological mobilization[119] of the masses (particularly wage workers and rural poor)[120] against the capitalist class relation and the propertied class as such, *and* from a proletarian, internationalist, and socialist standpoint. And this mobilization is seen as politically *independent* of the agents just mentioned: individuals, groups, political parties and movements of the petty bourgeois, regional bourgeois, 'national'-bourgeois classes or indeed of this or that faction of the bourgeoisie (e.g., agrarian, industrial, or financial fractions), the groups which deal with this or that appearance or excess of capitalism. This means that no alliance/support of working masses is necessary and possible with any petty bourgeois and bourgeois movements/parties/governments.[121] Such an alliance is the seed of self-decimation and/or class-collaborationism, no matter what cheap popularity or democratic respectability it may bring in temporarily. It is another matter that *individuals* belonging to these classes and defecting from these classes may help the masses in the anti-capitalist movements.
6. Socialism is about the self-emancipation of working masses and by these masses, and not by communist party bureaucracies or another form of intermediary. However, large sections of the masses currently do not possess proletarian, anti-capitalist consciousness. This is because of the ways in which the capitalist system works (its dull economic compulsion, its ideological and repressive system, the capitalist reality itself being a source of mystification, always naturalizing exchange relations and private property[122]). This is also because of the ways in which supposedly anti-

---

thinking including Stalinism and its peasantist-version, Maoism, according to which classlessness could be achieved in particular parts of the world in abstraction from a revolution at an international scale, from the international law of value. As Lenin said: 'we have always urged and reiterated the elementary truth of Marxism—that the joint efforts of the workers of several advanced countries are needed for the victory of socialism' http://www.marxists.org/archive/lenin/works/1922/feb/x01.htm

[118] As Panitch (1997:1) argues: 'There is popular resistance, people continue to fight back, they hold on to values that assert our humanity in the face of global commodification. But ... socialists [must not] ... shrink from a ruthless criticism of the limits of this resistance in so far as it is not socialist, even not yet fundamentally anti-capitalist; nor should we desist from criticising those socialists who still blithely imagine that every popular resistance has it in its genes to become socialist. What we know now, more clearly than ever, is that what is on offer, by either neoliberalism or social democracy today, does not provide solutions to contemporary capitalism's problems and injustices, let alone acceptable alternatives in terms of socialist goals and values of the defeatist and confused 'post-' intellectuals of our time, who would leave us with no analytic capacity, let alone with no commitment, with which to contribute today to the eventual relaunching of socialist politics'.

[119] Political mobilization of these classes is necessary against the ruling classes because the latter and the state controlled by them will not give up economic and political power which is necessary for lasting solutions to the problems class society creates.

[120] An alliance between these classes is made possible by the development of transportation and communication technologies linking villages and cities. And an alliance is necessary in part because peasants' livelihood, like workers', is undermined by capitalism, that a large proportion of peasants functions, less as property owners and more as a rurally-located reserve army of labor (including when they work as seasonal migrants in cities, working alongside permanent workers) and therefore they increasingly belong to the working class as such.

[121] From the *correct* claim that masses are not yet sufficiently class conscious, many *wrongly* infer that masses and their leaders should collaborate with ruling classes. The correct inference is: increase the level of their class-consciousness through ideological education and practical struggles informed by a class-conscious perspective.

[122] Although capitalism ruins small-scale producers, it also constantly generates them. This happens through gradual proletarianization of larger property owners: labor-employing property owners start losing their means of

capitalist forces have contributed to reformist consciousness, including bourgeois trade unionist and electoralist consciousness. The masses should be mobilized by democratically-organized but disciplined parties led by theoretically and politically advanced elements of the working class, initially for/around people's immediate needs, the satisfaction of which society has the resources for, and which have been created by the masses (under the tutelage of the bourgeoisie), but which are not used for the masses.[123] These needs include: a living wage and decent income for self-employed people including middle and poor peasants, an income that is determined by socially defined needs and not by an absolute poverty line; free and decent housing, education and health care, and free transportation; benefits for physically and mentally impaired and for older people past the retirement age; *complete* equality between men and women and people of different sexual orientation; return of childhood to children and complete stoppage of child- wage-labor; pollution-free environment; freedom from violence by state and hired musclemen and private agents of property owners; and opportunities for cultural advancement. The patent failure of the states, in both imperialist and imperialized countries, must be politically exposed. It is possible that the masses' anger against the system will force the system, which becomes fearful of worse things, to meet some of these needs. The process of mobilization of people, including self-mobilization informed by a proper, conscious, theoretical perspective, for these immediate demands will raise their level of political consciousness. This will happen due to a contradiction: between their needs and the system's imperative, between *their* needs and capital's needs (for profit and domination). The contradiction will be experienced when masses see that the current system cannot meet their legitimate needs because of the system's objective as well as subjective constraints (e.g., excessive boundless greed of those with animal spirits; ideas in the minds of political managers that the masses do not deserve a life of dignity and security). The Marxist perspective demands that 'class-conscious workers must win the majority of the masses to their side' (Lenin 1964:40) and the present conditions must be overthrown, as Marx says, because they cannot be reformed, for this is a society characterized by 'A mass of antithetical forms of the

---

production and reach a stage where they work as self-employed, with their own private property, which is reproduced through individual/family labor as opposed capitalist private property. Some property-less workers by virtue of below-average level of consumption (personal savings, etc.) and/or through remittance income from family members and such other personal strategies can become small-scale owners. The interests of small-owners are antagonistically related to capitalist interests due to competition, so at times they turn against big business, only in order to protect their own private property. The ideas (e.g. cultural superiority of small-scale ownership) and interests of small-scale owners are reflected in ideas/actions of petty bourgeois, opportunistic parties, movements, theories as in muchordinary commonsense.

123 'The revolution that modern socialism strives to achieve is, briefly, the victory of the proletariat over the bourgeoisie and the establishment of a new organisation of society by the destruction of all class distinctions. This requires not only a proletariat to carry out this revolution, but also a bourgeoisie in whose hands the social productive forces have developed so far that they permit the final destruction of class distinctions. ...Only at a certain level of development of these social productive forces, even a very high level for our modern conditions, does it become possible to raise production to such an extent that the abolition of class distinctions can constitute real progress, can be lasting without bringing about stagnation or even decline in the mode of social production. But the productive forces have reached this level of development only in the hands of the bourgeoisie. The bourgeoisie, therefore, in this respect also is just as necessary a precondition for the socialist revolution as is the proletariat itself. Hence a man who says that this revolution can be more easily carried out in a country where, although there is no proletariat, there is no bourgeoisie either, only proves that he has still to learn the ABC of socialism'. http://www.marxists.org/archive/marx/works/1874/refugee-literature/ch05.htm

social unity, whose antithetical character [class character] can never be abolished through quiet metamorphosis'.[124] If the current system does not meet the needs of the working masses, then the workers, who have the ability to develop the productive forces further and use them for their need, will gradually demand that the current exploitative and undemocratic class system be replaced by an economically and politically democratic system at national and global scales, and they will make this demand with the assistance of the supporting party-organizations coordinating their activities nationally and internationally, both inside and outside the legislative spaces.[125]

Conclusion

Marxist explanatory critique must be dialectical (it must see society as changing and as internally contradictory). It must be materialist, i.e., it must not only emphasize an objectively existing reality but also that that reality is material in the scientific sense: important aspects of that reality are both the biological-physical character of human bodies, the physical-biological nature existing independent of human actions, *and* human relations with one another and with nature that are necessary for the reproduction of life. [126] It must not ignore how the objective reality is seen/perceived by people (by different classes and groups) and reacted to. It must be mindful, in both explanatory and political sense, of the reality of non-class oppression (both in material and discursive terms), which always interweaves with, and complicates the effect of, class relations and class struggles. The Marxist critique must be multi-scalar, and especially internationalist, emphasizing the international nature of both capitalism and the fact that a potentially successful anti-capitalist struggle must be ultimately international. It must show that people's fight for autonomy and democracy including gender and racial equality and for democratic transparency, to be genuinely successful, cannot but be a part of the fight against capitalism itself. And it must be emancipatory. 'The primary task of the 'Marxist critic' [in the broadest sense] is to actively participate in and help direct the cultural [and political and economic] emancipation of the masses' (Eagleton, 2009:97).

A Marxist critic cannot blur crucial class distinctions and other social distinctions closely associated with these, and cannot obscure that moment within radical, working-class, popular and resistance movements, which is against the ruling class. A Marxist critique is one that is genuinely in the tradition of social critique/analysis begun by Marx and Engels. Being in this tradition does not mean that one must spend time on when Marx or Engels had their breakfast and what they wrote after dinner on such and such a date. Nor can one merely resort to this or that statement from Marx, Engels or Lenin to prove one's point. It cannot also be that: Marx or others in his legacy are beyond theoretical and empirical criticisms (of the type that are

[124] http://www.marxists.org/archive/marx/works/1857/grundrisse/ch03.htm

[125] The idea behind these spaces is spatial fetishism of sorts: that representatives of a *geographical* area (a parliamentary constituency) represent the interests and ideas of a *social* group, the masses, or the majority defined in class terms. This way – and there are other ways such as use of money power and muscle power, etc. -- parliamentarism neutralizes the class character of the masses.

[126] Trotsky (1939a) writes: 'Marx's method is materialistic, because it proceeds from existence to consciousness, not the other way around. Marx's method is dialectic, because it regards both nature and society as they evolve, and evolution itself as the constant struggle of conflicting forces'. http://www.marxists.org/archive/trotsky/1939/04/marxism.htm

mentioned in Chapter 1). 'Marx is the beginning of the radical critique of modern times, starting with the critique of the real world… To be a Marxist is to *continue* the work that Marx *merely began*, even though that beginning was of an unequaled power. It is not to stop at Marx, but to start from him', says Amin (2010: 9-10; italics added). There is indeed a need to continue the work which he merely began because 'capital's power today is less challenged than in the nineteenth century' (Dowd, 2002: 2), when Marx was critiquing it. And, there are numerous things he did not talk about or did not adequately talk about (e.g., imperialism; under-development of the periphery; nature of the state; gender and race relations; spatial unevenness inside a country and between countries; ethics), and this applies to major critics in *his* tradition. The spirit of ruthless criticism applies to Marxism as well. There must be a Marxist analysis of Marxism. To put it more dialectically: given the *present state* of knowledge about society and given the way society is organized, what is called Marxism has the best method of analysis and the strongest set of empirically verifiable propositions about the world; and to the extent that it may and does contain errors, these can, and should be, corrected but such a process of correction is unlikely to undermine the central categories of Marxism.[127] Some of the statements about more changeable aspects of society may need revision indeed, in the light of changes in material conditions and in the ways in which these are thought about.[128] What Marx and others do talk about must be critically examined partly from the vantage point of what they do *not* talk about: perhaps what they do talk about requires a certain revision, which is necessitated by the consideration of what they do not talk about. What about non-Marxist work (critique), work that is not Marxist? If non-Marxist work – including non-Marxist critique – is not good, it is not because it cannot be given the label Marxist[129] but because it is inadequate on philosophical, social-theoretical and scientific/explanatory grounds as well as on practical grounds. [130] But elements of non-

[127] Non-Marxist critique of Marxism is an *external* critique, which is not be conflated with the strong tradition of *internal* critiques. Similarly, Marxism (e.g. Marx's work) is an external critique of bourgeois thought (e.g. classical political economy), while there are numerous internal critiques of bourgeois thought (e.g. John Stuart Mill; in today's world, people like Raghuram Rajan); the internal critiques reflect contradictions within the ruling class and reflect the different strategies (including enlightened self interest and reformism) of ruling class elements about how to save capitalism from itself.

[128]Althusser (2005) talked about an epistemological break between young and mature Marx. It is possible to argue another 'epistemological break', between economic analysis (political economy) and analysis of state and ideologies, etc., which cannot be analysed in the same rigorous way as the more economic aspects of society, in part because they are more 'overdetermined', more concrete; political processes (including conflicts between 'people' and between them and the state, and how they are responded to in action) emerge out of, but cannot be reduced to, the economic. 'With the change of the economic foundation the entire immense superstructure is more or less rapidly transformed. In considering such transformations *a distinction should always be made between the material transformation of the economic conditions of production, which can be determined with the precision of natural science*, and the legal, political, religious, aesthetic or philosophic — in short, ideological forms in which men become conscious of this conflict and fight it out.' http://www.marxists.org/archive/marx/works/1859/critique-pol-economy/preface-abs.htm.

Even with respect to economic issues, statements may require revisions. Consider this. Analysing the dynamics of capital accumulation, Marx pointed out that in its most basic form its driving force was the transformation of money into an even greater quantity of money, with the process of production appearing simply as a "necessary evil for the purpose of money-making." This explained, Engels noted, why all capitalist nations are periodically "seized by fits of giddiness in which they try to accomplish money-making without the mediation of the production process." What was a "fit" in the days of Marx and Engels has now become a permanent condition of the global capitalist economy.

[129] To believe *that* will be to agree with non-Marxists who dismiss Marxist arguments by just saying 'that is a Marxist a view'.

[130] It should also be said that in non-Marxist analyses and critiques of society, and partly given the widespread revolt against scientific thinking, the economic (the articulation/combination of productive forces and relations

Marxist work, including about those features of the human material and discursive condition which are true about all forms of class society, can be, where necessary, incorporated into the Marxist analysis. Yet the crucial difference between the Marxist and *all* other forms of critique remains: the Marxist critique is a critique of the objectively existing system from the standpoint of the possibility and necessity of transcendence of the system and from the standpoint of the property-less toilers, while other traditions of critique are critical of merely this or that part of the system or this or that appearance or remediable imperfection of the system, and are, 'at best', from the standpoint of small-scale producers (and weaker capitalists and bureaucratic -- governmental and non-governmental -- managers and middle-class intellectual supporters of the system). The Marxist critique is system-transcending. The non-Marxist critique is ultimately system-reproducing, and this fact ultimately 'explains', and comes from, the uncritical character – or inadequately critical character of -- of its critique.

As argued in this chapter and in this book as a whole, Marxism – the Marxist critique -- *is* about class. It is about relations and divisions. It is about class struggle. But it is *more* than that. It is also about the abolition of class and the establishment of the democratic rule of the working masses, the majority of the population, who will self-rule and will not be ruled by any other force. This idea – about the necessity of abolition – comes from the first idea: that class is the fundamental cause of humanity's problems and that *within* the class system these problems of the masses of the world, including of the imperialized countries, cannot be resolved, and therefore the existing dictatorship of the property-owning oligarchy and undemocratic class-rule must be replaced by the democratic rule of the world's masses, initially organized through a state of their own. Here is Lenin from his *The State and revolution*:

> It is often said and written that the main point in Marx's theory is the class struggle. But this is wrong. And this wrong notion very often results in an opportunist distortion of Marxism and its falsification in a spirit acceptable to the bourgeoisie. For the theory of the class struggle was created not by Marx, but by the bourgeoisie before Marx, and, generally speaking, it is acceptable to the bourgeoisie. Those who recognize only the class struggle are not yet Marxists; they may be found to be still within the bounds of bourgeois thinking and bourgeois politics. To confine Marxism to the theory of the class struggle means curtailing Marxism, distorting it, reducing it to something acceptable to the bourgeoisie. Only he [or she] is a Marxist who extends the recognition of the class struggle to the recognition of the dictatorship of the proletariat. That is what constitutes the most profound distinction between

---

and associated accumulation process, and exchange and distribution mechanisms) is no longer subjected to the kind of rigorous analysis that is necessary. What appears to be – or what is offered as -- economic analysis is really a tasteless and nutritionally deficient soup of bits of the economic, the political and the cultural, a soup in which the latter two ingredients are more heavily present relative to the first. As mentioned earlier, only poor economic analysis is the result, one in which the economic is wooly; it, more or less, concerns market (including labor market) relations and consumption, and increasingly their cultural/ideational/discursive aspects. As soon as an economic process is mentioned, it disappears into the thin air of the discursive. Another trend, typical of postmodern economic narratives, is this: terms are lifted from Marxism (because one gains from Marxism' prestige) -- the *terms* which signify serious *concepts* -- but are used, mixed with random phrases of some esoteric philosophers, in such ways as have little resemblance with the terms original meanings. By falsely appropriating ideas from Marxism, one, at the same time, goes beyond Marxism in a critical and innovative way. This sort of malpractice – indeed academic dishonesty -- does not even leave such concepts as value and capital alone. This is a travesty of conceptual rigor. And because the economic -- and class -- underpinnings of the political and the cultural are, more or less, lost sight of, political and cultural analysis is also impoverished. The overall result: social critique – social analysis – suffers. [See also footnote nos. 68 and 84]

the Marxist and the ordinary petty (as well as big) bourgeois. This is the touchstone on which the real understanding and recognition of Marxism should be tested. And it is not surprising that when ... the working class [encounters] face to face with this question as a practical issue, not only all the opportunists and reformists, but all the ....people who vacillate between reformism and Marxism...prove to be miserable philistines and petty-bourgeois democrats repudiating the dictatorship of the proletariat.[131]

[131] http://www.marxists.org/archive/lenin/works/1917/staterev/ch02.htm

PART 2: CRITIQUING EXISTING CRITICAL IDEAS

Chapter 3

UNPACKING POLITICISM AND IDEALISM IN STATE THEORY: A CRITIQUE OF POST-MARXIST CRITIQUE

The state has been at the center of much theoretical discussion in social sciences. The debate on the state intersects in interesting ways with concerns of broader social theory, including those about class, and the relation between the economic and the political. The state has been looked at from the standpoints of major social theories (including feminism, Marxism, and liberalism). The map of state theory indeed reflects major arguments in social theory as such.

The 1970s and the 1980s marked the high point of 'meta narratives' on the state, of grand state theorizing, which aimed at making broader generalizations about the nature of the state, about the ways in which it works and produces effects. The famous Poulantzas-Miliband debate and its various derivative discussions on that debate were an important part of the discussion during this period. It should be added that thanks to the postmodern theory and its lingering impact on social science research, the passion for state theorizing of this type has been dampened a bit. In postmodernism, the focus is switched away from political economy and towards more cultural issues as these are manifested at the *local* scale, including the body-scale. By conceptualizing power as a diffuse and noneconomic relation, postmodern epistemology shifted attention away from the state, an apparatus that embodies a centralized form of class power. Yet, state theory remains a fertile area for many progressive social scientists.

In state theory, the state is seen as a complex entity with multiple aspects (see Das, 1996). A study of the existing literature on the state – and most of this has focused on advanced countries -- indicates that, broadly speaking, there are three kinds of analysis. One is the 'society-centric' approach, which looks at how the state must create conditions for accumulation, and how it reflects the interests and ideas of particular socio-economic groups within a given social formation. The state is perceived as implementing policies in furtherance of such interests. In Marxist circles, class interests and actions – those of property owners and lower classes -- have been emphasized. Feminists have stressed the interests of men vs women; the state is inherently patriarchal. Other social theories have stressed the influence of other non-state actors/agencies' (races, castes) on the state. Another is the 'state-centric' approach, which argues that the state shapes society in ways that do not necessarily reflect the interests of any single non-state socio-economic group. In the (left) liberal tradition (which overlaps with the post-Marxist and Weberian traditions), for example, government agencies – state-managers -- are said to take 'initiatives well beyond the demands of social groups', and are 'the most prominent participants in the making of policy decisions' (Skocpol, 1985: 4). The state – its organizations and managers -- discharges a role that many characterize as autonomous. Indeed, it is argued that state managers look after their own interests, which do not necessarily coincide with those of any group outside the state. In some contexts (e.g., some less developed countries), as emphasized in the developmental state literature, state managers are seen as able to discipline even fractions of the propertied class, and make them contribute to the national development agenda set by the former. Many scholars stress corrupt practices of state officials/politicians and deficiencies in the organizations and rules of the state as the major cause of many problems, including low economic growth and poverty. Indeed, the shift in focus has been from the government to governance.

Putting together these two broad approaches (i.e., society-centric and state-centric approaches), one can say that the state can be looked at in terms of economic structure (the imperative of accumulation) and in terms of the agency of dominant classes, lower classes, and state managers, and the various fractions of each of these groups. [132]

John Hoffman is a major state theorist. His book *Beyond the State* – along with many of his other works on this topic -- is an important contribution to the literature on the state, and speaks to some of the issues just mentioned. The present chapter is a critical assessment of this important work of Hoffman, who is now an Emeritus Professor of Politics at Leicester University. An assessment of his influential work would indirectly shed light on, and speak to, the kinds of work (mainly in the *post*-Marxist genre) with which his research shares some common ground (e.g., in terms of its anti-Marxist critique; and an under-emphasis on class). In a sense, this chapter[133] is a critical commentary on the post-Marxist thinking about the state via a discussion on Hoffman's work.

Beyond the State

In this book Hoffman discusses three issues: definitional problems concerning the state; statist and anti-statist assumptions in social theories; and the possibilities for realizing a stateless world. Hoffman accepts Weber's definition of the state as an institution that claims monopoly over legitimate force within a given territory. However, the more the state approximates to this definition, the more problematic its identity becomes. For example, the very need to exercise a monopoly of legitimate force arises only because states are challenged by rebels and criminals. And, the state that succeeds in imposing this monopoly thereby makes itself redundant (65) (unless otherwise noted, the page references are to Hoffman, 1995).

[132] Yet another approach is the 'state-in-society' approach, which seeks to combine these two approaches. It maintains that relations between each element are not given but constructed and – thus – fluid: the state influences society and society influences the state (Migdal, 1994, 2001). The thrust of much this work is, however, Weberian.

[133] This is a aevised version of Das (1999b).

Hoffman maintains, quite ingeniously, a distinction between coercion and physical force (88). People are not free outside society: all relationships involve coercion. But coercion does not prevent people from making choices. Force does. This distinction between coercion and force allows him to distinguish between government and state. Government is a process that resolves differences through coercive practices such as ostracism, economic pressure and moralism, all of which fall short of the use of force. Government, unlike the state, is essential in all societies. This is because without a degree of predictability and regularity, people cannot live together. For Hoffman, the distinction between government and the state is useful in challenging the idea that the state is indispensable to securing order. I think the emancipatory potential of the book lies in this point, a potential which, however, remains unrealized, as I will show.

Having discussed the conceptual character of the state, Hoffman turns his attention to the critiques of the state in major social theories. In particular, he discusses liberalism, anarchism, Marxism, feminism and postmodernism. Liberalism opposes and yet presupposes the necessity for the state. Individuals are naturally free and the state is unnatural. Yet, individuals (have to) accept its force. Anarchism is also both anti-statist (i.e., it rejects the state) and statist. For many anarchists, individuals are individuals only outside society. How then will they cooperate to secure their freedom? And, if individuals are naturally cooperative and their self-activity is inhibited in any social relation, as communitarian anarchists say, then coercion and force are to be opposed. But since all forms of political organizations are unacceptable, anarchists may use force to energize "skeptical masses." For some anarchists, free markets can provide a social cohesion that makes the state redundant. But how will this work, given such problems as political-economic disparities and externalities like pollution?

Marxism aspires to statelessness. But it is also inherently authoritarian. This is because of its: absolutist view of history, its monopolistic view of the working class as the leader of the revolution, and its dismissive approach to morality (141-142). Feminism argues that the violence that is central to the state is ultimately the violence of men who control the state. But its critical character is blunted by its assertion that the state has no specific significance, because male dominance is everywhere.

Postmodernism is a critique of logocentrism - the notion that binary terms are "adversaries which confront each other in a `zero sum relation'" (164). But logocentrism lies at the heart of the state in that the state seeks to impose monopolistic conformity upon pluralistic diversity. Thus postmodernism has anti-statist implications. But postmodernism is also nihilist. This nihilism makes a critique of the state impossible.

Aspirations to stateless societies expressed in the major theories, if not unambiguously, seem to be realized practically, however. This is the theme of the last part of the book. Hoffman shows that a post-statist world order - an international society - is emerging owing to the existence of common interests. Global problems such as nuclear weaponry, refugees and pollution mean that we all have a common interest in settling our differences governmentally, i.e., through institutions that negotiate, arbitrate and forge consensus (191), rather than use force.

Universal acclamation for democracy works to strengthen the case for statelessness. Democracy can exist in conditions of real pluralism and diversity only if it looks beyond the monopolistic institution of the state (202). However, states are needed to create statelessness. But so long as statist violence helps in pursuing policies to provide resources that empower individuals, it has a self-dissolving role.

Hoffman's work will surely appeal to many, especially (neo-)Weberians and post-Marxists. Indeed, *Beyond the State* seeks to develop a "radical view of the state which goes 'beyond' Marxism" (vii). Hoffman joins the ranks of Laclau, Mouffe, and others in seeking to establish the autonomy of politics and the state from their class roots. The most important contradiction in the book is this: Hoffman's political philosophy is one of anti-statism, but he has a politicist theory of the state and a statist theory of social change. Let me illustrate this.

Whatever Happened to the Class Character of the State?

Hoffman says that the state exists because "rebels and criminals" oppose the state (65). But underlying this idea is the assumption that the state already exists for some causally prior reason. What is that reason? Why is there opposition to the state from "rebels and criminals" in the first place? What is their class character, and why cannot their demands be met "governmentally," as opposed to in a "statist" way?

Hoffman argues that force has to be used because people cannot resolve their differences through negotiation and arbitration alone (79). The question is: "people," or "classes"? Once again, why can't Hoffman's "people" resolve their "differences"? Isn't it that the statist use of force is necessary because *class* "differences" cannot be reconciled through negotiations (and the decentralized use of force)?

In an earlier work, *Marxism and the Theory of Praxis*, Hoffman had said that the state "is and always has been the institutionalized expression of irreconcilable class struggle" (1975:220). But class struggle seems to be underemphasized in his later works, including not only *Beyond the State* but also *State, Power and Democracy* (1988). In the latter, the state "exists only because its monopoly is continually being challenged" (1988: 45) (a theme that continues in *Beyond the State* as well); the state "monopolize[s] legitimate force only because it institutionalizes a division between rulers and ruled" (1988: 33). There is nothing about the class nature of the rulers and, especially, the ruled, or correlatively about why the state's "monopoly is continually being challenged."

This leads to a related point: *Beyond the state*, which could be easily called *Beyond the Marxist theory of the state*, is consistently Weberian, but this consistency comes at the cost of a class analysis. Hoffman's definition of the state is admittedly Weberian, as is his view of society. Like Weber, the Hoffman of *Beyond the State* has a gradational view, as opposed to a Marxist class-relations view, of social differences; "disparities" are consciously privileged over class exploitation (142). His affinity to Marxism is mainly located where he argues - and he does not argue this always - that the state exists because of "disparities" and that there can be statelessness. Disparities are not unrelated to class, because class is a condition for disparities, but there is a world of difference, theoretically/scientifically and ontologically, between class and disparities. And when class is not given the emphasis it requires, the material basis for statelessness cannot be definitively argued for.

However, I want to stress that the class character of the state is not totally missing in *Beyond the State*. Hoffman does accept that "if the state system operates in the interests of a capitalist minority, then a good deal of force, deception and manipulation is required to ensure its cohesion and stability" (43), and that the state is a class-biased institution (205). So, his work is surely not one of complete neglect but rather of huge under-emphasis on, and under-theorization, of the relation between the state and class relations, with respect to both their origins and their reproduction. The class character of the state and the relation between the working class and the capitalist state are extremely controversial issues. I do not want to say that Hoffman is alone in under-theorizing these issues. He is echoing the arguments of many others, including the so-called post-Marxists (an euphemism for ex-Marxists or non-Marxists whose main connection to Marxism is via critique with an intent to replace Marxism (Marxism-as-class-analysis, as discussed in chapter 2) with various other ways of thinking about the world).

Against Hoffman's Post-Marxist Critique of Marxism

Hoffman's under-emphasis on class, among other things, allows him to make many indefensible criticisms against Marxism, especially his argument that Marxism is inherently authoritarian. This argument has two parts, each of which raises numerous questions. His failure to address these weakens his argument.

First, he argues, the capitalist circumstances that compel workers to resist capitalism may also compel Marxists to make untimely leaps, and take political standpoints that contradict the emancipatory thrust of their theory (140). Untimely leaps result in authoritarian political practices (141). Does Hoffman object to the "untimeliness" of the revolution or to the "leaps" involved in it? He seems to assume a necessary causal relation between the timing of an event (the untimeliness of the revolution) and its nature (authoritarian practices). But why should there be such a relation? Besides, authoritarian for whom? (More on this later.) If Hoffman is, on the other hand, objecting to the leaps involved in the revolution, he is assuming not only a necessary relation between reformism and democracy and between revolution and authoritarianism, but also that historical change occurs only in a gradual, incremental fashion as opposed to a revolutionary one. These assumptions are left unexamined. Further, in saying that revolutions inevitably concentrate power and create illiberal political institutions (p.135), Hoffman not only advocates reformist social change but also wrongly assumes that the consequences of the revolution - what happens in a post-revolution society -- can be determined from the nature of the revolution (so-called "untimely leaps"). The birth of capitalism in Britain - a revolutionary change, in the Marxist view, from pre-capitalist to capitalist social relations - was highly undemocratic, as it involved forceful dispossession of the direct producers; yet few will doubt that Britain is now more democratic than it was in feudal times.

The second part of his argument against Marxism is that a theory of emancipation must allow people to make mistakes, and I agree. Hoffman, however, sees three crucial deficits in Marxism; these prevent Marxists from discouraging certain tendencies -- those resulting in authoritarian political strategies and systems - that work against the post-liberal logic of Marxist theory (132, 141). First, emancipation for Marxists is not simply a possible end that a political movement might achieve, but a unique destination in which inexorable laws guarantee the working class its final victory. This implies that revolutions are part of the natural process of history, and must ultimately succeed. This position ties historical development to only one thinkable option -- socialism - and forces Marxists to support untimely events even if these have authoritarian consequences. This raises many questions. If revolution must succeed, how does it matter if Marxists support untimely events or not? Further, Hoffman has problems with the Marxist idea that there is only one result of the revolution (socialism). But what are the other thinkable alternatives to it? Why doesn't he defend these? Or, should people pursue socialism, barbarism, capitalism, and all other options as well?

Marxism's second deficit, Hoffman complains, is that for Marxists the political struggle has to be the class struggle, in which industrial workers have a leading role (141). This limits an emancipatory project to a particular constituency with a privileged position, a stance that makes it easier to justify authoritarian measures when these are taken either against non-proletarians or against those proletarians who do not listen to Marxists. Hoffman here appears to miss the distinction between primary and secondary contradictions or conflicts, as discussed by Mao. These types of conflict are handled differently. Differences in interests among members of the proletarian class (secondary conflicts) will exist. But why can't these be arbitrated through non-authoritarian measures, through coercion as opposed to physical force (a distinction Hoffman himself maintains)? Conflicts between proletarians and non-proletarians are primary conflicts and must develop differently from the way in which secondary conflicts are managed. In all societies, some restriction is imposed on freedom, as Hoffman rightly says in *Marxism and the Theory of Praxis*. And, to the extent that non-proletarians are exploiting classes, their rights in a post-revolution society have to be curbed, just as the rights of direct producers are curbed in class societies. *Beyond the State* has just about the same abstract concept of democracy/authoritarianism that Hoffman was rightly arguing against in *Marxism and the Theory of Praxis*. His views about class struggle and revolution, like those of many others, are largely -- and implicitly -- based on the conjuncture of the former Soviet Union, where the failed attempt to establish economic and political democracy – socialism – was enormously, if not entirely, due to the failure of revolutionary projects outside of that country and the consequent isolation of the Russian revolution internationally.

The third deficit, reinforcing the second, is that Marxism has never justified the struggle for emancipation in moral terms. Hoffman argues that what makes exploitation repressive is not the technical fact that workers create surplus value, but the disparities of effort and reward which characterize an in-egalitarian unjust society, so that people other than workers are also interested in their emancipation. But privileging workers leads to an authoritarian tendency.

First, this is a highly one-sided way of reading Marxist texts. One finds numerous references to morality not only in Marx's scholarly works, but also in his popular discussions (as in his Confessions to his daughters in 1865).

Second, the idea that workers producing surplus value is a technical fact completely misses the Marxist argument that capitalist production is an ensemble of *social* relations, and that capital is a social power. As Marx explains in *Capital I*, the capitalist labor process involves capitalist despotism. In part due to this, production and extraction of surplus value are subject to class struggle. The question of disparities emphasized by Hoffman is a distributional one; he is not alone here. This is a part of his post-Marxism, which is very popular among so-called critical social scientists of many hues. He fails to see that distribution of product is subsequent to, and heavily conditioned by, the production of (surplus) value. Hoffman's understanding of exploitation as a technical fact makes for his under-emphasis on the working class and its struggle, which I have discussed earlier. Disparities in the sphere of distribution may be proximate reasons for many struggles, but finally, as far as emancipation from capitalist social relations is concerned, it is struggles aimed at eliminating the capitalist form of production – and underlying property relations -- that matter. When Hoffman refers to exploitation as a technical fact (and he is not alone), what he implies is that ordinary people – workers – do not see them being exploited in the sense in which Marxist theory explains exploitation scientifically. For him, because workers do not see exploitation as exploitation (and that they see and experience merely disparities in distribution), therefore exploitation as a concept is less potent. This is idealism, pure and simple. As stressed in chapter 1, the real is not the same as what ordinary people or experts see or experience. Marx (1976:37) made a distinction between 'scientific truth' (and a deeper level of reality) and 'everyday experience'.

Third, no-one is denying that people other than workers may be interested in emancipation. But interests and the power to fulfill them are different things. The power to overthrow capitalism is not equally possessed by all groups interested in its overthrow (because of their differential location in relation to capitalist production). Hoffman seems to be unaware of Wood's argument (1986) that: the proletariat's importance as the revolutionary agent is derived from the fact that it is the class that is exploited and that has the power to halt capitalist production. Wood also argues that while capitalism creates a necessary condition for the communist revolution the latter necessitates political action; the revolution does not happen automatically because of some "inexorable law." In the language of critical realism, workers have the power to stop capitalist production and overthrow capitalism, but whether that power will be activated and how is a contingent matter. Finally, if workers are not to lead the socialist movement, who then will, and by virtue of what power? Why doesn't Hoffman offer suggestions?

Given the numerous unresolved questions Hoffman's argument raises, he cannot prove that Marxism is inherently authoritarian. Besides, his argument is quite idealist. Let me give one example. Although Lenin – as well as Trotsky – argues that unpropitious historical circumstances- isolation, civil war, cultural and material backwardness - have bequeathed a bureaucratic twist to the workers' state, for Hoffman 'this state derives from a political model which is basically illiberal and authoritarian in character' (emphasis added). Thus authoritarianism is due to Marxist *ideas*, not to *material* circumstances, in the place where those ideas were sought to be implemented (Russia) and internationally. Marxists do believe in the unity of (democratic) theory and (democratic) practice, as Hoffman rightly notes. But this unity takes place not in mind, not in theory, but under the constraints and opportunities embedded in particular material conditions and the balance of class forces. Working for private property-owners in a class society is the greatest constraint to democracy (although capitalist class relations create conditions for certain forms of democracy unimaginable under feudalism). A class-based revolution only removes that constraint- thus proving the democratic credentials of Marxism - but does not automatically guarantee democracy in a post-revolutionary society. There are numerous other constraints, emanating from the history of class societies and especially, capitalism, which have to be removed. These include: illiteracy, poverty, the possibility of the overthrown classes coming back, imperialist threat, gender and racial ideologies and associated discriminatory practices, and so on. By removing all these and other constraints, Marxism seeks to encourage democracy in every corner of society, a democracy which is more substantive and which is both economic and political and cultural and which is therefore qualitatively different from (a slightly upgraded version of) liberal democracy that is often the fetish of post-Marxist thinking that Hoffman represents.

Let us shift focus and consider Hoffman's model of a post-statist world. This is an illustration not only of his politicism, but also, once again, of idealism. There are two aspects to this model, although Hoffman does not present it this way. First, the state that is successful in imposing a monopoly of legitimate force (vis a vis all "criminals" and "rebels") thereby makes itself redundant (65), leading to a post-statist world. On the surface, this seems to be true. But looking at the state this way ignores the class character of those subjected to state force and is therefore politicist,[134] as I have said earlier. Why will the opposition to the state wither away? In a society where the oppressed and exploited classes are the majority, there is only one way for the state to disappear: it must be overthrown by working masses and replaced by a transitional state controlled by them, the majority-class. The state has to be *made* redundant. The state maintains conditions for class exploitation and therefore secures the existence of the exploited whose objective interests are opposed to the state. Thus paradoxically, the state secures the opposition to itself. When the state fails to maintain conditions for exploitation - or is made to fail in a revolutionary leap -- necessary conditions will be gradually created for its disappearance and redundancy. Thus, an unsuccessful state will be, in this sense, a redundant state. Second -and this is more important in Hoffman's model of a post-statist world but is equally politicist- the state can be redundant in an economic sense: it can redistribute material resources (212) to empower individuals so they can self-govern and hence will not require the state. But why and how will the state do this? The most important question Hoffman fails to address in the book is: can there be statelessness before classlessness? Can we look 'beyond the state' until and unless we can look 'beyond class'? Can the state be involved in redistribution beyond the point where, e.g., the need to work for wages under capitalist domination fails to work as a discipline on workers? Further, who is the primary agent that will (make the state) carry out this radical redistribution? Hoffman will answer: the 'people'. This, however, is a gross misunderstanding of the class character of the state and the 'people'. The emancipatory potential of the book alluded to earlier remains unrealized because of its politicism and idealism.

Finally, Hoffman's concept of democracy fails to transcend that of liberal democracy; the class character of the latter hardly receives any treatment at all. This is what Lenin said in his critique of Kautsky about the class character of democracy, in spite of his (Lenin's) justifiably positive view of liberal democracy's useful role in educating workers: 'Kautsky has renounced Marxism by forgetting that every state is a machine for the suppression of one class by another, and that the most democratic bourgeois republic is a machine for the oppression of the proletariat by the bourgeoisie.'(Lenin, 1965:107). One should repeat this for Hoffman and post-Marxist scholars like him. For Hoffman, democracy is representative democracy of the type we have in bourgeois society. His ahistorical and technicist reason for claiming this is that people do not have time for being full-time legislators. Democracy is also reduced to legislation, to an aspect of governance, and is conceptualized merely politically.

---

[134] An approach that is not politicist and that takes seriously the class character of the state can nonetheless argue that the state can influence the class relations and class conditions in ways that cannot be immediately and always be reduced to class relations and conditions. Within limits set by class relations, the state does indeed have much autonomy, although the degree of that autonomy is influenced by class relations (and other factors which are more conjunctural). These ideas are explored in Das (1996).

He does not reflect on the possibility of popular democracy (in both the 'political' and the 'economic' spheres), a possibility that is historically created under classlessness, which would increase the amount of time not directly devoted towards production and struggle for subsistence allowing people to devote time towards the day-to-day affairs of the state, or of what Hoffman would call government. [135]

[135] The critique that is presented here should not, however, detract from Hoffman's truly vast amount of scholarship on the state, on democracy and on social theory. The book is highly accessible and extremely well-written. It is a book that the reader would like to engage with, at least to confront the criticisms Hoffman makes of various social theories, even if one might not agree with all of his ideas and the politics they entail.

Chapter 4

THE DISCOURSE ON THE POLITICAL AND THE ECONOMIC IN THE WORLD'S LARGEST DEMOCRACY: WHERE ARE THE FAULT(LINE)S?

Economic processes are everywhere political in that in order to operate they require political conditions, both at local level and from the state (Caporaso and Levine, 1992). These processes are also political in that their inegalitarian and exploitative character leads to political struggles over the ways that the economic processes work and over their distributive outcomes. Similarly, the political conditions require, and are influenced by, economic conditions. For example, economic processes (e.g., rate of accumulation and economic growth; presence of mobile capital) influence the extent to which the state can be involved in redistributive projects and the conditions under which the lower classes can struggle for better living standards (Wright, 1978). In this essay, I examine selected works[136] on India's political economy and discuss how they investigate the interrelationship between the economic and the political processes. Where possible, I also try to relate these works to the existing literature on political economy.

BACKGROUND: ISSUES IN INDIA'S POLITICAL ECONOMY

The Sathyamurthy (1995a) collection analyses the agricultural, industrial and technological policies of the Indian state. The overall outcome of these policies has been a development process which is skewed in favor of certain regions and classes at the expense of other regions and classes. In the process, contradictions of a vertical nature (for example, between dominant and dominated classes, upper-middle castes and lower castes) have come to coexist with horizontal (for example, intra-ruling class) contradictions. In sum, the Indian political process has been characterised by two significant trends. These are a growing

[136] These are: collections of an enormous number of articles in Sathyamurthy (1995), and in Rao and Linnemann (1996), and Dreze and Sen (1995). These articles reflect the state of political economy in two time periods: a. between the early years of independent India and the beginning of what is considered a neoliberal era, and b. the early stage of neoliberalism itself. This chapter may be read in conjunction with chapter 7 which talks about ideas concerning a 'more mature neoliberalism' in India as reflected in the work of an influential writer, and with chapter 8 which presents my critique of neoliberalism.

regionalisation of the polity and the emergence of new social groups as significant actors on the political scene.

One of these actors is the 'class' of farmers. Their political action and their relation to the state are the thrust of Varshney's (1998) work. He argues that a democratic system introduced *before* an industrial revolution has led to a rise in farmers' political power. All political parties, including the Left parties, support their demands for higher farm prices and subsidies. Farmers have therefore succeeded in preventing the worst-case scenario from taking place, this scenario being the fall in producer prices that normally accompanies an accumulating grain surplus. But the best-case scenario, that is, *continual* increases in farm returns *irrespective* of the rhythms of technical change, remains unrealised. That is because rural power is subject to serious constraints. On the one hand, the farmers' organisation, which aimed at putting pressure on the state for more resources, is impeded by crosscutting cleavages within the farming community (for example, caste, ethnicity and religion). On the other hand, millions of poor Indians cannot afford costly food. Besides, there is also a limit to the extent to which the state can subsidise the rural sector, which is very large compared to that in more developed countries. State subsidy is especially a problem because farmers are only one group among many competing for the state's resources.

Drèze and Sen (1995) point to a different type of state failure in India, namely, its failure to remove poverty, illiteracy, disease and inequality of opportunity. Nevertheless, they argue that the state, or more generally public action, can contribute to a people-centred economic development aimed at the expansion of human capabilities. They suggest that economic development requires the mutually supportive interaction of public action, including state policies, and market stimulation.

The pro-market (or neoliberal) reform policy of the Indian state is the theme of Kurien's (1994) book. Since the introduction of these reforms in 1991, the Indian economy has been increasingly connected to global capitalism. Kurien discusses the nature and the implication of that connection. Reforms have been sponsored by a tiny minority to promote its specific interests, although neoliberalism has been promoted politically as being in the national interest. India's balance of payment situation has improved, but its debt situation has worsened. Industrial exports have not significantly increased. This is partly because of quota restrictions imposed by western countries, and because exports have remained concentrated in traditional areas such as textiles.

Finally, the way that neoliberal reforms have impacted the poor is the theme of the Rao and Linnemann (1996) collection. It draws our attention to the significant rise in absolute poverty in villages in the immediate post-reform period, reversing the earlier trend of a decline in poverty. The claim is that the reduction in public investment and social expenditures as part of neoliberal policy has contributed to poverty.

In the remainder of the chapter, I will critically consider a few selected issues. These are: the class character of Indian society; the nature and actions of the state and its 'democratic' form; and concepts and explanations of poverty and development. I have chosen these issues because they are all important political-economic issues and because they are common themes in more than one book being examined.

CLASS CHARACTER OF THE INDIAN SOCIETY

The class character of either Indian society as a whole or only the countryside is considered in almost all the works. But their approach to the issue varies. For Varshney, India is a predominantly peasant land. He uses the terms 'peasantry' and 'farmers' interchangeably because both peasants and farmers produce for the problems. First, his work suffers from an *under*-conceptualisation of class relations. His discussion of rural India and, in particular, his characterisation of India as a peasant land, which is consistent with the view of the Rudolphs (Rudolph and Rudolph, 1987) completely ignores the celebrated mode of production debate that looked at the class character of India's agriculture (Patnaik, U. ed. 1990). Indeed, he rarely refers to the vast literature on the radical political economy of agrarian India that deals with the capitalist nature of Indian agriculture. This neglect is partly a reflection of his overall theory of India's social change as industrial–technological change, rather than a change in class relations effected by the socially and spatially uneven development of capitalism. Second, to the extent that he does discuss class, his discussion has three flaws which I will itemise briefly. Partly, it is that his view of class is sectoral. Varshney talks about class relations as if industrial classes do not exist. He points to the linkage between agriculture and industry, but rarely talks about their capitalist character. This neglect leads to his inadequate analysis of the Indian state, as I will show later. Partly too, it is that his view of agrarian class relations is primarily based on the exchange view of class as opposed to the production/property relations view.[137] *Exploitation* of labor is not a part of Varshney's intellectual vision. Production for *market* is. Finally, he has a static view of class, for he ignores class differentiation processes, including the unevenly occurring agrarian immiserisation and proletarianisation to which Harriss, among others, has drawn our attention (Harriss, 1992).

In the other works under review, there is a good discussion of India's class map in several chapters of the Sathyamurthy collection and also in Kurien. During the last four decades, says Sathyamurthy (1995b), the Indian capitalist class has vastly expanded. In addition to the national industrial large bourgeoisie, the capitalist class also includes the agricultural bourgeoisie, the provincial industrial bourgeoisie and the non-resident Indians. The non-capitalist class includes the poor peasantry, the landless, agricultural workers, the urban petty bourgeoisie and the industrial working class, including its semi-skilled and unskilled segments and the casual and contractual laborers.[138] However, the regionally important feudal, semi-feudal and the feudally exploited people (for example, bonded laborers) are not discussed. Given that *feudal* elements existing in certain localities tend to impede the exercise of *bourgeois* state power, this is an important omission.

Several writers stress the significance of the political actions of classes. Thus classes are seen as both classes in and for themselves. This is to the good. The political action of farmers, in particular, has received considerable attention. But there is also some discussion of the urban working class to which I will turn first. Indian labor, according to Basu (1996), is one

---

[137] In the exchange view of class, classes are defined in terms of surplus production for sale in the market (landowners are defined as a class because they produce marketable surplus). In the production/property relations view, as briefly discussed in chapter 2, classes are defined in relation to ownership/control over means of production and the resultant processes of exploitation (in this view, landowners are a class primarily because they get their land cultivated through hired labor and/or tenants).

[138] T.V. Sathyamurthy, 'Introduction', in: Sathyamurthy, 1995. pp. 27, 31.

of the most expensive in the world. This is not because wages are high but because of high indirect costs of labor (for example, strikes). Clearly, Basu wants a quiescent labor, waiting to receive adequate wages by virtue of the sweet will of employers.[139] This is, of course, somewhat different from Drèze and Sen's general acceptance of the role of public action, which, significantly, includes working class organisation, in economic development, although they do say that too much adversarial public action can hurt economic growth, as in Kerala. Turning now to farmers' political action, for Varshney the claim that the new farmer agitations are class-driven is weak. Rather than having a narrow class base in the surplus-producing rich peasantry, the new farmers' movement has the support of *all* sections of the landed peasantry. For example, there is widespread support by small farmers for higher prices for cash crops as well as for food crops and lower input prices. Marginal farmers (that is, the food deficit farmers) can also be expected to support higher prices for cash crops and lower input prices, but they do not do so unless visible employment effects and strong political reasons (for example, organisation as a check on the bureaucratic abuse of input delivery) are simultaneously present. Laborers tend not to support these agitations, but, where they do, it could be mainly due to their dependence upon the rich farmers for wages and loans (Varshney, pp116;137-8).

I believe that Varshney's claim, that price agitations cannot be considered class-driven and are thus multi-class, can be challenged by the use of the concept of hegemony. As defined by Jessop:

> [H]egemony involves the development of a specific 'hegemonic project' which ... involves the mobilization of support behind a concrete, national-popular program of action which asserts the general interests in the pursuit of objectives that, explicitly or implicitly, advance the long-term interest of the hegemonic class (fraction).... Normally hegemony also involves the ... flow of material concessions to other social forces mobilized behind the project.[140]

I would argue that capitalist farmers are trying to build a hegemonic project which includes some concessions to non-hegemonic fractions of the landed (for example, poor peasantry) and perhaps even laborers (the view that 'higher prices will increase wages', which he himself refers to). A movement does not have to be *exclusively* about the interests of the capitalist farmers to be (called) a capitalist farmers' movement. Indeed, and in contrast to Varshney's stance, Patnaik and Hasan (1995) say that the farmers' movements represent the interests of the new rural capitalist producers *clearly* and *consistently*.[141] They explicitly argue that those poor peasants and laborers who are substantial net purchasers of food grains are the classes who stand to lose from farmers' agitations and are therefore entirely outside their support base. Varshney, however, asserts that marginal farmers can support the price agitations on non-economic grounds (see above). But he never problematises the so-called non-economic benefits of new agrarianism, such as making the bureaucracy more accountable. Its bureaucratic character is an inherent aspect of the capitalist state, partly, at

---

[139] Kaushik Basu, 'The impact of structural adjustment on social sector expenditure : evidence from Indian states', in: Rao & Linnemann (1996: pp. 228–54).

[140] Jessop, 1990. pp. 161–2.

[141] Patnaik and Hasan (1995: 287, 274–5); and Srivastava, 'India's uneven development and its implications for political processes', in: *ibid.*, p. 233; emphasis added.

least, aimed at keeping the masses away from state institutions (Das, 1996). It is true that the state is an arena of struggle, which means that it can be made more democratic, within limits, through political action. But lack of recognition of the obstacles to making this possible can lead to politicism, that is, the explanation of things solely in terms of political variables and especially in abstraction from economic processes.[142] On the other hand, Patnaik and Hasan never even entertain such a possibility and thus smack of mild economism.

For his part, Varshney suggests that, while the normative order of patron–client relationships has been gradually disintegrating, class conflict has not always replaced it. Laborers are increasingly conscious about their rights, induced by continuing social deprivations and indignities. But this increasing political awareness has not generally been translated into organised collective action. This is because, unlike the landlords or rich farmers, those who mobilise laborers are unable to provide credit, insurance or employment. Further, over time, even the organisers, including the communist parties, have been trying to mobilise on multiclass lines, not concentrating exclusively on laborers' interests. Varshney's discussion of laborers' organisational issues gives a semblance of balance to the treatment of rural class politics in his book. On the other hand, there is relatively little in the Marxist works, for example, the Sathyamurthy collection and Kurien, on the topic. To generalise, while Varshney tries to combine structural and agency-oriented analyses (although his view of structure and agency is far removed from *class* approaches to these matters),[143] the Marxist works are more structuralist and unfortunately pay only lip service to agency.

However, Varshney's analysis of class politics, like his analysis of class relations as discussed above, has several problems. First, he says that both mainstream parties/movements, as well as the communist parties, organise on a multiclass basis. But he does not ask *why* the leadership of these multiclass organisations is usually in the hands of capitalist farmers or rich peasants. Can there not be a multiclass mobilisation led by laborers and poor peasants, who constitute 70 per cent of the rural population? To the extent that the communist organisations are based on the support of multiple classes, including both exploiting and exploited classes, what is the contribution of state repression to this form of organisation? Second, Varshney says that there are obstacles to laborers' organisation and that farmers' power is also self-limiting. But, if both farmers and laborers are constrained in their political organisation, why then do the state policies benefit farmers, the rich farmers especially, while there is little attempt at (for example) implementing minimum wage legislation? More specifically, if farmers have a surplus commodity, the state ensures its sale at a profitable price (especially prior to the economic reforms), but, if laborers have a surplus of the only commodity they have (that is, labor power), why does not the state guarantee its sale and at an adequate price? What does this differential treatment of farmers and laborers say about the *nature* of the Indian state? Asking the sorts of questions I have raised is beyond Varshney's centrist world view and, for that matter, is beyond the theoretical horizons of even the more radical works under review, with but few exceptions.[144] Varshney (and others) seem to suggest that what farmers and laborers get depends on their political organisation, but they

[142] As I will show later, the work of Dreze and Sen is also politicist. Of course, politicism is a problem not confined to their work. It is a problem in a large part of state theory (see chapter 3).

[143] Callinicos (1988).

[144] See, for example, Bagchi (1995: 46–95); also Kurien, *Global Capitalism and the Indian Economy*.

neglect the *prior* issue of the structural source of the power of these classes: their class power and its relation to the state.

The Nature of the Indian State and its Interventions

Several types of state interventions have been discussed in the works under review. These include policies aimed at processes of socioeconomic change such as land reforms, poverty alleviation, the Green Revolution, industrial development and economic liberalisation. The discussion of the policies aimed at these changes is important in its own right, but it also sheds light on the ways the authors look at the nature of the Indian state. I will focus on this aspect. In particular, I want to discuss the class character of the state and the determinants of the state's actions and their effectiveness.

Class Character of the State

The class character of the state points to the classes that are the primary beneficiaries of state actions (or in-actions). Chaudhuri (1995) says that 'Indian planning was meant to benefit the industrial capitalists and the rich farmers'.[145] This is a premise that is indicative of the class character of the state and which is supported by Byres,[146] among others. Exercise of power over the state is facilitated by, although it does not necessarily require, the instrumental control by the dominant classes over the state apparatus. Instrumental control occurs both in terms of these classes actually occupying positions within the state apparatus and also in terms of their capacity to influence ideologically the actions of state actors (Miliband, 1977). There is considerable discussion of instrumental control in the works under review. In India, the state apparatus, says Bandyopadhyay (1995), is controlled by the propertied classes.[29] For example, as Varshney rightly observes, the local level state apparatuses (e.g., the local police and village-level bureaucracy) are dominated by upper caste landowners and share their biases. This fact, he says, was responsible for the failure of the attempt to nationalise the grain trade and also to promote land reforms.[147]

However, Varshney's discussion of the nature of the state is inadequate on several grounds. In the main, his sectoralism – his sectoral view of society, referred to earlier, leads to his sectoral view of the state, even when he discusses the role of the landed interests: any conceptualization of class is subordinated to sectoralism. He suggests that only some parts of the state, such as local level apparatus and the CACP, the agency that recommends farm prices, are influenced by the landed class or their politicians, but these institutions are less powerful than institutions such as the finance and defence ministries. The state in Delhi therefore might not have been a preserve of landlord power, but Varshney does not say which dominant class has the primary influence over the finance, defence and other ministries. He is also often quite uncritical of state actors and institutions. This is evident in his treatment of (for example) Nehru and the Planning Commission. But readers get quite a different view

[145] Chaudhuri (1995:110).
[146] Terry Byres, 'The state and development', in: Byres (1994).
[147] Bandyopadhyay (1995:325).

from Sathyamurthy's contribution to his own collection. Let me quote in detail. One learns, for example, that 'Nehru entrusted all the economics (i.e., finance, trade and commerce, and industry) portfolios to non-Congress "experts"—[who] would have won the enthusiastic approval and unqualified trust of a latter-day World Bank or International Monetary Fund! From 1957 onwards, the Prime Minister appointed [Congress] "experts" to these ministries.... These largely consisted of men who were themselves industrialist s or traders, or who enjoyed the confidence of the Indian national bourgeoisie.' The post-Nehru period was no different. 'In all the central ministries that have been in power since 1977, economic portfolios have been held by ministers openly committed to free market, capitalist, pro-liberalization, and denationalization policies.' The Planning Commission has the same story. '[W]ith the partial exception of ... Mahalanobis and Gadgil ... none of the executive heads of the Planning Commission ... had a vision of India's economic development that could be deemed to be a genuine alternative to that projected by the successive ministers of the central government in charge of economic portfolios.'[148]

Not surprisingly, the policies of the Indian state have been basically in favor of the propertied classes, especially the capitalist class, as seen in its current neoliberal policy. Baru (1995) says that the post-independence industrial policy sought to create the basis for an independent capitalist economy in India (even though, in practice, it was forced to yield considerable space to foreign capital).[149] The state has also promoted capitalism in rural areas in several ways. Consider land reforms. The thrust of these reforms was the attempt to push and cajole *rentiers* to turn themselves into capitalists.[150] Land reform measures simply created a suitable institutional framework for the growth of capitalist production, which in the last resort required the stimulus of profitability. This was provided in several ways. First, with the state-promoted Green Revolution, richer landowners could reap a profit of 50 per cent or more, which was more attractive than merely renting out land and usury business.[151] Second, the implementation of a strategy of planned investment and other expenditures by the Indian state on a large scale from the mid 1950s onwards created an expanding domestic market for necessities, particularly food grains. This, in turn, substantially raised the profitability of food grain production. The ratio of prices of food grains relative to manufactured goods rose (an issue Varshney also documents well). The problem with Varshney is that his exchange view of class and his sectoral view of the state ignore the land reforms' (limited) success in creating conditions for the emergence of a class which would pressure the state for (the continuation of) a favorable price policy, the issue on which he focuses.

Determinants of State Actions and Their Performance

A general question is: why does the Indian state do what it does? The works under review give different answers to this. Drèze and Sen, for example, say that what the government does can be influenced by public pressures. But much depends on what issues are politicised and

148 Sathyamurthy, 'Introduction', pp. 29–30, 32.
149 Baru (1995.24). Also Kurien, *Global Capitalism and the Indian Economy*, p. 32.
150 Patnaik & Hasan, 'Aspects of the Farmers' Movement in Uttar Pradash', p. 276.
151 Patnaik & Hasan, 'Aspects of the Farmers' Movement in Uttar Pradash', pp. 278–9.

what is, or is not, politicised depends on the visions and pre-occupations of *opposition* parties (Dreze and Sen, p 87-88). This is, in my view, politicist for (non-communist) *opposition* parties do not *oppose* ruling parties on crucial issues such as payment of compensation to landlords in the land reform laws. In other words, on class-related issues that do matter to the lower classes, opposition parties do *not* matter. This happens, in part at least, because both ruling and opposition parties work within the framework of a state that supports the fundamental interests of the propertied classes and share an anti-lower class ideology which, in turn, contributes to the de-politicisation of the crucial issues. Drèze and Sen ignore the fact that the ideology of the propertied classes and the coercive character of the state, among other things, influence what enters into political debates and what does not.

Varshney's explanation of Indian state interventions is marred by statism, another form of politicism. He assigns the state more causal power than it can possibly possess. The state, he says, introduced a price- and technology-oriented strategy (the Green Revolution) in the 1960s when the countryside was actually less powerful in the polity than it has been in the period since then. Varshney (49,111) notes that this 'change in agricultural policy in the mid-1960s had been primarily a state initiative', which indicates that he has an under-conceptualised view of the class character of the Indian state. His approach is sectoral in that he ignores the national class context of the state. He does not consider the fact that there is an imperative on the state to reproduce class relations in the country (not just country*side*). The capitalist state has generally to create conditions for capitalist accumulation and for the reproduction of capitalist property relations. Here cheap food is crucial. One major reason for the pro-farmer policy is to help richer farmers produce food cheaply, since this is important for industrialisation, private capitalist profits and industrial peace. Indeed, the surplus production from the developed regions of north India has been used by government in purchasing urban peace.[152] If cheap food is not provided, urban discontent and unrest on a mass scale may be confidently anticipated as Patnaik and Hasan point out happened in the early 1970s. Thus what is, for Varshney, an autonomous state action to a large extent emanates from the *overall* capitalist context of the state. No matter how autonomous it appears to be, 'the state power does not hover in mid-air', as Marx (1973) correctly recognised. The state, in short, must be seen in its class context, although not everything it does can be reduced to that context.

There is much discussion too of causes of failure in the implementation of state policies. Varshney, for example, provides two explanations of the failure of the land reforms policy: factional struggle at the top levels of the Congress party and the absence of political mobilisation of the intended beneficiaries. Local governments (*panchayats*) were supposed to help in the political mobilisation of the poor. Instead, the local 'notables' captured them. How this happened is explained by the imperatives of 'party building in a new nation'. The lower wings of the Congress party—the district and *taluka* (sub-district) levels—came under the control of landlords and substantial landowners. These groups saw the advantages of entering the party in power. For me, this is again statism. More specifically, Varshney tries to explain the failure of state *actions* entirely in terms of the failure of *state* structure (local level of apparatus; political parties). Varshney's modernisation theory of Indian politics fails to ask: is party building a class-neutral project? Is not party building in a class society such as India's largely about creating the political institutional framework within which the masses can be

[152] Patnaik & Hasan, p. 283.

controlled so that inegalitarian property relations can be safely reproduced? Varshney' politicist/statist discourse is a part of a more 'general statist paradigm' in (India's) political economy literature. This paradigm is the widespread assumption that the Indian state is an autonomous active agent which impinges on a passive society, galvanising it into appropriate responses as desired by the planners and policy makers. In sum, Varshney, like Drèze and Sen (and most authors in the Rao collection as well), does not look at the necessary class character of the state, especially the fact that large landowners are a part of the class base of the state (Das, 1998). They all ignore the fact that the state seeks to ensure that property relations are not attacked.

In contrast to Varshney's approach, there *is* a class approach to the failure of state policies. Bagchi argues that the failure of such policies as land reform and cheap loans for poor farmers is generally seen by planners and others as merely a defect of implementation. It is not seen as the integral, constitutional birthmark of a society in which landlords, usurious moneylenders, privileged bureaucrats and policemen thriving on criminality remain in control of change. Varshney, as well as Drèze and Sen, all share this premise which Bagchi criticises. Commentaries on land reforms by these authors fail to observe that 'policies towards land reform were never part of any Plan *strategy*, in spite of the pages devoted to it' (Chaudhuri, 1995, 106). Indeed, as the constitution stood, land reform was not a sphere of activity for the central government, although, according to Chaudhuri, it is difficult to believe that a government that took the matter seriously could not have made a better show of progress. Indeed, he complains, the Five Year Plans never provided for an alternative set of policies that would be contingent upon a failure to implement land reforms.

Consider too in the same light the state's unsuccessful attempt to promote balanced industrial development. This also shows the importance of the class context of state actions. The state has intervened more effectively in favor of industrialisation where the regional capitalist class has been strong (as in the north-west, western and southern parts of the country) and where it has traditionally played a more important political role along with the rich peasantry (Srivastava, 1995, 237-8). Obversely, support given to industrialisation has been less in areas (such as the eastern states) with a weak indigenous capitalist class.

Nature of the Democratic State-Form in India

India is considered to be the largest democracy in the world. Drèze and Sen, Stuijvenberg (1996), and Varshney, among others, all characterise the state and the political system as democratic. But how democratic is India, and with what consequences for the masses?

Varshney discusses the ways in which India's democracy facilitates what he calls 'democratic peasant mobilization' against state policies. He argues that, if the state can repress farmers without any electoral or political sanctions, rural mobilisation can be easily stilled at its birth. However, a democratic system places serious constraints on the state's repressive capacity *vis a vis* farmers, particularly as they themselves are well represented in the upper tiers of the polity. Additionally, opposition parties have a vested interest in embarrassing the government and a free press puts further constraints on the government (Varshney, 98,114,199). Very similar points were made by Drèze and Sen. Readers will also know that Sen is a long time admirer of India's democracy. A government that has to face criticism from opposition parties and free newspapers, and that has to seek re-election, cannot afford to neglect such problems as famines, Dreèze and Sen note. Similarly, Stuijvenberg (1996:52) asserts that mature democratic institution s and the freedom of press (along with numerous eminent economists) are safeguards against too reckless an implementation of neoliberal economic reform (Dreze and Sen, 87-88; Chaudhuri, p 112). It is only in the Sathyamurthy collection that one (occasionally) hears about 'the authoritarian practices of a quasi-democratic state apparatus' and their implications, such as the fact that women are among the worse victims of predatory capital and the repressive state apparatus (Bagchi, 1995, 86).

In short, in the conventional literature the democratic character of the state-form is not problematised and, in particular, the *class* character of its particular democratic form is not treated critically. Varshney (p45) says that, in a democratic system, it is unlikely that 'drastic measures', such as repression, could be taken against protesting farmers. But how did the state repress the famous Telengana peasant resistance? How does the state repress the day-to-day struggles of the masses for better living conditions (Desai, 1987)? He ignores the fact that the power of farmers is mainly due to their control over property. Their power does *not* stem from democracy, although they may have received some concessions from the state through mobilisations that are facilitated by democracy. In my view, democracy in India has been mainly reduced to the resolution of conflicts, through elections and otherwise, between dominant classes/class-factions and their electoral representatives.[153] At the risk of generalising, I would say that Indian society and the Indian state are more *un*democratic than democratic from the standpoint of the underprivileged *majority*. Go to urban neighbourhoods and rural areas and you will see that lawlessness is ubiquitous; laws are up for sale and/or in musclemen's pockets nearly everywhere. If *democracy* could empower people irrespective of their *class* background, one must wonder why the majority of Indians are below or very close to the line of absolute poverty.

Poverty and Development: Concepts and Explanations

Drèze and Sen argue that poverty lies not merely in the impoverished state in which the person actually lives, but also in the lack of real opportunity to choose other types of living. Poverty is thus, ultimately, a matter of 'capability deprivation'. The 'expansion of human capability [such as ability to read, live a long life and so on] can be, broadly, seen as the central feature of the process of development' (Dreze and Sen, p.10)' Development is also seen as a gendered concept. Economic progress on its own does not necessarily reduce the gender gap significantly. Indeed, India has an exceptionally low female–male ratio. Adult men have disproportionately benefitted from improvements in living conditions and medical care. The fact that professional attendance at birth remains so rare in several Indian states, while modern medical treatment is very often used to cure diseases that are not specific to women, is a good illustration of this point. As Drèze and Sen again rightly argue, the emancipation of women is an integral part of social progress, not just a 'women's issue'

[153] I am saying 'mainly', because I do not want to ignore the intrinsic value of democracy nor certain real political-economic benefits from democracy for the population at large and for its less privileged sections, although the benefits the latter have received, especially economic benefits, are certainly minimal. On positive and negative aspects of democracy in India, see Das, 'The Social and Spatial Character of the Indian State', p. 793.

(p142, 154, 159). Nor is, in their view, the growth rate of GNP to be regarded as the ultimate test of developmental success, although at the same time one must not reject the importance of economic growth itself. There has to be growth for it to be participatory or redistributive. In sum, Drèze and Sen offer a people-centred concept of development, which may be appropriate for India and other less developed countries, given their multiple aspects of deprivations, including income deprivation (Dreze and Sen, 184-5)

While poverty and economic development have been somewhat appropriately conceptualised in Drèze and Sen, the causes of poverty and the causes of slow economic growth in India have been discussed in the other books as well. Let me look at economic growth first. Varshney (p20) notes that agriculture may not have contributed a significant amount of savings to the industrial sector, which may partly explain India's slow industrial growth rate until the late 1970s. More important, though, it seems, have been the actions/inactions of the state. As Drèze and Sen (p40) argue, the state has neglected primary education. This is important because inequality in basic education translates into inefficiency, as well as further inequality, in the use of new economic opportunities. This *distributive* failure supplements the effect of educational backwardness in restricting the *overall* scale of expansion of skill-related modern production. The Indian state has also presided over a decline in public investment. There are many reasons for this. First, the allocation of resources by the state has led to a proliferation of subsidies and grants to placate different competing groups. This reduces the surplus available for public capital formation, an issue Bardhan (1999) has also pointed to. Second, the state has been unable to raise adequate resources from the affluent. The decline of investment for all these reasons, in turn, has led to disincentives for private investment, given the existence of a direct relationship between public investment and private corporate investment (Roy, 1995, 138-9).

However, for Drèze and Sen (181, 203), the cage that most effectively keeps the Indian economy tamed is that of bureaucracy and governmental overactivity. Bureaucratic control, says Basu (1995, 257-8), emanates from the particular nature of India's democracy. This is based on a system of overlapping rights: everyone has the right to decide on every matter in contrast to a system of partitioned rights where everyone has a domain over which he or she has the full right to decide. Indian-type democracy thus allows many to exercise veto power and presents individuals from effective decision-making because they need clearance from others at every stage. This system impairs flexibility and stifles economic development. In my view, this latter argument is but a softer version of the neoliberal explanation of state failure to promote development, which is 'based on ... the assumption that an all-powerful state has been the root of all economic evil and the progenitor and promoter of all unproductive ("rent-seeking") activities'. According to Sathyamurthy (1995b:34-5), this presupposition ignores the numerous devices at the disposal of dominant elements in the ruling classes (including the bureaucratic apparatus of the state itself) to manipulate the state apparatus.

A final point in relation to economic growth which emerges is the skewed distribution of demand. The fact of unequal distribution of land and assets in agriculture has meant that demand originating from within agriculture for domestically produced industrial goods only grows slowly. The limited demand base for these goods is evident from the fact that the poorest 50 per cent in rural and urban areas account for only about 20 per cent of industrial consumption.[62]

Let me now turn to the suggested causes of poverty. The state is again seen to be central, with neoliberal policy contributing in several ways. In order to limit the quantum of food subsidy at existing levels so as to contain the fiscal deficit (Nayyar, 1995:175), issue prices of food grains have been revised upwards consequent upon the upward revision of minimum support prices fixed by the government. Of course, the higher price of food adversely affects the poor who are net buyers of food. There has also been a further compression of demand following reduction in government spending and restrictions on the import of raw materials and capital goods. This slows down the general rate of growth which means slow employment growth. The poor are especially dependent on public expenditure for employment and so cuts in public expenditure have hurt them. In general too, high inflation, caused partly by devaluation and the rising revenue deficit which are parts of the neoliberal reform package, has eroded the real incomes of the poor (ibid., 172-3). Indeed, the vocabulary of poverty alleviation is absent from the rhetoric of liberalization (Roy, 1995, 146).

But even historically according to Chaudhuri, it seems 'unlikely that government policy has from the beginning been consciously designed to benefit large sections of the rural population' (Chaudhuri, 1995, 107). 'No influential person in government has suggested that the anti-poverty programmes should be given priority in the same way as power generation.' (Roy, 147)˙ Programmes that directly benefit the poorest communities in India tend to have been sacrificed at the altar of growth. Drèze and Sen and Gupta (1996,147) point out that growth is necessary for poverty and that growth does trickle down. But notes that percolation to the poor from growth only becomes effective when growth accelerates to at least 7–8 per cent per annum. To the extent that growth is slow for the reasons just discussed, it contributes to poverty. Until growth reaches the level identified, positive poverty alleviation policies are needed. Yet these policies also have had only limited success, in part because they have largely been administered 'from above' without any proper assessment of needs and resources at the local level and partly because of leakages (major benefits from these programmes have gone to the non-poor) (Nayyar, 1996, 188; Gupta, p 146).

Several writers in the Sathyamurthy volume suggest that the state has promoted capitalism (for example Baru, Patnaik and Hasan). But, as Kurien (37-8) rightly suggests, the vast majority of the people have very little resource power to take advantage of the 'prosperity' that capitalism has brought about; they can, at best, be passive participants in it. They frequently find that the only commodity they have for sale—their labor power—is not saleable. As is usually the case, the benefits of growth have accrued to those who control land and capital at the expense of the poor (Chaudhuri, 111-2)

Finally, the lack of pressure from the masses is considered to be a cause of poverty. Drèze and Sen (p. 87) comment that 'successive governments in India have had reason enough to rely on the unending patience of the neglected and deprived millions in India, who have not risen in fury' about their socioeconomic problems. In a similar vein, Varshney (p176) says that the rural poor are not organised enough to pressure the government to allocate more resources to rural development, This last argument does seem rather to smack of a 'blame-the-poor' approach since little consideration is given to the way absolute poverty itself can impede organisation.

CONCLUSION

Taken together, these books shed considerable light on many aspects of India's political economy and state-society relations. Clearly, Varshney's is one of the best recent commentaries on rural political economy in India from a centrist (a liberal) standpoint. Its merits include the fact that it exploits quite well the complementarity between theorisation and empirical investigation and between interviews and textual documentation. It sheds much light on how the state institutions work and impact on the society. However, apart from its politicist /statist assumptions, the major problem is its underconceptualisation of class and, in particular, its assumption that one can look at class relations in rural areas without looking at the class context at the national level. The other two centrist works—the Rao and Linnemann and the Drèze and Sen volumes—are also important, the former for shedding light on the link between neoliberal policy and poverty and the latter for highlighting the state's neglect of social development. The Sathyamurthy volume and Kurien's work are major contribution s from the Left in drawing attention to the class character of state policies, but they are weak on the political response to the state's class biases.

Chapter 5

CAPITALISM AND FREE LABOR IN THE WORLD ECONOMY: A CRITIQUE OF MARXIST VIEWS

Freedom is an important concept in critical social theory. It means *being free to do* certain things (that satisfy human needs). It also means *being free from* certain things (that frustrate the satisfaction of human needs). At a lower level of generality, i.e., in class societies, freedom – or unfreedom – can be seen as that of specific classes. In capitalism, freedom can be seen from the angle of business or labor. Indeed, freedom in the realm of exchange relations, to buy and sell a commodity as one wishes, a freedom which presupposes relatively unfettered property-ownership, is a basis for much of what we call freedom – and discourse on freedom – in capitalism, including in political arenas. Freedom to buy and sell – free market – is in line with capital's need for profit-making. The idea of free market has been challenged on several grounds. For example, one scholar says, 'it defies reason in this world of supercorporations to see markets as free – when, for example, in the US the 500 largest industrial companies (out of millions) normally do about 80% of all sales' (Dowd, 2002: 7; McNally, 2006). Freedom of some companies means the relative absence of freedom for other commodity-buyers and commodity-sellers? But what about the freedom of ordinary people as sellers of their only commodity (labor power) and as direct producers of these?

The nature of labor freedom and unfreedom in capitalism is a highly controversial topic. A fundamental thesis in the Marxist critique of society is that 'wherever a part of society possesses a monopoly of the means of production, the worker, *free or unfree*, must add to the labor time necessary for his [her] own maintenance an extra quantity of labor-time in order to produce the means of subsistence for the owner of the means of production' (Marx, 1977:34; italics added). This means that all workers as direct producers experience this un-freedom: they are *not* free not to surrender surplus value, which the property-owners freely appropriate. They must surrender a large part of what they produce to property-owners, who have the freedom to control the production process. They have no freedom not to work under the control of any employer for a wage,[154] neither do they have the freedom to decide how the production process happens and what purpose it serves. They have little freedom *as direct producers* of commodities. But laborers are considered free to choose which employer they

[154] Correspondingly, in the political sphere, working masses as citizens may have the freedom to choose who is going to govern, but their freedom to choose people who will satisfy their demands and run the affairs of the government in their interests is extremely limited to the point of being non-existent.

will work with. Capitalism is indeed considered progressive as compared to pre-capitalist systems in that ordinary people have the freedom to choose their employer. Or, is it? Is labor's freedom in the above sense as real as it looks?

One of the best-known specialists in radical development studies and political economy,[155] Tom Brass (2011) in his book *Labour regime change,* as in many of his other numerous publications, has consistently called attention to the fact that a fully functioning capitalism is compatible with unfree labor. Indeed, whenever it is in the economic and/or political interest of capital, capital dispossesses labor of its freedom to freely sell the only commodity it possesses (i.e., labor power), resulting in the emergence of unfree labor. Unfree labor is a medium, and a product of, struggle between capital and labor. It is not just that capitalism happens to use unfree labor where it is found, but capital actively seeks unfree labor and creates it where it does not exist out of free labor. The scenario is similar to political freedom. Political freedom is curtailed, and indeed a democratically elected regime is gotten rid of, whenever it is in the interest of a powerful section of the (global) capitalist class. Regime change, Brass says, highlights the contradiction between the lip service paid by (western) capitalists to democracy and the routine undermining or even ousting of any political regime which they do not like. Brass's use of *Regime change* in the title of the book is deliberate therefore.

Citing textual evidence from a range of Marxists (e.g., Marx, Kautsky, Lenin, Trotsky, Plekhanov, Mandel), Brass says that accumulation does not necessarily require free labor-power, and can do without this. If this is not the case, he asks: 'why currently do 'fully-functioning' capitalists in so many different global contexts accumulate quite adequately using workers that are unfree?' (p.51).[156] Anyone with a familiarity with the topic will know that a vast amount of work on unfree labor is historical (Kolchin, 1987; Menard, 2001; Montero, 2011) or concerns the present-day LDCs, including Asia. This might indicate that unfree labor is a thing of the past or happens in the LDCs only, not the advanced world. Such a conclusion would be simply unfounded. And this Brass shows so effectively.

Labour regime change is an attempt to answer one of the central theoretical questions in social sciences: about the way a capitalist labor regime develops and changes, why and with what implications for the workers. Unlike some of the earlier work of Brass on unfree labor, the main focus of the book is theoretical: to trace and assess the epistemology structuring different interpretations of the link between capitalism and unfreedom. The book exemplifies the idea that social science research must be 'critical' and 'difficult' (see Das, 2012a). Brass assesses ideas on the basis of empirical adequacy, conceptual consistency and coherence, as well as political-practical implications of an argument. Brass, characteristically, is ruthless in the Marx's sense. He is doubly critical: of ideas about unfree labor, and of the objective world of unfree labor. As a consistent critique of postmodern idealism (and populism), readers will not find confusing and meandering discussions on (unfree) labor regime as a social construction or that unfree labor can be transcended through micro-political interventions.

The aim of this essay[157] is to analyze, critically and in some detail, the discussion on unfree labor as contained in Brass's book, and is guided by the belief that Brass's work on

[155] Tom Brass, who taught at Cambridge University, was closely associated with Journal of Peasant Studies from 1980 until 2009. He was a member of the JPS editorial board from 1986 to 1990, when he became the third editor, a position he held for almost two decades.

[156] Unless otherwise noted, references to Brass' work are from Brass (2011).

[157] This is a revised version of Das (2013).

unfree labor such as *Labour regime change* needs to be widely discussed, including in Asia, given the importance of unfree labor in this part of the world (see Brass, 2008; Derks, 2011; Martin, 2009).[158]The essay is divided into three main sections. In section two is the relation between unfree labor and capitalist social relations discussed. In the third section is dealt with the relation between unfree labor and the development of productive forces under capitalist social relations. The fourth section presents a brief comradely critical assessment of Brass's treatment of unfree labor, posing several questions to him (and others working on unfree labor) for further consideration.

Relation between Unfree Labor and Capitalist Social Relations

On the relation between capitalism and labor unfreedom, Brass identifies several theses or bodies of literature, which is indicative of his vast command over a massive amount of global scholarship, both historical and theoretical. These are: Semi-Feudalism Thesis (SFT); Disguised Wage Labour Thesis (DWLT); and Accumulation by Dispossession Thesis (ABDT). I will counterpose these to Brass' De-proletarianization (DPN) thesis (the acronyms are not Brass's).

According to adherents of SFT (and he includes Byres, U. Patnaik, Prasad and Bhaduri, among others): if a place or a country is identified as having made the transition from feudalism to capitalism, then capitalists must be using free labor. The transition from feudalism to capitalism is considered a one-off stage. The product of this transition is a free worker. Once a worker is free, she is assumed to *remain* free. When unfree workers *are* encountered, one of the two solutions is adopted in SFT, says Brass. Either the labor process in question is declared to be pre-capitalist, awaiting a transition to capitalism; or, the fact of accumulation is accepted and the workers employed are described as free labor (p.96). With respect to the latter point, when/where workers are hired by capitalists to use machinery, they are treated as free (p.85)

The first solution requires some elaboration. According to SFT: if property owners use unfree labor, there cannot be capitalism, but semi-*feudalism*. Since unfree relations are *pre*-capitalist, their presence invariably signals either the absence, or incompleteness, of a national transition to capitalism (p.87). Employers using super-exploited migrant workers or bonded laborers are semi-feudal *like* the landlords extracting money-, or labor-rent, from tenants (p.76).

In SFT: capital is opposed to unfree labor. Where unfree labor is found, capital invariably strives to replace it with free labor power (p.76). Employers using tied labor arrangements are anomalies. The possibility that capitalists might prefer workers who are unfree to free labor is excluded *ab initio*. In this vein, the semi-feudal social relation (of Third World agriculture) will be metamorphosed into social relation of agriculture of core countries. The next stage after semi-feudalism is therefore seen as a fully functioning capitalism. The latter is conceptualized thus: a group of permanent workers enjoying trade union rights and employed

---

[158] There can be no innocent (non-'symptomatic') reading of any text, however. So the Brass text itself (as well as some of the texts which form the raw material for that text and for this essay) will be interpreted on the basis of Marxist theory and critique as I understand it.

for a good wage under one roof in a big factory or on a big farm. Imperialism and feudalism are considered to be obstacles to the installation of a fully functioning capitalism. The political implication is that political energies should be spent on not fighting capitalism but feudalism and imperialism and on bringing a more democratic capitalism. Socialist struggle will happen in some distant future.

While SFT says that unfree labor is incompatible with capitalism, according to the Disguised wage labor thesis (DWLT) (of Banaji, etc.), all production relations are free, all the time. Banaji subsumes different kinds of workforce – tenants, sharecroppers, artisans, lumpen proletariat—into free wage labor (p135). In certain contexts (e.g., 19th century colonialism in south India), capital can integrate peasants through forced commercialization. The latter does not require dispossession of peasants by capital, because direct producers can continue to work on their own land (p.109), albeit at the behest of capital, and not as independent units of production (p.106). In this view, 'the process of labor remain[s] the process of small producer[s]' (p.107). These were/are quasi-enterprises performing what is wage-labor, and the price for the enforced sale of what they produce is a concealed wage (p.106). Thus rural households are peasants-as-cultivators, who receive a hidden wage for growing crops on their own land (p.106). The smallholders are treated as the proletariat even though they are not free in both the senses of Marx [e.g., even though they are indebted to moneyed capitalists]. Because the proletariat are composed of peasants performing disguised wage-labor, so all relations are free and capitalist (fn 10, p.107). Politically, the fight of this heterogeneous workforce (tenants, sharecroppers, rich peasants; etc.) cannot be a proletarian fight against capitalism but for their own interests in various forms of property and income-from-own-labor. As the concept of class is confusing, so does that of class struggle (p.135).

According to Harvey's ABDT (accumulation by dispossession thesis), the contemporary capitalist system is dominantly a form of primitive accumulation where there is a new round of dispossession, a new form of enclosure of commons, including government services/provisions (p.147). New imperialism entails a shift from capitalism as a system of production to one that is engaged simply in appropriating already existing assets. Primitive accumulation continues in a capitalist system where labor is free, for Harvey. If there is unfree labor, it is a part of primitive accumulation, not capitalism proper. Unfree labor is acceptable to capitalism but is not reproduced by capitalism proper, which does not actively seek out and reproduce unfree labor (p.146). Harvey says that accumulation by dispossession in the sense of creation of a proletariat out of dispossessed peasants allows over-accumulated capital to be invested (Harvey 2003:149), but he says nothing about any connection between over-accumulated capital and the fact that workers are dispossessed of their freedom to be just proletarians. Politically, ABDT is more about a fight for capitalism which stops dispossessing and privatizing rather than a system without class exploitation as such.

Having carefully and critically discussed many of these views on the link between (un)freedom and capitalism, including their underlying political agendas, Brass offers his alternative view. It is best to discuss his De-proletarianization thesis under two sub-sections.

What is Unfree Labor and What is Free Labor?

According to Brass, when Marx talks about labor power as free, he is simply contrasting the feudal serf with the capitalist wage labor. The former was still not separated either from the means of production (land) or from the control of its owner (feudal lord), but the latter is now compelled to provide the capitalist with labor power. For Brass, labor power is the personal property of the worker. 'for a worker to conform to the Marxist definition of free labor, s/he must have and retain permanently the capacity to commodify or recommodify his/her own labor power' (fn 35, p89). Workers may not be proletariat if they are not free. Unfree workers are de-proletarianized: they were free but have become unfree. Unfree laborers – including prison laborers and indebted bonded workers as well as those who are seasonals, local, casuals -- receive wages and do confront capitalists as a pure use value. They get paid and appear in the market and move from one place to another, but not *as* sellers of their *own* commodity.

Against Banaji's view that if you can freely enter into a contract – whether or not you are able to exit – you are a free worker (p.131), Brass says that freedom involves *the freedom to enter into and exit from the sale of labor power*. Otherwise self-sale into slavery will be freedom. Presence of a debt relation between employer and employee compels the latter to borrow from the former in order to survive thereby extending involuntarily the duration of both debt and employment (p.132-133). For the rural poor, borrowing leads to debt and debt to unfreedom (e.g., sale by indebted parents of children into slavery).

Freedom in Capitalism and in Different Capitalist Contexts

To systematically discuss Brass' views on the capitalism-unfreedom link, it will be useful to deal with these first at a general level (capitalism as such) and then at more specific level (agrarian capitalism; advanced capitalism and globalized capitalism), although Brass does not necessarily *present* his views this way.

Brass distinguishes between two forms of transition: systemic (from feudalism to capitalism) and relational (unfree to free labor). The former can be realized without the latter necessarily being accomplished (p.87). According to Brass, labor power is neither always and everywhere free, nor is it always and everywhere unfree. Labor power is unfree not because capitalism is at its beginning but because it is mature (and maturing) (p.271), and this is in contrast to a large amount of literature which sees unfree labor as a thing happening in the past.

Brass's theory of unfree labor is partly based on: Hegel's concept of labor as private property, and Marx's concept of labor power as a commodity that is bought and sold. This appropriation has an economic dynamic: it fuels accumulation. It also generates 'conflict between the parties to the exchange'. This is the conflict between 'owners of means of production who purchased labor power, and owners of the latter'. Unlike Hegel's, Marxist theory says that in the process of class struggle, the individual subject as owner of his/her estranged labor power is formed into a collective subject. This in turn signals a dual transformation: from the laborer-as-individual to a component part of a class-in-itself, and from the concreteness of self-hood to the abstract/universal otherness of a proletariat. 'In the course of this struggle', while capitalists attempt 'to force down wage levels and increase the intensity of labor', workers 'seek to improve pay and conditions', and they can do so as long they remain free (p.73).

If labor is a property, it must be protected, but there is the need of capital to drive down wages and conditions (p.50), so labor as freedom is an *obstacle* to capitalist economic development (p51). 'The capacity of workers -- once free -- not just to combine and organize in furtherance of their class interests but also to withdraw their labor-power, either absolutely by going on a strike or relatively by selling their commodity to the highest bidder', this capacity poses a challenge to capitalist discipline and profitability (p.162). One can easily see how three aspects of *capacity of the worker* are dialectically, although implicitly, brought together in Brass: capacity to produce more value than is embodied in it (this explains capital's interest in exploiting and oppressing/disciplining labor); capacity of the worker to commodity-recommodify the labor-power; and the capacity to fight against capital's boundless thirst for surplus value as well an unceasing attempt to dispossess it of its freedom where necessary.

Because labor tries to improve its conditions, which can only happen at the expense of capital, capital limits or curbs the ability of workers to commodify / recommodify labor power. This kind of action on the part of capital is a weapon deployed by capital in its struggle with a proletariat seeking to improve pay and conditions. The process of class struggle subsequent to class formation results in proletarianization giving rise to its opposite, de-proletarianization (p.163). 'De-proletarianization [DPN] involves the reproduction, the introduction, or the reintroduction by capital of unfree labor, and corresponds to a workforce decomposition/recomposition frequently resorted to by employers in their struggle with labor' (p.68).

Brass's theory of DPN links reproduction of unfree relations to class struggle between workers and employers *once capitalism is well established* (p.82). De-proletarianization refers to a process in which a worker who *was* initially free has been *made* unfree. It refers to not just permanent and/or local debt bondage relations but also to one that extend to include migrant, seasonal and casual workers. Employing a waged migrant is doubly advantageous: since employed only seasonally, capital does not have to pay for her annual reproduction cost. Since migrant workers do not have the right to work for the highest bidder (p.164), their presence is used to intimidate free workers contemplating or undertaking strike action (p.8).

As long as bourgeois expropriators avoid their own expropriation, and therefore class structure is intact, capitalists retain the weapon of class struggle. If during one time they give some concessions including citizenship rights and free labor relations, they can withdraw these anytime where profitability and or competiveness requires it: 'labor regime change cannot but involve the reversal of gains' received earlier through struggles (p.262).

There is not an inherent tendency on the part of capital therefore to replace unfree production relations with free relations, particularly when cost/control considerations – vital in the class struggle – favor the continued employment of unfree labor. This is true historically and in contemporary times. Brass's DPN thesis goes right against the SFT, DWLT and ABDT which downplay, or do not adequately (in terms of theory and otherwise) recognize, unfreedom of labor employed by capital.

Brass is thus able to move the significance of the distinction between free and unfree labor *from* the site of transition from feudalism to capitalism and locates it as a process *within* capitalism itself (p.71). From the standpoint of capitalism as such, deployment of unfree labor is a serious and recurrent possibility. One may now consider the issue in the specific contexts: capitalist crisis; capitalist globalization, and specific sectors within the social division of labor within capitalism (e.g., agrarian capitalism).

For Harvey, economic crisis and associated over-accumulated capital seeking greener pastures is behind the dispossession of people from their assets and commons (in the imperialized periphery) (Harvey, 2003). In Brass' view, however, where and when further accumulation is blocked by overproduction, economic crisis may force capital to restructure its *labor* process: replace free workers with unfree workers or converting the former into latter. Unfree labor helps capital combat economic crisis by cheapening labor cost. Presenting an original critique of Harvey[159] for not talking about laborers being dispossessed of their capacity to re/commodify the only commodity they have (p.148), he notes that 'This is [indeed] a logical final step in class struggle waged by capital, one that would ensure that workers are deprived of the sole remaining weapon in their conflict with owners of the means of production: making or not making available their labor power, according to the conditions stipulated by the market (p.148).

Many associate globalization with freedom: apparently globalization spreads democratic practices to all places. Is it possible that unfree labor is a thing of the past, a property of the world *before* globalization? For Brass, globalization has actually created some favourable conditions for the use of unfree labor. 'As accumulation... becomes international in scope, capital frequently replaces free worker with unfree worker' (p.74). Globalization of free markets means that unfree labor is not just an option but in *some cases a necessity*, as competition cuts profit margins which in turn force down labor costs. For example, Marks and Spencer, the fashion retail giant based in Britain, publicly eschewed outsourcing in search of cheap labor but then resorted to it when it was undercut by rivals (p.7). This example shows why nationalist and moralist strategy – including that of NGOs or international institutions such as ILO -- aimed at the abolition of unfree labor will not work, as Brass notes. Where accumulation has a global reach, as now, capital has the confidence and the power to dispense with the compromise with labor it has had to make in the past. Because employers can draw on the global reserve army they no longer have to accommodate the wishes and interest of workers (in advanced countries where labor had won some concessions through struggle).

One can say that globalization – or imperialism -- has taken practices of advanced capitalism to what are/were otherwise backward countries. In reality: the pattern currently

[159] Harvey's view about accumulation by dispossession has produced a little cottage industry (which includes land-grabbing studies). There are numerous problems with this concept. It is, first of all, a chaotic concept, for it includes so many things under its scope, which are not necessarily connected. What conceptual advantage does one gain by clubbing privatization of government-owned companies, mortgage fraud by banks, and dispossession of small-scale owners together? More concretely, a central problem is that: Harvey, oversealous to popularize marx's primitive accumulation dispossesses the power of that original concept; he indeed under-conceptualizes both dispossession and capitalism. He generally stresses accumulation by dispossession and its politics *at the expense* of 'accumulation by exploitation', its anti-capitalist class politics, which he thinks the 'old Left' has over-emphasized. He ignores the fact that: both forms of accumulation (i.e., accumulation by dispossession and accumulation by exploitation) and their associated politics must be seen as parts of a dialectical whole, the global capitalist-class system, and one in which the ways in whch surplus labor is appropriated colours other aspects, including, the nature of extra-economic relations. He confuses the extra-economic aspect of dispossession with economic (market-mediated) aspects (and this is something Fine and Brenner have also pointed out). The process of people losing land and other assets is only partly through extra-economic coercion: Leninist class differentiation, which he hardly talks about, is another, when smaller-scale producers lose their assets because of their economic unviability, i.e., because of competition in a market dominated by big business. This is the process of accumulation by class-differentiation. Thus what capitalism is really marked by three logics of accumulation rooted in relations of production and exchange. A one-sided stress on extra-economic dispossession is not acceptable. One must also ask: is a capitalism without dispossession a better capitalism and worth fighting for? Many people – on the Left -- have uncritically jumped on to the bandwagon of so-called accumulation by dispossession; lurking under this and related ideas are the intellectuals' sympathy for, and the actual interests of, small-producers.

takes the form of subcontracting of production by large MNCs to many small scale sweatshops (often located in rural areas of Asia and other less developed world regions), where coercion and bonded labor relations are rife.[160] This is not semi-feudalism = absence of a fully functioning capitalism, SFT would like us to believe. Instead of the factory system that SFT associates fully functioning capitalism with, what we are witnessing is decentralization of production, increased importance of outsourcing and downsizing and use of casualized female work force (p.76). The regime of unfree labor is not limited to a context of backward capitalism (or indeed to backward countries, as Wallerstein wrongly thinks (p.165; p.145). Brass provides empirical evidence to emphatically show that: advanced capitalism does not get rid of unfree labor; indeed, it creates a condition for the use of unfree labor, i.e., deskilling which allows the use of unfree labor.

Now consider unfree labor in capitalism in the specific context of the agrarian sector. Unfree agrarian labor is rampant in the agrarian sector of both advanced countries as poorer countries. Advanced country agriculture is increasingly looking like agriculture in Asia and other parts of the less developed world. Let me stress the latter context here. Capacity of capital to use unfree labor is facilitated by two conditions. For one thing, because rural producers – like producers in general -- can draw on a large global reserve army (p.163), the use of unfree labor allows capital to work the laboring animal to death, without having to worry about the health and living standards of their workers (fn. 71, p.163). Also: because agribusiness companies can produce things using cheap unfree labor in a country and sell the commodities in another country, the fact that use of cheap unfree labor is a barrier to establishment of *national* market (as SFT says) and will be discouraged does not hold.

The role of debt bondage has also changed. Under primitive accumulation, debt is used to force peasants off the land which is then acquired by agrarian capitalists. Under capitalism proper, however, the object of debt is to have control over *labor power* itself, which leads to unfree labor. What is involved is not separation from means of production but from the ownership of labor power, preventing its subject from personally commodifiying it. It is unfree labor, not primitive accumulation *per se*, that is a contemporary phenomenon.

The de-proletarianization concept has extended the debate on unfreedom in two ways beyond the original focus on small cultivators: firstly to those who are no longer cultivators but who rely on the sale of labor power for their livelihood, and secondly to workers who are not permanent or local (e.g., migrants, seasonal workers, temporary workers) (p.237). This it has done by focusing both on conditions impeding commodification of labor power by its owner and by highlighting that unfree relations are reproduced as the result of class struggle waged from above.

Un-freedom of the direct producers has existed at different times. But its role has changed. It is used not by semi-feudal landlords in a context where capitalism has not developed. It is rather used by capitalists (e.g., capitalist farmers) themselves. The class struggle generated by an accumulation project in Third World agriculture *on occasion* requires an employer to replace free production relation with an unfree one (p.91) in order to prevent/pre-empt conditions (e.g., proletarian class consciousness) that are favorable to the coming of socialism (p.81). Brass notes that 'bonded labor is in particular circumstances for

[160] To the extent that MNCs signify advanced capitalist operations and to the extent that sweatshops operated by MNCs use unfree labor, this fact shows that unfree labor is not incompatible with advanced capitalism.

rural capital the preferred relational form, so it will increase as economic development happens (p.252).

Contrary to the view of SFT that landlords and peasant capitalists are economically (and politically) different, Brass argues—rightly—that for cost and discipline reasons, rich peasants, no less than landlords, engage in restructuring the agrarian labor process and thus seek to replace free labor with its unfree equivalent (p.98). The economic advantage of such restructuring is that it enables landowners first to lower the cost of local workers by importing unfree, more easily regulated and thus cheaper outside labor, and then to lower the cost of the latter if/when the original external/local wage differential has been eroded. Thus it is possible for employers to either maintain wages at existing (low) levels or even to decrease pay and conditions of each component of the workforce, thereby restoring/enhancing profitability within capitalist labor process (p.69).

One might argue that only a small part of world workforce is unfree and that unfree worker is not employed on a regular basis. Brass's correct reply is that neither numerical smallness of free workers nor the seeming infrequency of their deployment is a true measure of their economic impact, which is felt throughout the free workforce, including free labor (Fn32, p.148). Unfree relations are not marginal, either temporally (that it was a thing of the past) or spatially (that it happens only in poorer countries).

Much existing research (SFT, ABDT, etc.) argues that class struggle should aim at making capitalism use free labor and thus democratizing capitalism, which NGOs, etc. believe could be achieved by the state. Many believe that in the current stage the fight should be against (imperialist) dispossession of smaller owners and privatizations (and, I may add, possibly *for* the establishment of a small holder friendly economy, if necessary by cooperative associations able to compete against imperialist capital).[161] In contrast, Brass thinks that class struggle should aim at making labor free, but this process should include in its agenda, socialism. Capitalism will not meet the demand for free labor *because* it depends on unfreedom. The fight for freedom – as the fight for an adequate living standard more broadly -- can only *succeed* if it is a part of the fight for socialism itself. I agree. The inability or unwillingness of capital to solve the agrarian question is terms of production relations (and not surplus generation and transfer) stems from the fact that to do so would adversely affect its own economic interests as much as those of feudal and semi-feudal landowners. Because of this an agrarian bourgeoisie (or more accurately, the bourgeoisie with agrarian interests) does not and will not sweep away unfree labor, a task which falls on the proletariat (fn 38, p.252).

[161] Utsa Patnaik says this: 'the small producer in this country is one of the lowest cost producers in the world, and there is a good prospect of small production stabilizing and facing international competition, *provided the advantage of large scale production are reaped through producer associations*' (2007:31; italics in original). This means that, intellectually, the problem of development is a problem of small scale of production at the national scale and of the absence of policies against international competition, and that politically, there is no need to launch a struggle against the existence of international competition itself including by mobilizing small farmers as an ally of the world working class.

Unfree Labor and Development of Productive Forces Under Capitalism

Whether or not unfree labor promotes development – development as the development productive forces as manifested in a long-term systematic increase in labor productivity via technological change – has been at the center of the discourse on development. The idea that an unfree labor regime is not conducive to – is incompatible with -- the development of productive forces under capitalism has a long history. The linkage between unfreedom and development – like that between unfreedom and capitalism itself as a class relation as discussed in the last section – can, in my view, be looked at a more general level (e.g., capitalism as such) and at a specific level (e.g., backward capitalism; agrarian capitalism).

First, the more general level. It is said that the unfree worker has no incentive to work efficiently (Adam Smith) (p.16), and therefore the product produced by it is expensive (Mill) (p.20). It is also said that unfree labor itself is more expensive and therefore irrational because it is not hired and fired according to business needs (Weber) (p.18).

But why must unfree labor be necessarily incompatible with the increased level of productive forces? Brass is rightly critical of the incompatibility idea (p.24). If it is the case that unfree labor will not show care and efficiency, this is also true about free workers when they engage in class struggle (p.25). [162]To the extent that unfree workers are hired for a season or a year and can then be fired after the contract has expired, this insecurity of contract can make them work hard, just like free workers. Also, like free workers, they will work hard to avoid punishment for non-compliance – violence, coercion (p.26), if not for pecuniary incentives. Note that, and this is something Brass does not stress, un-free workers, like free workers, must work for a wage under dull economic compulsion (they have been dispossessed of their property, so they must work hard to keep their jobs). And, because they cannot bargain over their price, they are cheaper than free labor. Unfree workers are more profitable to employ and no less efficient.

The objection that unfree labor lacks skills and inefficient may be racist. Unfree labor (slaves, but also South Asian and South East Asian immigrants working in the Gulf States where their right to change employers is severely restricted) may have technical skills, but may be reluctant to work as hard as possible (p.20). Brass says: 'a consequence of increasing the level of the productive forces through the installation of machinery and the application of technology… results in the deskilling of the workforce' (p.29), so unfree laborers (e.g., rural migrants) with the least skills *can* be employed. To the extent that deskilling is a tendency under capitalism, workers' particular skills are less important, so the idea that unfree workers are less skilled, even if it is true, is immaterial. Installation of machinery can happen through unskilled workers who are replaced by skilled workers. Unfree workers – including women and children whom Marx considered unfree -- are an important part of the reserve army that capital draws on (p. 32.1). Deskilling allows hitherto unutilized elements from the reserve army to be deployed.

It is said that capitalist development is accumulation of capital, which is premised on agrarian transition that licenses the generation of surplus, which is transferred from agriculture to industry (fn40, p.92). In the context of poor countries, several barriers to

---

[162] Skilled workers were used in the American whale industry who were made unfree through cash advances and purchases from ship's store (p.25).

national-capitalist development were identified (p94): lack of the home market to raise consumer demand for industrial products, which would provide investment opportunities to local capitalists. This lack of the home market – an issue which Lenin studied in his *Development of capitalism* – was connected to unfree relations. Firstly, landlords, who use unfree labor, were an obstacle to expansion of buying power (p.94). This class appropriated labor-rent from tenants, so unfree relations of production were equated solely with landlord/tenants relations (95.1). Also unfree labor restricts the national market because semi-feudal employers keep wages of unfree workers low.

The question is how will a transition to capitalism happen based on a regime of free labor? Many scholars (e.g., Byres), says Brass, restrict their analysis of the agrarian question and its process of systemic transition (from feudalism to capitalism), to individual nations. That is: capitalist development as simply and everywhere an endogenous (=national scale) process: 'capitalist development, surplus extraction, and its transfer from agriculture to industry, are all said to occur within the confines of the (boundary of the) same nation state' (p.87). Brass is correct in his critique of a closed economy (nationalist) model and over prioritization of the nation scale. Capitalist development and agrarian question (whether and how it is resolved) must be considered at the international scale as well, and not just at the national and regional scales, which must be seen in the context of the international scale. He argues that capitalists -- agribusiness enterprises – working in an international capitalist system break the link between consumption and production (p.87). Surplus extracted by agribusiness from agriculture here is reinvested in industry there, not least through keeping wages of agricultural labor lower (by means of unfree labor relations, among other things) (p.88). Surplus is also realized 'in the form of lower food prices, which in turn permit the cheaper bundle of wage goods that register as costs of industrial accumulation in other contexts to be lower, thereby contributing to the process of capitalist development elsewhere' (p.88). Capitalist development, Brass says, can and does take place where the rural workforce is unfree and impoverished since both accumulation and availability are determined not by the home market which may be non-existent or negligible but by an international one (p.87-88).

Labor Made Unfree or Formally Subsumed? A Comradely Critique of Brass

Ever since I read *Capital 1* back in the early 1990s, I have understood that while capitalism is *generally* based on free wage labor, the *actual* degree of freedom in a time and in a place – just as, for example, the degree to which wages conform to the value of labor power -- must be, at least partly, a product of the balance of power between two different classes, within the specific context of the development of productive forces. Brass's detailed theoretical exposition of the connection between capitalism and labor (un)freedom – including his attempted history of the concept and a critical examination of various Marxists have conceptualized unfree labor -- has enriched my own understanding as it undoubtedly would that of many others. Anyone who wants to comprehend the nature of labor regime must read his work. I am in fundamental agreement with him that in the course of class struggle and whenever it is necessary in the interest of accumulation and profit making, capital can, and does, resort to labor unfreedom: it replaces free workers with unfree ones and/or it makes existing workers unfree. This happens in countries of the core and the periphery. However, I will raise a few questions for Brass (and other scholars of unfree labor) to consider.

1. Relative Surplus Value

The real and ultimate aim of capital (i.e., productive capital) is, strictly speaking, not to hire cheap labor *as such* (or whether free or unfree), but to appropriate – and maximize -- maximize surplus value. This can happen in *two* ways: appropriation of absolute surplus value and that of relative surplus value. These two forms of surplus value correspond to formal and real subsumption of labor under capital (Marx, 1977: 1025-1029; 762). [163] Now: appropriation of absolute surplus value – labor being formally subsumed -- is *one of the two ways* in which surplus value can be produced/increased. And hiring cheap labor is *one* way in which absolute surplus value can be raised. Then: hiring unfree labor is *one* way in which labor-power can be cheapened. [164] There are many other ways, including gutting previous wage concessions through trade unions which themselves increasingly impose cuts. [165] Therefore the central problem is situated at a higher level of abstraction: absolute surplus value (formal subsumption of labor) vs relative surplus value (relative subsumption of labor), and the time- and place-specificity of the dominance of one over another. The crucial issue of free vs unfree labor must be placed in (relation to) the *problematique* of (the dual forms of) surplus value.

2. Reserve Army

Connected to the issue of relative surplus value is that of the reserve army, which Marx (1977) discusses in chapter 25. Brass associates unfreedom with the reserve army: elements of the reserve army (e.g., unemployed people) are vulnerable to being made unfree, which means that one form of vulnerability (un-employment) leads to another form (un-freedom in the employment-market). To cut costs capital makes use of unfree unemployed/under-employed people. But why is the second form of vulnerability (unfreedom) *necessary*? Why

[163] Capital makes workers work longer hours (it also pays lower than the rate that reflects the value of labor power, although Marx assumes that capital pays labor at below). This is appropriation of absolute surplus value. Capital also appropriates surplus value through productivity-enhancing technological change making workers produce more in less time. This is relative surplus value. Both these methods can coexist, although one method may predominate over another in specific contexts.

[164] Note that strictly speaking, in Marx's theory of absolute surplus value (formal subsumption of labor), wages cover the value of labor power, on an average, and that the worker is a free worker who experiences no extra-economic coercion.

[165] It is widely known among genuine Marxists that the current economic crisis has been used by major companies and their political representatives to slash workers' wages and impose speedup. For example, the Obama administration's expensive bailout of the auto industry, which has earned him support from many workers in the 2012 election who mistakenly think Obama and his party will protect them, was based on massive wage-cuts. The United Auto Workers union supported Obama's demand for poverty-level wages. Wage-cuts and speed-ups with the help of unions are a part of the strategy of insourcing – bringing back jobs to the US. Workers generally have the juridical freedom both to choose their employer and to join unions, and yet wage cuts are possible.

is the reserve army of *free* labor itself not enough to keep the wages down and undermine the political power of currently employed and free workers (see p.32-33)? Is it possible that because there has been so much unfounded opposition to, or inconsistent/vacillating thinking about, unfree labor within capitalism, Brass has felt the need for bending the stick in the opposite direction 'a little too much' so the incorrect view can be adequately corrected, a Leninist tactic?

3. Specificity of Capitalism

When one says that capitalists use unfree labor, that means that we are assuming that using free or unfree labor is not a part of the *definition* of capitalism. Capitalists using unfree labor are capitalists, but what makes them capitalists *in the first place*?_According to Brass, Marx says that capitalism and feudalism both represent servitude of labor. This implies that there is little relational distinction between direct producers in a feudal society (e.g., peasants) and in capitalism (wage-workers).[166] Clearly, this is an exaggeration, which Brass himself might not want to consciously make. Identity-difference is an important principle of dialectical thinking, which Brass himself practices. Capitalism, like a feudal society, is a class society; both are characterized by servitude of labor to ruling classes. That is identity. But there is a difference: the 'specific economic form, in which unpaid surplus-labour is pumped out of direct producers' (Marx, 1981: 927) such as slaves and feudal peasants is uniquely different from how wage laborers are generally exploited.[167]

Might one not consider the following proposition? Theoretically, capitalism is based on the exploitation of free wage labor (free in the Marx sense), and the use of coercion to appropriate surplus is dominantly extra-economic. But that in actual contexts, the *extent* of freedom is a contingent question and that, more specifically, many laborers, as Brass correctly asserts, can be made unfree because that is in the economic-political interest of their employers. In a context of, for example, a rise in development of productive forces and successful labor struggle, labor *may* have more freedom than otherwise. At the limit, of course, *all* laborers can become unfree labor. But then would the society where that is the case be/remain *capitalist*? When some laborers are unfree labor, that is one thing. When the number of unfree laborers crosses a given magnitude, the society in which that is the case, where that is the main trend, becomes a different society. The law of quality-quantity is an important law in dialectics, one which Trotsky (1995:117-118), among others, gave much importance to. One is here reminded also of what Lenin (1905:178) says: 'the theoretical proposition that capitalism requires the free, landless worker… is quite correct as indicating the *main trend*, but capitalism penetrates into agriculture particularly slowly and in extremely varied forms.' (italics added). Clearly, and as Brass himself is aware, Lenin, like Trotsky, does not rule out capitalists' use of unfree labor, but one must distinguish between the *main* trend and something that is truly not that.

---

[166] One may note that direct producers can be without the power to sell their labor power personally and freely due to two forms of coercion: extra-economic and economic. Brass appears to make no distinction between the two.

[167] There is also another question here: what is the conceptual difference between the real semi feudal landowners/employers who use unfree labor and capitalists who use unfree labor, the capitalists whom some Marxists call semi-feudals?

Consider an analogy. An average laborer is paid at the value. *Capital* is more or less written on the basis of this assumption. But Marx assumes that in concrete conditions, millions are paid under the value[168], which, like the degree of labor freedom, is partly a product of class struggle.

4. Development and Underdevelopment

For Brass whether labor is free or not has little connection to the development of productive forces under capitalism, for unfree labor can promote accumulation, like free labor. But as relevant works of Brenner (1986), among others (e.g., Ellen Wood)[169] have suggested, labor freedom does promote systematic capitalist development via technological change.[170] Brass supports Marx's idea that the bourgeoisie constantly revolutionizes means of production.[171] If this is the case, why will capital use unfree labor? In other words: if labor is cheap -- and capital can make labor cheaper by making it unfree -- why will it use technology to develop the productive forces (which can be combined with unfree labor)? Accumulation and development always happen in specific places. So, and from a geographical standpoint, the question is, if the currently developed countries are developed, has the free labor regime there not played an important and systemic role, as Brenner has suggested?[172] What indeed is the role of a) technological change (as well as relocation to areas where labor is cheaper and nominally free) as a strategy of accumulation and economic development and of b) other methods of accumulation than unfree labor?

Let us now turn to *under*-development, of the periphery. Brass is right in arguing against semi-feudalists who say that producers employing unfree labor cannot be capitalists. Then the question is: why are those *capitalist* countries backward? *If* unfree relations – including debt relations -- are not the barriers to economic development, then what *are* the barriers to the development of these countries? *If* unfree labor can promote development via accumulation, according to Brass, then what promotes *under*-development? *If* unfree relations can promote world accumulation, why it is that the majority of countries, including in Asia, suffer from low labor productivity and associated mass poverty? If unfree labor in a poor country attracts capital investment because it is cheap, why is it that close to 65% of FDI is in the global triad (Japan-Western Europe-North America), where the majority of labor are free, and why is the surplus thus generated not (always) re-invested in the poorer countries?

The regime of unfree labor *can* have adverse consequence on the development of productive forces, and specifically, at an early stage of capitalism. Consider Lenin here: 'an inevitable consequence of the ... labor-service system is low productivity of labor: methods

---

168 In his rather relatively-neglected *Wage, labor and Capital*, Marx says: while it is true that 'The price of [workers'] cost of existence and propagation constitutes wages', this statement applies to the whole 'race' of laborers, for 'Individual workers, indeed, millions of workers, do not receive enough to be able to exist and propagate themselves' (1976: 27; also 1977: 747-748]

169 Brass does not discuss the work in the Brenner (1977) genre (see also Wood, 1999).

170 A capitalist must find other ways (e.g. technological change) of cheapening commodities than just paying lower wages and making workers work longer hours than the average, for laborers are free to leave that capitalist for another competing capitalist.

171 This is true as a general statement. Whether capitalism revolutionizes means of production at a particular point in time and in specific areas is a different matter.

172 The fact that Brenner severely under-emphasizes the importance of imperialism in the development of the currently developed countries is a different matter.

of farming based on labor-service can only be the most stereotyped; the labor of the bonded peasant cannot but approximate, in quality, to the labor of the serf' (1905:204). Interestingly, Brass would agree on the point about unfreedom and (under-)development. '[I]t may indeed be true that the existence of unfree labor *inhibits* the *development* of the productive forces'. But he is quick to add that: 'However *once* established, there is no intrinsic reason why capital should not employ unfree workers in conjunction with advanced productive forces' (p32; italics added).[173]

The question is precisely this: what explains the 'once established' scenario, the scenario of 'advanced productive forces' in conjunction with unfree labor can be used? In the vast majority of countries in the global capitalist system, advanced productive forces are not established which would generate the kind of on-going technological changes and labor productivity that western Europe, for example, experienced. Why not?

At the risk of repeating one may say this: Brass explains well how capitalist *development* can take place through the deployment of unfree labor. But what he fails to address is this vital question: why does the opposite – capitalist *under-development* – happen, whether or not there is free labor? If it is the case that capitalism is reproduced at the international scale, which is true, and that backward and advanced economies are reproduced simultaneously, as parts of the same (imperialist) system, then what are the *linkages* between the two parts and between the imperialist system as a whole and the backward parts, such as in Asia? Why is it that in the majority of the countries, 'the more advanced capitalist elements' (which *combine* with less advanced elements) are present to a *less* extent than they are in a few (mainly Euro-American) countries? Yes, capitalism is about world accumulation and that it is a *global* system, but does the capitalism of economically backward countries of that global system (=imperialist system) not have any specificity at all in terms of the ways in which surplus labor is pumped out of direct producers, including from labor that is (made) unfree? To the extent that a vast reserve army (without government protection) in the periphery allows employers to appropriate absolute surplus value through a regime of low wages and long hours via the deployment of politically unorganized labor (which includes unfree labor), will employers be under any necessary and structural imperative to go for systematic productivity-enhancing technological change of the form that has been typically seen in imperialist centres (see Das 2012b for a detailed discussion)? In one sense, the class relation of capitalism, including the use of unfree labor must be seen at the level of the whole system. At the same time, this relation must have specific properties and specific consequences (for economic development), in the core and the periphery, which must be carefully assessed, and more so as the tentacles of imperialism and the force of internationally uneven development are getting stronger.

Conclusion

Much scholarly work, including that of Marx, generally assumes that workers are economically free, i.e., they are free to choose their employers and bargain over their wages. This chapter, revolving around the theme of workers' freedom performs a double critique. It

[173] What is being claimed here is especially true where, as just mentioned, advanced productive forces result in deskilling which allows capital to draw from the reserve army which includes unfree elements.

examines the work of a Marxist scholar – Tom Brass -- on the topic of freedom and unfreedom. It examines the critique by this author of existing work on freedom/unfreedom. The chapter then subjects Brass's own views to my (sympathetic) critique.

Brass offers a thesis of de-proletarianization on the capital-labor relation. According to this: capitalist accumulation is compatible with unfree labor, and it thrives on it. Historically, capitalists have indeed actively sought out unfree labor. By offering this thesis, he challenges three shibboleths: that the capitalism/unfreedom link is contradictory; that it is in some sense accidental and not imposed by employers, and that a benign state (or a moralist-nationalist strategy) can eliminate unfreedom. Brass says that 'As long as unfree labor yields profits, its reproduction by capital is guaranteed' (p.9).

The issue of unfree labor in relation to the capitalist class relation and to capitalist economic development is an absolutely important one, both in more or developed and in less developed countries. Brass' work will hopefully encourage much productive research on this topic outside the boundaries of such theories as 'semi-feudalism' and 'capitalism as accumulation by dispossession'.

Brass's de-proletarianization theory, however, raises new questions. For example, what happens to the nature of capitalism *if* all or most of its workers become free labor?; will it be still *capitalism*? How could it be distinguished from *pre*-capitalist class relations, or indeed, *non*-capitalist relations (e.g., Stalinism)? What implications of that possibility (of all workers being unfree) there will be for the relation between the political and the economic? It is one thing to say that capitalism is based on the exploitation of free workers, but that in concrete conditions and in specific places and times, employers can and do make use of unfree workers, including by making currently free workers unfree. But can one argue that: whether labor is free or unfree makes no distinction to the fundamental character of capitalism-as-a-whole, the totality of the class-process called capitalism. Further, and moving to a part of that totality, why is it that the vast majority of capitalist countries, including the ones where capital does make use of unfree labor, have remained economically backward with a very low level of labor productivity, and without any systemic tendency towards technological change?

Chapter 6

DEVELOPMENT OF CAPITALISM AND CAPITALIST DEVELOPMENT IN INDIA'S RURAL AREAS: A CRITICAL REVIEW OF SOME ARGUMENTS

As discussed in Chapter 2, the Marxist critique identifies classes, their relations, and the ways in which these relations (as well as class struggles) block or further productive capacities of society. While neo-liberals and postmodernists continue to downgrade or ignore class, important works on the topic have been produced of late in the political-economy tradition. In terms of the *origin* of capitalist class relations (or the transition from pre-capitalist to capitalist relations), whether in western Europe or in the global periphery, rural areas have been at the center of critical research on the topic, as it is widely recognized that capitalist relations originated in rural areas (Hilton, 1976; Aston, 1987; Harman and Brenner, 2006). By examining the arguments concerning capitalist agrarian conditions in India made by some of the experts in the field – Patnaik, U (1999) and by Sinha and Pushpendra (2000) from India, and Heller (2000) from the US -- the chapter[174] will demonstrate the continuing salience of class relationships to an understanding of rural areas in India (and indeed in the periphery). It will examine: first, the *concept* of class and the relation between class differentiation and class struggle, employed in the literature; second, the actual relation of agrarian transition to class relations and class struggle. It will not only discuss how the class nature of agriculture has been fruitfully explored, it will also point out the inadequacy of the class analysis. A major inadequacy concerns the ways in which class relations of capitalism are conceptualized (i.e., how the *quantitative* level of development of productive forces is conflated with class relations, which is a more qualitative issue, and how class struggle is inconsistently thought about). The literature also suffers from an inadequacy by under-emphasizing imperialism, which can block the development of productive forces in rural areas.

---

[174] This is a revised version of Das (2001b).

Agrarian Class, Class Differentiation and Class Struggle

According to Utsa Patnaik, who is probably the most well-known Indian radical scholar working on agrarian issues in India and the global periphery, three criteria are used in Marxism to identify classes in rural areas. These are: resource endowments, or possession of means of production; the nature of labor use (whether exploiting, self-employed or exploited), and the production of a retained surplus above subsistence needs (Patnaik, 1999: 212–13). Arguably, exploitation (the second criterion) is the most important of these three internally related criteria. She constructs an exploitation index that captures the class status of an agricultural household. It measures the extent of the use of outside labor or conversely the extent of working for others, relative to the extent of self-employment (p.211). The index for a household is defined in the following terms: labor-days-hired-on-the-operational-holding-of-the-household minus family-labor-days-hired-out-to-others plus family-and-hired- labor-days-used-on-leased-out-land minus labour-days-similarly-worked-on-land-leased-in-by-the-household, all of which is then divided by labor-days-worked-by-the-household-on-its-operational-holding (p.212).[175]

Rural households belonging to the exploited classes are those in which the category of work-for-others exceeds that of work-for-self (or self-employment). These classes consist of *poor peasants* working as poor tenants and landed laborers, and *landless laborers* working entirely for others (Patnaik, p.236). By contrast, the exploiting classes are *landlords* who do not undertake manual labor on their own account, being much rather employers of large quantities of the labor of others, and *rich peasants*, who are involved in at least as large and employment of others' labor as self-employment. In between these two categories are found the self-employed classes, which for her consist of *middle peasants*, whose manual labor on their own account exceeds the labor of others they employ, and *small peasants* who neither employ labor nor work exclusively for others, but nevertheless whose work-for-self exceeds work-for- others (Patnaik, p.236). Clearly, by including self-employment in her definition of class, Patnaik's analysis can be said to operate at the level of social formation rather than mode of production.

The class approach to agrarian structure has itself to be differentiated from non-Marxist discourse about the peasantry. In contrast to Marxism, therefore, neo-populists like Chayanov [1966] have argued that how hard family members work on peasant family farms is wholly/mainly determined by family consumption need (the household consumer-worker ratio); that peasant family farmers are more efficient and have a higher degree of stability than larger, capitalist farmers; and that there is an inverse relation between the size of landholding and productivity/efficiency (Patnaik, p.17). But the class approach suggests, as Patnaik (pp.209, 216) says, that given class differentiation *within* the peasantry, not all households operate family farms, and that different classes have different production functions, because of which (and for reasons discussed below) labor-hiring and thus exploiting households show greater output per acre, greater use of modern techniques per acre, and greater per-acre use of commoditized modern inputs when compared to smaller and

[175] Operational holding is conceptualized as land owned plus land leased in minus land leased out; labor is defined as manual labor. The index is a ratio which can be positive or negative, depending on whether the household is a net employer of outside labor (in the form of the labor-power of a laborer or a tenant) or is itself on balance working for others (as a laborer, or a tenant, or both).

poorer peasants. The inverse relation holds *within* the class of small-scale tillers (who do not buy or sell labor power), poor peasants and laborers with some land, and their so-called efficiency, which wrongly informs the populist rationale for land reforms, really 'reflects the desperate struggle to wring a livelihood from absolutely inadequate bits of land' (Patnaik, pp.44, 45). It is also the case that with technological modernization, poorer farms tend to be disadvantaged and the inverse relation tends to disappear (Patnaik, pp.45–6; see also Dyer [1996]). Class analysis also questions the usefulness of concepts frequently encountered in development literature (Patnaik, pp.3, 6–7, 210, 324): for example, terms common in the study of agrarian change, such as 'typical tenant', 'homogeneous peasantry', 'the poor', and even 'endowment' [as in Sen's [1981] analysis of famine/poverty]. In terms of class composition or class-specific modes of acquiring means of survival, therefore, all these concepts are internally diverse.

Class is not just an economic but also a political concept. Because class relations are relations of exploitation, their reproduction (or dissolution) occurs as a result of class struggle. The latter process is in turn enabled/constrained by the structure of class relations, along with the labor process on which the class structure is based. Consider, for example, how changes in class structure or class differentiation can affect class struggle. As state intervention in the form of tenancy reforms gave ownership rights to some of the former richer tenants, they became capitalist farmers or rich peasants. In political terms, this broke the anti-landlord unity of the peasantry. Of particular interest in this connection are rich peasants, of whom Patnaik (p.206) says: 'The rich peasant minority constitutes a developing peasant bourgeoisie primarily producing with hired labor.' Politically, the class interests of a rich peasantry diverge from those of agricultural laborers. Not only are the interests of this peasant stratum opposed to those of laborers, but the struggles conducted by the latter can be weakened by the influence rich peasants exercise over self-employed cultivators. As Patnaik says: 'Since in its cultural level and habits of life the rich peasant minority is not divorced from the rest of the self-employed peasantry – the middle peasants and small peasants – and is further linked to these classes through ties of caste, it can exercise a strong ideological influence over these classes', who are laborers' potential allies (Patnaik, p.206; see also Varshney [1995]).

The success of the class struggle conducted by rural labor is undermined by another fact. Capitalist contradiction has not been deep enough, Patnaik (pp.205–6) claims, leading to a situation where the exploited classes (poor peasants and landless agricultural laborers) are not yet a decisive majority in most regions of the country, which weakens potential organization against the exploiting classes. Another crucial aspect pointing to the incomplete nature of agrarian differentiation is for her the existence of a large self-employed peasantry. This, along with the fact that the agrarian labor process is nature-dependent, means that the practice of labor-hiring is not confined to exploiting classes: even middle peasants (and some small peasants) use hired labor, especially during transplantation and harvesting seasons in the agricultural cycle (Patnaik, p.204). Consequently, political relations involving the mainly self-employed peasantry and rural workers become problematic. This is particularly true of wage struggles, which have a more adverse affect on middle peasants than on the big exploiters of labor (Patnaik, p.204). In the Tanjavur region of Tamilnadu during the late 1960s, for example, the struggles conducted by rural workers succeeded in raising wages. Whereas larger landlords were able to avoid paying higher wages by recruiting cheap migrant laborers from outside the state, middle peasants were unable to do this. It was for this reason that wage demands made by rural workers were opposed not just by rich peasants and landlords but also by middle peasants. As Heller's study of Kerala shows, the process and success of class organization is further complicated by the *small-scale* nature of *capitalist* agriculture: that is, the existence of *small capitalists.*[176] Unlike large-scale agricultural units (estates, plantations), small-scale agriculture does not have the formal and permanent features conducive to the regulation of employment conditions and wages. This problem is itself compounded by the nature of the labor process, a consequence of which is that most agricultural employment is seasonal: in the case of paddy, for example, labor demand fluctuates dramatically between periods such as harvesting – when there is strong competition for workers – and periods when no labor is needed. A seasonal and casual labor force working for a large number of small capitalist farmers does not lend itself to organized and regulated wage bargaining (Heller, p.93). It is also the case that the existence of a substantial self-employed peasantry plus a mass of small agrarian capitalists makes the ideological gulf separating workers and exploiters less apparent, and is for this reason fertile ground for the emergence of populism ('we are basically all the same') which frequently blunts the edges of class struggle (see Brass [1999: 266]).

Despite the problems these kinds of class relations pose for the successful outcome to the process of class struggle, the latter has taken place. Kerala is in fact a classic example. A necessary condition for class struggle is class formation: given class structure, class formation – that is, the transformation of classes-in-themselves (Patnaik's main interest) into classes-for-themselves (Heller's focus) – is not necessary but contingent. In the case of Kerala, it was a product of agrarian discontent, anti-imperialism and social reform movements against caste-based oppression (Heller, p.243). In this particular state, as in others throughout India, rural class formation was facilitated by the Communist Party (Heller, pp.95, 243). Processes such as the erosion of caste-based forms of social control (which was an outcome of struggles by lower castes/classes), the increased literacy among *dalits* and the bureaucratization of local authority have all undermined the vertical ties of dependency between rural property owners and agricultural workers, which has in turn facilitated their struggle (Heller, p.95).

Discussions about class struggle, however, often suffer from an imbalance between class structure and class agency. Like many others, therefore, Patnaik assumes – but does not empirically show – that poor tenants and laborers are not a decisive majority, and that consequently it is this which constrains class struggle. A number of awkward questions cannot be avoided: could it be that capitalist contradiction in rural India is deeper than Patnaik's concept of capitalism allows her to recognize (I will return to this later), and that therefore class structure is much less constraining of class struggle than she thinks? Given that class organizational *strategies* affect class *struggle* (as work by Przeworski [1985] and others suggests), could it not be the case that the fact that most parties/organizations that mobilize these classes are class-collaborationist – thus the 'subjective' factor (political discourse of parties/movements) -- is a more important constraining factor? By contrast, while Heller rightly stresses non-economic factors facilitating class struggle, he underestimates the role in this of Kerala's agrarian *class structure*. It is a truism that in explaining something one has to stop somewhere in the causal chain, but stopping at the

[176] Much the same point is made by Banaji [1999] who, in an analysis of the findings contained in the ecological and agrarian atlas produced by Daniel Thorner and Cheng Han-seng [*Thorner*, 1996], shows that agrarian capitalism – albeit composed of small-scale capitalist producers – was already present in parts of India (and especially Gujarat) during the 1930s.

*non*economic level is problematic. Indeed, classes struggle under certain objective conditions. In Kerala these conditions included a greater degree of polarization in the distribution of leased-out land (large lessors), a high proportion of landed laborers in the class of farm laborers, and a high ratio of laborers to cultivators (Das, 1999b: 2119–20). All these elements of the agrarian class structure need to be linked to the fact of (and forms taken by) class struggle. Furthermore, Heller's highly optimistic claims (e.g., pp.115, 140) about the favorable relation between the state/bureaucracy in Kerala and lower-class struggles often come close to the social-democratic view that the capitalist *state* could operate as an instrument of the lower classes. These claims are far removed from much of the Marxist debate about class, which has shown among other things how the structure of the capitalist state and bourgeois democracy much rather weaken working class struggle over the long term (Das, 1996, 1999; Clarke, 1991). This has indeed happened in Kerala, one of the most social-democratic places on earth. If the reification of constraints is theoretically and politically unacceptable, an idealist-politicist approach to enabling conditions is no less so.

Class, the State and Agrarian Transition

Class analysis is doubly important: not only does it tell us what society is like at a given moment (= structure), but it also sheds light on how society is changing (= process). Having referred briefly to the former aspect of class analysis, it is now necessary to focus on the latter, and one aspect in particular, namely, the process of change (or transition) in agrarian class relations, and the accompanying issue of the development of the productive forces. Since the arguments are well known, it is necessary to provide here only a brief sketch of these interrelated elements.

As Marx himself maintained, and as many Marxists have argued since, class relations can fetter or further the development of productive forces: class shapes both incentive and ability to accumulate. This applies both to exploiting and exploited classes. Agricultural production, like 'production in general' [Marx, 1977: 347], requires investment, and the latter is a function of surplus. But – as Patnaik rightly points out – whether or not a peasant cultivator manages to keep the surplus s/he generates depends on his/her class position. A poor peasant tenant does indeed produce a surplus, but s/he can retain (at most) the necessary product: that is, that part of the net output sufficient to meet consumption needs (Patnaik, p.211). Since in these circumstances there is very little left to the direct producer for the purpose of re-investment, poor peasant tenants' class position impedes the development of productive forces. Similarly, class relations can fetter the emergence of capitalists from a pre-capitalist property-owning class. If landlords can earn a lot through renting out land and through usury, Patnaik and others argue, their class rationality will not favor the development of productive forces in agriculture. Indeed, according to Parthasarathy, a contributor to the Sinha-Pushpendra volume on land reforms, landowners in many areas are leasing out land because non-agricultural employment – such as petty trade in fertilizers and so on, or working in electrical shops – is more rewarding than cultivating land through hired labor (Sinha and Pushpendra, p.70).

But why is capital investment in agriculture *less* attractive? The answer, according to Patnaik (p.36), lies in the class relations linking a land-hungry peasantry and landlords.

Peasants are already paying the highest rent possible by cutting costs to the minimum (for example, cutting back on their own consumption, underfeeding their animals, maintaining inadequate equipment). This in turn raises the rent that a tenant who is a capitalist producer would have to pay. The capitalist farmer has to make a profit which is equal to average profit on money invested *plus* what Patnaik calls 'pre-capitalist rent', but a petty producer has to pay only the rent (Patnaik, p.37). To make such a relatively large profit, therefore, the capitalist farmer has to make investments, which will lead to a sharp rise in land productivity.[177] Thus, the required level of profitability is so large that capitalist investment is discouraged.[178] Evidence, however, suggests that the barriers that class relations pose to capitalist investment have now been overcome, and in some places the 'depressor' has ceased to work.[179] The ways in which this has happened are distinct in different places, meaning that the agrarian question (or the generation of a surplus in agriculture, and the transfer of a marketed surplus from agriculture to industry) has been resolved in varying ways. Here I will focus on two.

Agrarian transition in India – which is most applicable to the agriculture of the north-west region – is a process effected from above and mediated by the state. This is the Japanese path to agrarian transition, effected through state intervention (Patnaik, p.189) and couched in socialist/populist slogans. In fact, crucial aspects of the involvement by the state in the transition to a capitalist agriculture are discussed, by Patnaik and others. In the case of India, the state promoted capitalist development through land-reform laws. As the contribution by Dhar to the Sinha and Pushpendra volume (p.137) outlines with regard to Bihar – but which is true of most parts of India – *zamindari* (statutory landlords) abolition laws changed juridical relations of ex-*zamindars* from conditional ownership to complete proprietary rights. *Zamindars* used their own social and economic power at the village level, as well as existing state institutions and the land-reform laws themselves, to retain most of their land (Sinha and Pushpendra, pp.128, 137). Many landlords used the compensation money they received for minor parts of their estates being taken over by the state to make productivity-enhancing investments in agriculture (Patnaik, p.191). Furthermore, once the rent burden ceased to be an economic burden for some of the erstwhile well-off tenants who were given ownership of

---

[177]Given that average product per worker on poor peasant holdings affects wages paid to laborers, and if peasants are already cutting costs to the minimum, capitalists cannot further reduce wages to increase their profits.

[178]The argument holds as strongly if the cultivator is an owner-occupier because s/he can invest her/his money elsewhere and rent the land out (Patnaik, p.37).

[179]The argument about the economic impact of the 'depressor' is an old one, and concerns the extent to which it is more worthwhile for landlords to appropriate rent than to undertake direct cultivation with wage labor. In contrast to Patnaik's interpretation, where high costs of investment preclude capitalist entry into agricultural production, and landlords simply remain non-capitalist/'rent-seeking' agents – others suggest different reasons for the same phenomenon. Dumont, for example, attributed the persistence of 'rent-seeking' to a fear on the part of landlords that direct cultivation would lead to what for them were two negative outcomes: first, it would result in higher output and thus lower prices (and consequently lower profits they received as agrarian *capitalists*); and second, it would mean better-paid and thus more independent workers, a consequence of which would be diminished employer control over rural labor, a situation that might ultimately threaten existing property relations. On this Dumont [1973: 232–3] has commented: 'Like Dube in his [book] *Indian Village*, I noticed that many Indian landlords adopt a Malthusian attitude: to maintain ground rents at a high level, they prefer not to reclaim or irrigate new land. On the outskirts of villages, one sees large fields suitable for ploughing left undeveloped; these are the property of absentee landlords who fear that to bring more land under the plough would increase the work and thereby contribute to the raising of wages – which are at present absurdly low. Also, higher production would lead to a fall in prices.' For the argument that in India the 'depressor' has ceased to work, see Harriss [1992].

their holdings, they became rich peasants and capitalists in their own right (Patnaik, pp.191–2; Dhar in Sinha and Pushpendra, p.137).

If the land-reform laws aimed at reorganization of *property relations* along capitalist lines, then other interventions worked (more or less directly) at the level of *productive forces*. First, the state launched large-scale investment from the 1950s onwards, which resulted in the expansion of the domestic market for food-grains. This led to a greater inflation of food-grain prices relative to other products, and favorable terms of trade for agriculture (Patnaik, p.190). The sharp rise in agricultural prices benefited those – mainly landlords and rich peasants – who, as Patnaik (pp.168–71, 195) argues against Narain [1961], were major producers of marketable surplus, and provided the capitalist trend with a stimulus by raising the profitability of expanding agricultural output through the use of new techniques. Second, the state's procurement price was set at a level higher than the cost of production in areas of emerging capitalism (e.g., Northern India), which enabled farmers there to make huge profits. Indeed, the procurement price was calculated to cover not only production costs and profit but also an imputed rent on owned land (Patnaik, p.343). The price policy thus tempted landowners to make investments so as to develop the overall level of the productive forces. Third, the 'green revolution' policy, which provided cheap inputs and institutional credit to rich farmers, actually made it possible for landowners to make the investments. Accordingly, this particular policy worked even more directly at the level of productive forces (Patnaik, pp.193–4). In this way, technological modernization through the green revolution policy contributed to a high rate of profit, thereby undermining the 'pre-capitalist rent' barrier to accumulation (Patnaik, p.195). The resulting levels of profitability were higher than those which property owners could obtain by leasing out land, or engaging in moneylending and trade. Thus far, the story is well-known and uncontroversial.

However, the story of state-led agrarian transition as told by Patnaik (and others) is incomplete without reference to what I will call class-juridical interventions of the post-colonial state, and this reflects the *under*-theorized status of the class character of the state in the theoretical position on agrarian transition, including Patnaik's. In her case this is true in spite of the references contained in her book to state interventions. Like its predecessor, the post-colonial state enshrined in the Indian constitution the right of private property owners to appropriate surplus, not only in the form of rent and interest but also as profit [*Desai*, 1986]. Combining the formal political structure and discourse of bourgeois democracy with what were palpably undemocratic methods (violence, 'encounters', and so on), the post-1947 Indian state also successfully crushed/pre-empted any grassroots agrarian struggle (for example, the Telengana movement, Naxalism) which attempted to challenge private property relations and/or to effect a democratic, non-bureaucratic land-redistribution-without-compensation [Das, 1999b]. While the Indian state has done everything it can to make private property – including capitalist private *property relations* – juridically firm and well-protected, to put *means of production* in the hands of capitalists, and to ensure they sell their commodities for profits, it has by contrast done little to recognize the right of workers to fair employment, and to ensure adequate working conditions plus a decent living wage [Das, 2001a: 107, 114]).

In most parts of India, therefore, the state has allowed capitalist farmers to pay abysmally low wages (giving rise to rates of exploitation of more than 300 per cent in some places, as Patnaik herself points out), an objective secured in part by means of obstructing a worker's right personally to sell his/her own labor-power [*Brass*, 1999: chs.3–4]. [180]This, along with other kinds of state intervention (cheap inputs, price policy etc.), have contributed to a high rate of profit that Patnaik thinks is essential in order to persuade landowners to invest in raising the productivity of agricultural land. The problem with this view is that a near-exclusive stress by Patnaik on the role of price and inputs policies leads her to allocate primacy to exchange relations and productive forces over class relations, a view that is theoretically problematic. Indeed, to say that landowners respond favorably to these policies is to assume that there is *already* a class of capitalists prepared and able to accumulate, but this is a class, which she says does not quite exist because of pre-capitalist type class relations (the rent barrier). Patnaik's claim about inflationary planning per se being a stimulus to the emergence of agrarian capitalism is arguably (and perhaps inadvertently) a version of the neo-Smithian position associated with the exchange-relations-based argument of Sweezy [1976] in the 1950s agrarian transition debate. The question is: before the class of property owners favourably responded to state policies by starting to invest and accumulate, what was their class status? Were they *feudal* lords, who just switched to capitalist investment due to favorable interventions of the capitalist state?

I will argue briefly that when examining the process of the emergence of capitalist class relations, therefore, one needs to look at three transitions: from the pre-capitalist regime to formal subsumption; from the pre-capitalist regime to real subsumption; and from formal to real subsumption.[181] Formal subsumption is 'the general form of every capitalist process of production' [Marx, 1977: 1019], and it signals nothing more than the capitalist takeover of the pre-capitalist labor process. Money is invested to make more money and productive forces are developed in this stage (possibly at least at the same rate as under the pre-capitalist regime). But the systematic tendency to develop productive forces that characterizes what Marx calls a 'specifically capitalist mode of production', or the real subsumption of labor to capital, is absent under formal subsumption. An important issue that is overlooked by most writers on agrarian transition (and one to which Heller only alludes) is the extent to which rural/agrarian change at the all-India level – and indeed in the global periphery -- has been a transition a) *to* the formal subsumption of wage-labor under capital [with which Banaji (2010), mistakenly, conflates subsumption of *peasant* under capitalism], and b) to the real subsumption. This is a complex theoretical issue, which cannot be expanded on here (for a more detailed analysis, see Das 2012b).

Patnaik focuses on the transition from what she calls a 'pre-capitalist' regime. But is what she calls a 'pre-capitalist regime' really pre-capitalist? She assumes that because the portion of the total product retained by a poor peasant tenant is much smaller than the sum represented by capitalist rent, the rental payment is *ipso facto* pre-capitalist. But is this not allowing a mode of *distribution* of product to characterize a mode of *production* which refers to the way in which surplus is pumped out from direct producers?[182] To what extent could Patnaik's tenants be conceptualized as formally subsumed? In many areas of India, where

[180]It is clear, however, that Brass [1995b] and Patnaik [1995] disagree strongly over whether or not capital strives to reproduce unfree labor: he maintains it does, whereas she questions this. The significance of this distinction is that for Patnaik a transition to agrarian capitalism still lies in the future, whereas for Brass (in the sense of transition to capitalist class relations) it has already been effected.

[181] I am abstracting from the issue of hybrid subsumption (see Das 2000b).

[182]Patnaik's argument appears compatible with the notion that where laborers are paid below the value of labor power, their exploitation is pre-capitalist, because on average wages represent the value of labor power.

struggles for higher wages are successful, landowners respond by leasing out land to tenants, many of whom were/are indeed laborers [Das, 1995]. In such cases, is it correct to characterize the form of exploitation as *pre*-capitalist? Patnaik assumes that landowners are either a rent-appropriating class or a labor-hiring class making investments to increase productivity: but what about the landowners, probably outnumbering both these two groups, who employ laborers (and are therefore not appropriating rent) but who nevertheless undertake no productivity-enhancing investment?

This difficulty stems from the fact that Patnaik's stress is on *land*-productivity raising investment and its role in undermining a 'pre-capitalist' rent barrier to capitalist accumulation. But is it not the case that the real test of the development of productive forces under capitalism is an increase in *labor* productivity? A rise in land productivity in a given year does not necessarily indicate a rise in labor productivity. If landowners are not aiming at increasing labor productivity through technological change, and are thus not reducing necessary labor, to what extent has the transition to real subsumption (which is the only form of capitalism Patnaik recognizes) taken place at all? Given all these questions, the so-called transition in (north-west) India to what Patnaik would call 'capitalism proper' needs to be re-examined, as does the issue of whether landowners using hired labor and green revolution inputs are really capitalists while landowners just leasing out land are pre-capitalist exploiters. This is not a mere academic issue. For an assertion that pre-capitalist and capitalist systems of exploitation coexist can be compatible with and supportive of a collaborationist politics – that is, agricultural workers uniting with 'progressive' agrarian capitalists against so-called 'pre-capitalist' landholders – even if Patnaik would wish it otherwise.

The story of agrarian transition in India told by Patnaik, an economist (and similar writers) stresses class *structure* at the expense of class *agency*, especially the agency of lower classes. An alternative story of the transition exists, which takes 'from below' class struggle (and politics more generally) seriously. Patrick Heller, a sociologist from the US, tells this story, and it is about Kerala. In the latter context, therefore, class struggle waged against feudal landlords undermined a pre-capitalist agrarian economy, thereby creating a space for the development in Kerala of capitalist private-property relations and a market economy. On the one hand, land-reform laws which were implemented under pressure 'from below' led to secure proprietorship for erstwhile tenants, and also to the abolition of pre-capitalist rent (Heller, p.153). On the other hand, property owners were no longer able to exercise as before the 'extra-economic levers of landlordism', and thus secure surplus exclusively through the extra-economic and political subjugation of labor (Heller, p.136). Instead, they have to deploy the means of production more efficiently, in the pursuit of capitalist profit in the market. As important is the fact that the ensuing market economy was *contested* by rural workers. This process of contestation, and the resultant state intervention to control the proprietary function of capitalist farmers, has taken different forms throughout the state of Kerala.

In Palghat, for example, workers' struggle has been over the labor process, focusing on employment security. The consequent passage of a law gave legal sanction to laborers' customary rights to work: the erstwhile permanent workers were given a guaranteed right to employment (Heller, p.138–40). The law restricted owners' right to hire and dismiss labor as they wish, thereby slowing down the pace of proletarianization, and provided rural workers with protections against the virulence of the market (Heller, p.145). In Kuttanad, by contrast, class struggle resulted in wage increases which led in turn to farmers resorting to labor-displacing mechanization, especially tractorization (and this shows how class struggle is related to development of productive forces). Indeed, the first tractors were introduced in Kuttanad in 1954 by a few large landlords. But tractorization itself then became an object of class struggle (Heller, pp.147–8). Accordingly, the use of tractors 'was viewed as a direct challenge to labor. ... The [CMP-affiliated ploughman] union threatened to forcibly plough fields manually and demanded monetary compensation for tractor ploughing' (Heller, p.149; see also Tharamangalam [1981]). Laborers also burnt tractors in an undeniably Luddite fashion. Bowing to pressure from the union, the Kerala government decided in 1962 that 'hired tractors should not be used if as a result a worker is denied labor', thus effectively banning tractorization (Heller, p.149). After much negotiation, farmers were granted the right to use tractors, on the condition that a portion of ploughing work be set aside for manual ploughing (Heller, p.150). This meant that the ploughmen would receive financial compensation through what was in effect a social tax on capitalist mechanization.

But even with these additional costs of mechanization, the returns on tractor use from increased productivity and lower overall costs produced handsome profits for capitalist farmers in Kuttanad (Heller, p.150). In 1977, the Industrial Relations Committee (which mediates between workers and capitalists) worked out another compromise that was specifically designed to increase overall production. As improved pumping facilities, increased government subsidies and higher paddy prices had all made growing a second crop more attractive in Kuttanad, rural labor organizations allowed full use of tractors without compensation for the second crop, on the grounds that the cultivation of a second crop would itself increase productivity and employment (Heller, p.150). This class compromise over the use of tractors was repeated in case of threshers (Heller, p.152).

Thus Heller's story is one about agrarian transition from below. But the transition from below is not the usual *economic* one, in the sense of petty commodity producers differentiating into capitalists and laborers/tenants (Heller, p.137; Patnaik, pp.27, 35). Indeed, Heller states that in Kerala pre-capitalist relations did not crumble under market forces and succumb completely to the logic of capital (Heller, p.84). The agrarian transition, or transformation, as Heller would call it, was instead largely a *political* process. In this sense, the story of Kerala's agrarian transition looks very much like the one Brenner [1978] tells about Western Europe. But there is a difference. And it is that both the dissolution of the pre-capitalist social structure and the advent of a bourgeois transition in Kerala were not led by a commercializing landed elite. These processes were engendered (and later contested) by direct producers, i.e., tenants and laborers. The tenants freed the land and the laborers freed themselves from the clutches of pre-capitalist relations. Laborers also influenced the actual ways in which the ensuing capitalist economy has (and has not) worked. As we have seen, class struggle has meant downwardly sticky wages, with wages fixed above market clearing levels (Heller, p.119; Patnaik, p.201). This has happened in spite of a labor supply/demand situation that is not favorable to workers (Heller, pp.92–3). With downwardly sticky wages achieved, labor could relax control over the labor process without adversely affecting the aggregate terms of exchange (Heller, p.152). Heller firmly refutes the theory – held by Herring and others – about class-struggle-induced stagnation and capital strike. He argues that class struggle has promoted redistribution and furthered, not hindered, the development of productive forces (Heller, p.119). Moreover, unlike Brenner's theory of agrarian transition, Heller's is not one purely about class struggle. In the story Heller tells, therefore, state institutions have played an important role in class struggle and class compromises (Heller, pp.136–7, 153). There are several reasons why this has been the case. First, in the course of mediating class struggle, state interventions have strengthened the authority, legitimacy, democratic accountability and social embeddedness of public institutions. All these characteristics have improved state performance, and thus contributed to the state playing an effective role in promoting economic development through provision of institutional credit, extension services, state-assisted mechanization and so on. Second, with class struggle came the institutionalization of class conflict, and with that a more stable investment environment.[183] Wages have behaved more predictably than market forces would determine. Similarly, the law aiming at providing security to permanent workers with customary rights to employment reduced the recourse to militancy, thereby removing obstructions to the overall process of casualizing the workforce and rationalizing the production process (Heller, p.145).

It is true that 'social welfare, labor market control, and wage increases come at the expense of private investment' (Heller, p.154). But 'such limits ... do not rule out the *specific type of dynamism associated with capitalism* and do not preclude the creation of institutional forms that can, over the long run, nurture accumulation' (Heller, p.154, emphasis added). Given the stress on the role of the state in Heller's theory, his is what I will call a class-struggle-developmental-state theory of agrarian transition. This theory is an improvement over both the Brennerian view and the statist view (e.g., the Japanese path) of agrarian transition. While Kerala's transition from the pre-capitalist regime has been completed, its transition to a real subsumption of labor under capital is incomplete; a regime of a mass of small capitalists cannot possibly indicate a successful and genuine transition to capitalist agriculture based on real subsumption of labor. At the all-India level, the situation is worse: the 'rent' barrier to transition still exists, and extra-economic coercion in the sphere of production – which can block agrarian transition – does exist at the local scale. To the extent that Bhaduri's [1983; 1993] 'forced exchange' is prevalent, it too constitutes a further obstacle. And most importantly, even if the dominant class relations in agriculture are capitalist in nature, before an agrarian transition in the sense of the transition to real subsumption of labor could be said to have been completed successfully at the national and regional levels, a new obstacle has arisen. It is to this that I now turn.

IMPERIALISM, AND CAPITALISM IN RURAL AREAS OF THE GLOBAL PERIPHERY

The debate on agrarian question, and the whole issue of agrarian transition, examines how class relations in the rural areas of less developed countries either fetter or further the development of productive forces, both in agriculture and industry.[184] It is argued here that the usefulness of this debate hinges crucially on the clarification of an important concept:

[183] Indeed, the 1991 Minimum Wage Committee, on which the state as well as capital and labor are represented, recognized that '[I]f wages are too low, this will lead to tension in the agricultural sector' (Heller, pp.93–4).

[184] The classic Marxists texts on the agrarian question are those by Lenin [1964] and Kautsky [1988]. It is difficult not to agree with Watts and Goodman [1997: 16] when they observe that current approaches to the agrarian question are too narrowly focused 'on the internal dynamics of change at the expense of ... globalization', and, further, that the agrarian question itself is not something that can be 'resolved' once and for all. Their view about the continued relevance of the agrarian question (and hence its non-resolution) in the wider context of globalization is similar to the position taken here, except that the international dimension is identified by me not with globalization but with imperialism.

fettering. The latter term means that existing class relations block possible *further* development of productive forces (leading to a slow or slower growth rate, for example), a situation I will call 'development-fettering'. This is the traditional meaning that the agrarian transition debate has used until now.

But recent work by Marxists, including Cohen and Wright (see Sutton [1996: 11–15] for an overview), has revealed that fettering has another meaning which I will call 'use-fettering' and which, I argue, can be fruitfully utilized in studies on agrarian transition. Use-fettering means that rational use of *existing* resources is blocked by the current set of class relations. That is, productive capacities that have already been *developed* are at present un-*used* or under-*used* due to existing class relations. The discrepancy between capacity and use is not to be seen in an absolute sense, however. As Cohen says, the question is not under-deployment (or use) of resources, but 'grotesque over-deployment in some directions and injurious under-deployment in others', indicating an irrational deployment of resources. And (ir-)rationality of deployment must be judged in turn from the standpoint of human preferences/needs, which, as Sutton [1996: 14] states, determine what objective capacities are being fettered.

Scholars influenced by postmodernism and other forms of bourgeois discourse euphemistically refer to imperialism as globalization, free trade, and the like. It is in reality a form of class relations: relations between metropolitan bourgeoisie and Third World workers/peasants. Although Patnaik and some contributors to the Sinha-Pushpendra volume (Parthasarathy and also Pushpendra) all discuss the impact of imperialism on Third World agriculture, they fail to consider imperialism in terms of the broader question of *agrarian transition.*[185] Looking at 'use-fettering' in the capitalist system as a whole, those interested in agrarian transition need to ask whether, and how, capitalist relations at the world level – imperialism – lead to an *irrational* use of existing resources located in (rural areas of) the global periphery; that is to say, irrational from the standpoint of needs of the vast majority of the population at the margins of society who want, above all, a sufficient amount of food to eat. Given the latter preferences, the question is whether land and other natural resources that *can* produce sufficient means of subsistence – such as food-grains – are being 'use-fettered' by imperialism. I will argue that imperialism, which had earlier 'contributed' to the agrarian transition through the 'transfer' of green revolution technology in a pre-emptive response to class struggle and the possibility of a red revolution in the Third World countryside, has now, in certain ways, blocked agrarian transition, again in its own interest.

As Patnaik points out, the single most important effect on agriculture of imperialist liberalization is the inverse relation between food-grains production and agricultural exports, and the ensuing threat to food security (Patnaik, p.372; see also Pushpendra in Sinha and Pushpendra, pp.59–60). India's export-promotion drive in agriculture started in the late 1980s, and became significant in 1991. This process has led to changes in cropping patterns: cereals and pulses are being replaced by sugar cane, horticultural crops, aquaculture, and oilseeds – for example, soybean for feed export is displacing coarse grains in South India (Patnaik, pp.400, 407; Parthasarathy in Sinha and Pushpendra, p.70). Several of the

[185] Patnaik often tends to treat imperialism as if it is simply an unequal exchange between core and peripheral countries – and thus an exploitative relation involving nations and not classes, an approach which by inference categorizes workers in the core countries as beneficiaries of imperialism. This interpretation of imperialism can have unfavorable (and perhaps unintentional) implications for working-class internationalism. In fact, the agrarian objectives of imperialism need to be seen partly as a desire to increase relative surplus value capital extracts from the core working class through a reduction of necessary labor.

mechanisms underlying the inverse relation are considered by Patnaik. The first of these is that liberalization – neoliberalization -- is subjecting the economy of peripheral countries, such as India, to demand from imperialist countries, whereby land and resources of the former are being bid away by the pull of demand from the latter (Patnaik, p.404). Consumer tastes have changed in these countries because of rising real-income inequality, health consciousness and environmental movements. So there are expanding demands from these countries for vegetable oils, fruits, vegetables, fibre, sea food and so on. But only a small fraction of these can be produced there (or produced profitably), given the restricted growing season in their temperate lands.

These crops can, however, be produced in the developing countries such as India, given their climate–soil specificity and at a very cheap cost, promising very high profits for global agribusiness (and Third World capitalist farmers). Thus a growing proportion of agricultural commodities that the North needs and demands has to come from the periphery. This leads to pressure to open up its agriculture (Patnaik, pp.352–3).[186] There is also neo-liberal pressure to reverse land reform laws, which are said to be an obstacle to the flow of capital into rural areas (Pushpendra in Sinha and Pushpendra, pp.45–6, 54). Indeed, the reversal of these laws will pave the way for foreign companies (and also local capitalists) to own/control land, and thus enable them more easily to convert its use from food-grains cultivation to the production of agricultural commodities for export.

By contrast, these same neo-liberal globalizing polices of the IMF are in the context of Third World countries – and especially in the rural areas of such nations – income-deflating policies that create more inequality. These policies, which include wage restraints, direct tax cuts and cuts in subsidies for the poor, mean that in non-metropolitan contexts there is now a huge mass of people who do not have the money to buy grains. This market mechanism (i.e., lack of effective demand) in addition to the fact that foreign/domestic capital seeks to earn profits by supplying agri-inputs to farmers and by buying cheap farm-raw materials for agro-processing (e.g., potatoes for chips) makes sure that the *use* of land and other resources is diverted to production of things agricultural exports (Patnaik, pp.355, 386) and for local elites. This happens in many ways, including through contract farming mechanisms in specific localities, especially where larger-scale capitalist farmers exist.[187]

Surely, *in certain localities*, capitalist farming based on (very expensive) technological advancement comes to exist. But these resources could be invested to increase labor (and land) productivity in the production of farm-goods *in large parts of the country*, which will be used by the majority of the population and by local urban firms (e.g., cotton for textiles), thus producing an 'organic' growth process.[188] Arguably money for exports can be used for buying food, but there is an internal relation between export promotion and deflation of

[186]The story of how neo-liberalism is fettering agrarian development flies in the face of the Ricardian trade theory, which maintains that trade benefits all parties to the exchange (Patnaik, pp.370–78). This theory is based on comparative costs of items being traded, but since certain crops either cannot be produced in temperate lands but only in the tropics, or cannot generate sufficiently high profits for capital in the former contexts, comparative costs cannot be measured, and therefore the question of both sets of countries gaining an advantage does not arise (Patnaik, p.373).

[187] Ritika Shrimali is completing an excellent doctoral dissertation on contract farming at York University, Toronto, examining its class character, including its relation to different fractions of capital, both productive and financial.

[188] I am not suggesting that such a nationalist process will itself solve the problems of economic under-development in India. I am pointing to this process to contrast it with the imperialism-driven growth process in agriculture.

demand for food crops, so demand and supply of food shrink simultaneously (Patnaik, p.405). So foreign exchange earned from cash-crops exports is used for profit repatriation by transnational agribusiness corporations and for financing the export from imperialist countries of manufactured products destined for the exploiting classes and the middle class in India. Moreover, the price of agricultural exports declines (and with it foreign exchange) as the number of exporting countries increases.

It is true that the shift away from food-grains could be partly compensated for by a rise in yield – the development of productive forces -- through investment. But under IMF rules, public investment which earlier played an important role in agrarian transition (see Nanda [1995], and also Patnaik, p.189) has been cut back (Patnaik, pp.363, 372, 408).[189] If the area under food-grains is being converted to non-food-grains production, and with growing pressure on the Indian state to make land available for industrial and tertiary sector output, the required increase in agricultural yield to produce a sufficient amount of food-grains to compensate for the shift to export crops would be beyond the scale that is anyway achievable (Pushpendra in Sinha and Pushpendra, pp.56–7, 60). Indeed, what is observed is a decelerating yield, which is insufficient to compensate for the loss in area, leading to a slowing down in the growth rate of food-grain output, and falling per capita food production and food availability (Patnaik, p.408; Pushpendra in Sinha and Pushpendra, p.57). This suggests clearly a process of imperialism-induced use-fettering (=irrational use of resources) leading to a development-fettering (=fettering of the development of productive forces, leading to stagnation). The imperialist policy package will, it seems, be implemented in spite of its adverse effects, because it serves the interests of the metropolitan capitalist class and its allies in India, including capitalist farmers and sections of the middle class whose support has been bought by unfreezing consumer imports and direct tax cuts (Patnaik, pp.356, 366; Pushpendra in Sinha and Pushpendra, p.62). Thus imperialism must be an important part of the analysis of agrarian transition, in particular, the transition to capitalist development based on technological change which increases labour (and land) productivity.

CONCLUSION

In a general sense, and current disclaimers by postmodernists and others notwithstanding, class analysis is important because it contributes to an understanding both of the possibilities for change and also the obstacles to this. More specifically, understanding how class relations change in relation to the development or use of the productive forces in Third World agriculture is crucial to this broader process of societal change. How class relations (whether pre-capitalist or not) are an obstacle to agrarian transition in postcolonial societies is therefore an integral part of the agrarian transition discourse. Now, however, the epistemological parameters of this discourse need to expand, so that theory about the nature and impact of agrarian transition can accommodate the current stage of imperialism. The impact of the latter on Third World agriculture requires, in short, to be *retheorized* in terms of an ongoing agrarian transition. This in turn entails linking discussions about imperialism and agrarian transition with the new debate in Marxist social theory on the fettering of productive forces by class relations.

---

[189]This, too, demonstrates the extent to which imperialism has imposed 'development-fettering'.

Self-evidently the issues raised by agrarian transition are not ivory-tower topics circulating only within the academy. The uneven and 'incomplete' and 'combined' nature of agrarian transition (in the sense of both transition to capitalist class relations and to capitalist class relations combined with the development of productive forces driven by technological change) has, among other things, undermined grassroots political unity against the landed class, although the adverse current impact of imperialism on Third World agriculture makes it possible for new forms of political unity to emerge. Class analysis shows that those with little or no land – poor peasants, small peasants and laborers (with possible middle-peasant allies) – will gain from a unified political opposition to and struggle against imperialism, the object of which is to unfetter the use (and also the development) of the productive forces. Such an attack on the institutions of imperialism will also need to be linked to challenges mounted against forces within India, among whom the most obvious are traders looting food-grains in the government stores meant for the working class and the poor peasantry (neither of which are able to purchase this resource due to IMF subsidy cuts), rural and urban capitalists benefiting from the opening up of Indian agriculture to imperialist exploitation, as well as state actors and institutions supporting and facilitating this process of imperialist penetration.

If class relationships between imperialism and its internal allies have fettered the objective productive capacities of the vast majority of the rural population in economically peripheral areas of the Third World to satisfy their subsistence needs, then those affected in this manner must of necessity unite politically and mobilize to push through agrarian transition understood in the wider sense outlined here. In short, the development of 'from below' capacities in response to the current 'from above' onslaught against the Third World rural poor is a precondition for effecting agrarian transition based on democratic control over land and other natural resources, where the use and development of these resources will not be fettered by exploitative class relations.

Chapter 7

WHY POVERTY AMID PLENTY? A MARXIST CRITIQUE OF SOCIAL DEMOCRACY IN THE PERIPHERY

In the wake of the economic success of East Asian capitalist countries in the 1970s and 1980s, a debate ensued on how this success happened. Some (including World-Bank-ish free-market hawks) argued that these countries' 'success' was mainly due to free-market policies. More social democratic-minded scholars, however, argued that it was due to an activist state that guided and directed the market and the business groups, made targeted investments in the economy, including in social and physical infrastructure, and chose the winners and the losers in the market. This was the East Asian developmental state model. The larger conceptual—political canvas of which this model is a part emphasizes that significant improvement in the living conditions of the poor is compatible with the private sector, capitalist growth, and economic globalization. It is a different matter that the real differences between these two views are skin-deep, in that both accept the hegemony of capitalism as an economic system. The book under review, 'Poverty Amid Plenty in the new India' (2012) is written by a long-time and respectable commentator on Indian economy and polity, Professor Atul Kohli of Princeton University.[190] It employs a slightly modified social-democratic developmental state view of the new India. A firmly rooted democracy, a commitment to growth, national capitalism, and rapid economic growth, and, on the other hand, the rising inequality and consequently the political movements of the groups excluded from that growth and democracy are key features of this 'new India', or India's new political economy, which is the focus of the book under review. The book asks the same question as Amartya Sen does in many of his works including *Development as Freedom*): why does the production of wealth not satisfy needs of the humanity?

The book has three parts, which discuss the political changes that have made the state increasingly pro-business, the actual economic changes, and regional diversity in political economy, respectively. Kohli describes and seeks to explain the fact that whereas India's

[190] The book is a part of the tradition that argues against the idea that globalization has made social democracy impossible on the periphery; this tradition imagines that redistributive efforts at promoting justice and equality in the developing world can work, not at the expense of economic growth but along with integration into the national economy. Scholars in this tradition include Peter Evans, Dietrich Rueschemeyer, Michael Walzer, Richard Sandbrook, Patrick Heller, Amartya Sen, and Stuart Corbridge. There is no suggestion that there is complete consensus on social democracy in the periphery among them, however.

economy is growing briskly, relative to its pre-1980s past and to many other countries at present, millions of Indians are left behind. He is at pains to emphasize the increasing inequality between cities and villages, between provinces, and between the rich and poor. The situation with respect to poverty, literacy, and health is improving, but it has only done so modestly since the 1980s.

In other words, the 'new India' is characterized by want or poverty amid plenty. The reason for this, according to Kohli, is that the state is becoming increasingly pro-business (i.e., big indigenous business), which is not the same as being pro-market. And unlike many, Kohli believes that economic liberalization is only part of the process that created this new India, a process that began not in 1991 but in the 1980s. As the state became more pro-business, the economic and political power of business grew. And the more the private sector emerged as the main motor of capital accumulation and growth, the more India's political elite had to—and has to—create policies favorable to the private sector.

The private sector—in this case, big business—exercises its power in many ways in what is now called 'India, Inc.' Too much stress on redistribution or too much anti-business rhetoric/policy can be threatened with capital flight (akin to capital strike). In addition to the indirect constraints the private sector puts on the state, it also exercises power in direct ways: it influences politics by using media, changing people's attitudes towards private enterprise, running for and financing elections, lobbying for favorite policies, and putting pressure on the state via chambers of commerce that propagate a pro-business political economy. Given capitalists' control over parties through the financing of elections, all parties have become pro-business. Economic policy makers are now asking businesses what they want and how government can help. A narrow ruling alliance is producing the spectacular growth. This alliance is also producing social exclusion and inequality and, as a result, political problems—namely, those surrounding how to manage the excluded.

Unlike in earlier times (during Nehru and early years of Indira Gandhi) when socialism and populism were used as legitimating ideologies to manage the excluded and win elections, at present, the political system is using a variety of other tactics. These include the use of family lineage (e.g., the Gandhi surname), the illusion of inclusive growth, and the politics of religion, caste, and regionalism. These are used to serve narrow interests without alienating the majority—to get votes. A division of labor appears to have been created by trial and error: the national center, Delhi, has been focusing on growth and helping big business, while at the periphery, in the provinces, the Mayawatis and the like have been using caste and other forms of symbolic politics and demagogy to deal with the excluded (p. 68). There are also efforts to insulate critical economic decisions from mass pressure by creating a rational and technocratic apex: economic decisions are made by technocrats such as the Manmohan Singhs and the Montek Ahluwalias. As well, the state is attempting to decentralize the task of accommodating the noise in body politics by shifting responsibility for this task to lower levels of government. This tactic frees the national elite to take credit for India's shining, while the failures in implementation of pro-poor policies can be laid at the doors of lower-level politicians. Often, such failures can be used to justify cutting funding to welfare schemes.

However, the system is fully able to manage the excluded. This fact leads to desperate actions at the individual level (e.g., farmers' suicides), social movements such as Naxalism, and NGO-led movements (p. 76). Indeed, although support for private ownership of business has increased among educated and upper-income groups, support for public ownership has actually decreased among less-educated people and the poor (p. 50).[191]

Kohli's analysis is carefully crafted, meticulously utilizing facts culled mostly from government sources. For those who take democracy seriously, he does an enormous service: he demonstrates very well how the democratic state is being instrumentally controlled by Indian big business, which constitutes only a small fraction of the total population. The book is a damning indictment of democratic India, which has lately become the darling of western imperialists in terms of investment and strategic partnership (with the aim of containing the undemocratic and 'communist' China). In discussing the new India, Kohli correctly avoids empiricism, adding that '[h]ow facts are arranged and interpreted is deeply influenced by underlying theoretical assumptions and normative commitments' (p. 4). He rejects mainstream economics as well as what he calls 'strict Marxism' (p. 5). He uses the language of class within an overall left-Weberian perspective. The theoretical categories underlying his empirical assertions and their political implications deserve a serious and detailed critical assessment. This is the purpose of the remainder of this essay.

ECONOMIC GROWTH AND INEQUALITY

Like the state elites and business groups and their supporters, Kohli is very positive about India's fast economic growth. He endorses it. Growth creates the necessary conditions for the alleviation of poverty and has directly contributed to it.

Now, first of all, what *kind* of growth has happened? Kohli seems to be more concerned with the quantity of growth rather than its quality. He is oblivious of structural obstacles to a systemic rise in labor productivity, one of which is this: given a massive reserve army, entrepreneurs tend to hire people at low wages for long hours to produce cheap goods for an internal and external market, without much incentive to invest in productivity-enhancing technological changes. His nationalist outlook largely misses the fact that India is playing its role in the global economy as a low-wage platform of global capitalism. The stagnation in agriculture is actually much deeper than Kohli thinks: consider the declining per capita production of food grains caused by India's resources, including land, being increasingly used for high-value agricultural commodities for the global market. Consider also how the farming sector is increasingly controlled by indigenous and foreign big business through contract farming and other mechanisms (e.g., the sale to Indian farmers of expensive genetically modified seeds by foreign companies and their Indian subsidiaries). He is insufficiently critical of the fact that much of the so-called growth has been in sectors that hardly produce anything useful that ordinary workers can afford to consume, or that produce things that people usually do not consume. So the condition for an *articulation* between production and consumption—a hallmark of organic development—is missing. Furthermore, if one considers the depletion and destruction of resources in the last three or four decades, the real economic

[191] Kohli discusses the nature of state-business alliance at both national and provincial scales. He stresses that while the Indian state has entered into a pro-business alliance, this alliance has an interesting regional dimension: at the provincial level, it does not exist the same way it does nationally. While Gujarat is close to the national model, in Uttar Pradesh patronage-based politics dominate and growth suffers, while in West Bengal some kind of social democracy has worked, producing modest growth and a modest amount of redistribution.

growth rate may in fact be smaller than Kohli cares to think. Kohli does not say anything about all this. He, like the ruling alliance he criticizes, is too enamored by the 6% growth.

Now we should examine the other side of growth: inequality and poverty. Kohli accepts that some inequality is inevitable in a market society (p. 129). Markets are inherently hierarchical, he says. Higher rates of return on capital and scarce skills explain inequality (p. 129). There is more inequality than there should be, however, because of the pro-business ruling alliance. In other words, capitalistic growth, which is the growth that Kohli talks about without naming it this way, is good. It could reduce poverty. But because of inequality (for which this growth is only partly responsible), poverty alleviation has been modest. What he ignores is that the fundamental cause of inequality is differential control over the means of production and labor power, which is the other side of the fact that society's resources are used to meet the profit-imperative, and not human need. The most fundamental level of inequality in income and living standards is between the owners of the means of production and those who perform wage labor (both more skilled and less skilled). Then there is inequality between owners (that is, between owners of smaller and bigger operations) and between workers. Poverty simply means that on the ladder of unequal distribution of income, the people who are on the lower side of the ladder have less income than necessary for a non-poor standard of living. Poverty is essentially a question of inequality. Kohli does not consistently conceptualize the poverty—inequality relation this way. He also does not consistently connect growth, which he endorses, to inequality.

Kohli's view of capital is problematic. He has a physical view of capital; he sees capital as a thing, as something that produces a benefit or utility: the more one has it, the more benefit one derives. In reality, capital *is* an exploitative relationship. The fundamental reason for inequality, which any capitalist state, no matter how autonomous it is, cannot do much about, is made clear by the fact that an average worker receives at best a small fraction of what she produces, enough that she can survive and continue to work. Growth that produces profit for capital but little employment for workers is a major cause of inequality, and this Kohli pays lip service to because he endorses the growth record. Capital dispossessing peasants and taking away their minimal means of subsistence in the name of special economic zones, etc., as another major cause of inequality does not register in Kohli's conceptualization of poverty, nor does the increase in the price of daily commodities, the government subsidies for these having been withdrawn, nor does the near-stagnation in real wages for most people.

The so-called poverty decline that Kohli attributes to growth is more a statistical artifact than anything real. While the economy must be run along rational lines, there is irrationality in thinking about the poor, an irrationality of which he does not take note. An example of irrational thinking is the poverty line that Mr. Montek Ahluwalia, the Planning Commission's deputy chairman, defended. This was 26 rupees in villages and 32 rupees in cities per person every day. Such a cutoff per capita income level, he said, 'is not comfortable but it is not all that ridiculous in Indian conditions'; this is part of this irrational thinking.[192] But Kohli is not far off from this kind of thinking either. If one accepts that every person must have the right to a decent life—including enough nutritional food, clothes, health care, housing, etc.—the current definition of poverty (which is much less than a dollar a day) says that to be poor is to have far less than the level of income necessary for a decent living. But for Kohli, even '$2 per day per capita income [as a cutoff point for a daily poverty-line] is probably too high a

[192] Quoted in the *Hindu* (Oct 12, 2011).

standard to set for a country like India' (p. 132). If the poverty level is defined at a very low level, as it is, a very small increase in average income and a small corresponding increase in the income of poor people can potentially lead to some decrease in poverty, but does that decrease indicate any qualitative and significant improvement in their standard of living? A lower threshold for poverty, to which Kohli is not opposed, has served important functions for big business and its state. It influences perceptions of what constitutes a decent standard of living, and thus influences the value of labor power and reduces the wages that capital has to pay. A higher poverty line would put pressure on wages and thus on profit. A lower definition of the poverty line creates the illusion that poverty is decreasing, that growth is contributing to that decrease (because poverty has been decreasing since 1991), and that the state, controlled by big business, can intervene to make the poverty situation better. In other words, a modest social democracy is possible. This is the outer limit of much thinking on poverty in India, including on the right and the left, which shows the poverty of their thinking more than anything else.

THE CHANGING SOCIAL CHARACTER OF THE STATE: A PRO-MARKET (NEOLIBERAL) STATE OR A PRO-BUSINESS STATE?

Kohli recognizes that 'India, of course, is a private enterprise economy. In this limited sense, the Indian state has never been deeply anti-private enterprise' (p. 6). But the state has taken on a new attribute: it has been a pro-business (as opposed to pro-market) state in the sense that 'the primary commitment of the Indian state [was, and to a large extent, is] to *established* Indian businesses rather than to any general principle of creating free markets and a global opening' (p. 105). All pro-business governments are not pro-market. He argues that a state that is pro-market would not be an interventionist state, would cut spending, would not favor already-established businesses, and would promote new entrants. It would not favor indigenous enterprises over foreign businesses, nor would it favor big businesses over smaller businesses (p. 108).

The pro-business strategy—and Kohli's interpretation of it—is derived from the real-world experience of East Asia. But it is different from the South Korea-type state in that the Indian state has not done enough to help improve the efficiency of the private sector or to help the poor. It is more a facilitator than a direct doer. Elements within the state can make the lives of business-people difficult. So, the Indian state is a modified version of the East Asian developmental state. Kohli says that 'India's authority structure was and remains too fragmented, and given Indian democracy, the underlying class basis of state power could never be too exclusively pro-business' (p. 110) and that the capitalist class is not hegemonic in the Marxist sense (p. 40). This is seen in the fact that attempts to trim public expenditures, to privatize state-run businesses, and to reform labor laws face political obstacles due to pressures from groups other than big business (p. 40).

This is a part of thinking -- to which Professor John Harriss[193] and others (e.g., Amartya Sen, Jean Dreze) subscribe-- that the Indian state is not a paradigmatic example of neoliberalism (p.113), because it does not completely ignore the poor who engage in social movements to put pressure on the state for concessions. The merit of this way of thinking is

[193] Harriss, (2011).

that it is not 'strict': it is flexible; it does not look at the world as black or white! The problem is that it is simply absurd. It completely ignores a law of dialectics, which says that 'quantitative changes beyond certain limits become converted into qualitative' (Trotsky, 1939b). It implies that to be bald one has to lose all the hair on one's scalp. To be hot, water does not have to be at 100 degrees. Water at 95 degrees is really hot, as far as the human tolerance for heat is concerned. The last 5 degrees are not much of a consequence. Losing hair or the physical warmth of water, beyond a limit, beyond a *certain* level of tolerance, becomes a qualitatively different thing. [194] Using Trotsky's language, one can say that the Indian state, like the state in the USA, etc., has made so many concessions to the ruling class and withdrawn so many of the hard-own concessions to working masses that the nature of the state has passed a level of tolerance (of the masses). It is a neoliberal capitalist state.

I indeed find little real substantive distinction between the state being pro-market and the state being pro-business (i.e., pro-big business). A state that does not intervene in the economy exists only in the neoclassical economics textbook (case in point: the bailout of banks during the 2008 crisis), although the actual degree of intervention at a specific time and in a specific place is a different matter. A state that is pro-market must also be pro-business because the market is dominated by business and big business. The market process happens at the national and international scales. A state that allows its national market—in other words, its national business class—to slowly open up to the global markets is no less *pro*-market. It is pro-market at the national scale. All states try to protect their own businesses. It is difficult to argue that a state that would 'spend more, control labor more, and support capital more actively' (p. 102) is pro-business but not pro-market, unless the market as it operates concretely is (mistakenly) seen as not class-differentiated, as a market where competition does not give rise to monopolies (i.e., big business), and as a place where big business does not rule. The state in India—as elsewhere—is pro-business, pro-big business. It is *also* pro-market; this market is guided by the state, in the interest of the common affairs of the different capitalist fractions. Indeed, what is so unique about Kohli's idea that the state is a pro-business? Marxists have held that the state has always been an organ of—or has always been led by—big business and big landowners, which are increasingly colluding and compromising, when necessary, with foreign, imperialist capital. So what is novel about Kohli's assertion about the state being pro-business?

Underlying the idea that the state is pro-business rather than pro-market is what I will call Kohli's politicist notion of class. He thinks about class more in terms of what I will call 'political life chances': the capitalist class is one that is conceptualized less in terms of its control over the means of production and of the exploitation of the working masses, and more as the *beneficiary of state policies* and as a class that exercises political—strategic power through control over the media and political parties, for example. On the other hand, the working masses are seen less in terms of their lack of control over the means of production, less in terms of their status as exploited, and less in terms of the political power they have by virtue of their class status. They are seen more as excluded groups, that is to say, as groups that are excluded from the benefits of state policy, that are politically fragmented, that never have the power to mount a fundamental challenge to the state and big business, and that may get some crumbs thrown at them if state capacity is increased. It appears that classes, for

[194] 'Dialectical thinking analyses all things and phenomena in their continuous change, while determining in the material conditions of those changes that critical limit beyond which 'A' ceases to be 'A''.(Trotsky, 1939b)

Kohli, are more politically constituted and *not* constituted as 'large groups of people differing from each other by the place they occupy in a historically determined system of social production, by their relation … to the means of production, by their role in the social organization of labor, and, consequently, by the dimensions of the share of social wealth of which they dispose and the mode of acquiring it' (Lenin in *A Great Beginning*).[195] This sort of theory of class and of the state that it influences is reinforced by and expressed through Kohli's language of (social) exclusion (and marginalization), the language of the petty bourgeois left, which originally came from France, a place known for many other fashionable petty-bourgeois intellectual trends masquerading as radicalism. An objective consequence of Kohli's use of this language is to displace the language of class and exploitation.

The inadequate class theory leads Kohli to the idea that the apex of political economy has changed, but not the bottom half. Now: how can the apex (i.e., big business) grow without immiserizing the bottom three quarters or so? Classes are internally and antagonistically connected; how can things change with respect to the exploiting class but not to the exploited classes? If Kohli really did look at the bottom—the working masses—he would see corresponding changes in their *direct relations* with the business class, which are promoted by new state policies: their increased rate of exploitation, their dispossession from whatever little property they had, their insecurity, their increasingly unsafe working conditions, and so on. Kohli refers to political economy many times. In political economy, an important concept is the value of labor power. Wages, on average, as Marx explains in chapter 6 of *Capital 1*, should cover the cost of maintenance of labor power, including costs incurred daily on food and other basic needs, and other costs that have a different time frame and are incurred more infrequently, such as rent, education, and health care. Imagine this: let business pay the full value of labor power, and let workers pay their taxes to the government, which the government can then use to provide what Kohli calls the public goods (i.e., health and education). Kohli never raises the issue of wages or providing safe working conditions. It is a naked fact that capital pursuing growth (read: growth in its profits) does not pay a wage that creates a demand for high-quality education or health or the financial ability of the state, via taxes from the working masses, to provide these 'public goods'. Kohli appears to be oblivious of this. Poverty is mainly a political affair: it is a failure of the state. Not of business. Poor people, for him, are *people*, not classes.

Kohli's view of class is one of contingency. Class determines some aspects of society and not others (pp. 4-5). It is such an underlying theory of class, a theory that says that the state has significant autonomy vis a vis the capitalist class, that influences Kohli's (developmental statist and social democratic) interpretation of the state. That theory of class must be rejected as inadequate. The state must be seen as a capitalist state *tout court*. Kohli forgets that even the 'socialist' Nehru could not tolerate the *bourgeois* land reforms attempted by the Left parties, whom Kohli rightly calls social democratic. Why? A successful challenge to the private property of the landed might overspill to become a challenge to capitalist property as such.

The pro-business interventionist interpretation of the state is based on a fundamental conflation. For Kohli, the state intervening on behalf of capital signifies state autonomy, rather than the fact that the state is acting as a collective capitalist and under pressure from capital. He forgets that while the state can intervene on behalf of and for capital, it will not

[195]Lenin, V. 1919. *Collected Works*. Vol. 29. (http://www. marxists.org/ archive/lenin/ works/ index.htm)

necessarily intervene on behalf of and for the poor masses; he forgets that the hand that works for capital is not the hand that can work for the masses. Making the distinction between the state being pro-business and being pro-market—where business, or big business, is only *a part* of the market—creates the illusion that while the state acts on behalf of one part of the market, it has sufficient autonomy to intervene in the other part of the market, namely, the poor. Seeing the state as pro-business rather than pro-market creates the illusion that the state can heed business groups a little less, that the political power of big business can be countervailed a little, and that the state has significant autonomy vis a vis the business groups, which it can use to promote inclusive growth.

SOCIAL DEMOCRACY IN PRO-BUSINESS INDIA

Kohli is (slightly) critical of the free-market view that India's opening up of the economy will accelerate growth and produce inclusive growth (pp. 212—213). Such a view ignores the fact that 'economic changes are embedded in political and social realities' (p. 213).

Inclusive growth will not come via active civil society (that is to say, protest politics and perhaps some economic class struggle). Nor is revolution possible. This is because of the ethnic- and caste-based fragmentation of the masses and of the superior military power of the state, Kohli says. (Apparently none of these applied to Russia?) Revolutionary politics will not just happen in India (p. 74). Maoist revolutionary struggle will necessarily fail because of the military might of the state. Revolution is also not necessary, because there is nothing wrong with capitalism as such and some inequality is inevitable. Kohli takes capitalism for granted. It is here to stay. After all, he argues, markets (read: capitalist markets) increase efficiencies. (It is as if the 2008 economic crisis and the massive waste that it caused did not happen). However, some excesses of private enterprise have to be reined in: the level of inequality that is more than what is inevitable, as well as malnutrition, the low level of education, and the poor health of workers. This requires redistribution of resources that growth has made available.

Redistribution requires not electoral pressures and occasional farsighted politicians who can make a difference, but something else, namely, modest social democracy, which is the outer limit of possibilities (p. 47). This is the type of social democracy that India's communist parties have practiced: they have included excluded groups using class themes (p. 70). Kohli has been advocating 'well-organized representation of the underprivileged in the political sphere so as to facilitate a shift, not toward populism, but toward a real social-democratic politics' (p.213) since his 1987 book, *The state and poverty in India.* This will also require significant improvement in the capacity of the Indian state to deliver resources and services to the poor, a capacity that is lacking now. In this model, state interventions will remain critical for facilitating growth in the short and medium term. He does recognize the limits of social democracy: if politicians emphasize only the poor and near-poor, they will alienate private investors, hurting economic growth. The more they appease the latter, the more they will alienate the former (p. 71). But a modest social democracy is all that is possible.

Kohli's 'normative preferences' for social democracy, which are problematic, follow from his 'analytical ideas' about class and the state, which are no less inadequate; they follow from his:

> state-society frame of reference [that] shares an elective affinity with social-democratic preferences. This affinity is rooted in the core assumption that states and societies have their partially autonomous logics of action that, in turn, mutually influence patterns of political and social change. This assumption allows one to imagine the possibility of democracy in poor societies, to argue for a vigorous role for states in promoting economic growth and welfare provision, and at the same time to worry about the growing power of capital in political and social life. (p. 5)

This state–society autonomy/interaction perspective presupposes, and clears the ground for, a rejection of the class perspective and revolution. 'In the past... Marxists have often been sympathetic to the goals of revolution and communism' and neoclassicals believe in free market (p. 5). He believes that both are wrong. So are Marxists and neoclassical economists in the same category of wrong thinkers, are equally wrong? Kohli says that in the past, Marxists were sympathetic to revolution. So now they are not? Or is it that, for Kohli, one can be a Marxist and not be sympathetic towards revolution? Is it that one can be a Marxist and be, like Kohli, a social democrat? In fact, Marxists are not just sympathetic towards revolution. The possibility and necessity of revolution, for them, follow from their analytical ideas, including about class discussed earlier. For them, class—and therefore the capitalist class relation—is the fundamental cause of humanity's most fundamental problems, such as poverty and inequality and a lower level of human development, and class relations have to be abolished in order to put any significant and permanent dent in these problems. This is no less true about India, where, as Kohli himself notes, the population of poor people is more than the entire population of countries other than India and China.

Revolution against the state and capital is out. What is *in* is the idea of state autonomy vis a vis big business, which is very popular in intellectual circles (especially in state theory),[196] as well as the more general idea that repudiates the class reductionism of 'strict Marxism'. These refutations must be refuted. The state can be autonomous of capital only temporarily. The general tendency is this: the class that controls the means of production, whether its members are blacks or whites or browns, is the class that more or less controls state power (as well as the production of ideas). A class cannot control state power for too long if it does not have control over the means of production; this is an important part of the idea of Trotsky's permanent revolution. The idea that ordinary people, through some control over state power, can achieve significant and long-term control over economic resources is analytically as unscientific as it is politically useless. This idea might have had some validity before the 1970s, where productive and financial capital was much less mobile than it is now. But in the current time, the political control of capital to promote inclusive growth is a left-bourgeois illusion that reflects an unconscious fear of signs of the growing radicalization of the masses, who need to be contained through deception and trickery.

Kohli says that growth has made resources available that can be used for the poor. One should ask: if resources are available, why is the poverty line defined as being equal to destitution, a definition that Kohli does not unequivocally oppose? Kohli is forgetting several things here. In thinking that economic growth under the rule of *capital* makes available *resources* which can be used to benefit the poor, he forgets that these resources are potentially *capital* under capitalism: that they can be used to make more money. The resources are not mere physical things. They represent a social relation. The more working masses consume

[196]Joel Migdal and Peter Evans, among others, have written about this, as has Kohli himself.

(proletarian and semi-proletarian masses), the more limited is, generally speaking, the opportunity to make profit (assuming there are enough working bodies). This explains why there is a structural limit on how much of the available resource can be used for human welfare. Mere physical availability of resources – co-presence of resources and poverty -- does not mean much. In a capitalist economy, there are strong limits to public resources being used to better the conditions of the poor even if those resources are available, because the poor are also workers and when they live better, the balance of power on the ground changes in their favor. This is why welfare programs, such as employment generation schemes, are opposed by landowners (as Kohli is well aware). Even if resources are available, politicians and businesspeople are reluctant to use them for fear of inflation. Kohli sees the poor as low-income consumers; capital sees them as exploitable workers and as potential antagonists. For him, the poor are never active beneficiaries in their own welfare; instead, they get some crumbs from a state with increased administrative capacity and a social-democratic commitment. Kohli forgets that it is extremely unlikely that the poor will gain significant benefits outside of their fighting for a radical change in the system. His propositions that capitalist growth is making resources for redistribution available and that social democracy will make the lives of the poor better go directly against the idea, tested through experience worldwide, that the bourgeois class has an unyielding determination to give significant and long-term benefits to the masses, even if resources are available. This is especially so at a time of increased capital mobility. Kohli is aware of capital strike. He wants to ignore it.

Even if resources are available, state capacity to reach the poor is limited, Kohli says. But he forgets to ask how it is that the same state has the capacity to hold national and international sports events, conduct elections at national and provincial levels, test nuclear missiles, fight wars, build railroads (including even dedicated ones for business), invite foreign dignitaries, cut deals with foreign companies, jail/harm/kill striking workers, and do many other things. Where does that capacity come from? Does state capacity have a class character, or does it not? For Kohli, apparently it does not. If the state is so powerful as to be able to crush the movements of the poor (as he acknowledges) and if the state has the capacity to do all the things he mentions, what stops it from, for example, dispossessing the business class, which is a tiny minority, and creating conditions where the productive power of ordinary people, who are the majority, can be developed and resources used for their welfare? Once again, does the state's so-called administrative capacity have a class character? All those – post-Marxists and others -- who believe in the power of ideational articulation and autonomy of the political and of the state must ask these questions.

The agents of Kohli's social democracy – bearers of state capacity to help the poor -- are parties like the CPI(M) (Communist Party of India [Marxist]), for which, it must be stated, scholars like Amartya Sen, the Nobel laureate, also have some sympathy. Many people call CPI(M) communist. This makes as much sense as the Wall Street Journal calling Congress, a party of the big bourgeoisie, a centre-left party. Kohli rightly clips the wings of illusions that the CPI(M) and parties like it are communist parties. A communist party is one that mobilizes proletarians and semi-proletarians, independently of bourgeois and petty-bourgeois forces, around immediate economic and political demands, the goal being to fight for the overthrow of capitalism, nationally and internationally. Left parties, at most, want a more developed, slightly more democratic, slightly more egalitarian society. Kohli does well to call a spade a spade. He calls CPI(M) and the like social democratic. But what he takes away from CPI(M) in one hand, he gifts it in another hand. That is: he has been saying for decades that an organized, disciplined party such as CPI(M), given some ideological coherence, could obtain significant benefits for the masses. If the big business has too much voice, why can the subaltern not speak a little, and not have a little influence on the state? It is after all a field of democracy where people sit at the table to make their voices heard. Kohli forgets that Left parties such as the CPI(M) have been precisely the kinds of parties that have propped up one bourgeois government after another in India, including Congress-governments, and that have contained the revolutionary anger of poor peasants and the working class through bourgeois trade unionism and other mechanisms. These parties, while in power, have implemented blatantly pro-bourgeois policies, being responsible for the emergence of right-wing political puppets of big business and regional bourgeoisie to act as pro-poor imposters. Kohli's view of social democracy is undermined because the agents of social democracy are reified: they are given more power than they can have.

Kohli's view of social democracy also collapses when one assesses the democracy element of his social democracy. Recall that he says that state and society have relative autonomy and that this autonomy 'allows one to imagine the possibility of democracy in poor societies' (p. 5). Democracy will ensure that the benefits of growth reach the poor. Now, Kohli thinks that India is a vibrant democracy (and there is some truth to this; if this is true, the credit goes to the struggle of the masses for democracy). Elections are routine, fair, and competitive (pp. 24, 60). India is a noisy democracy. Many groups periodically press more or less organized demands upon the state for one valued good or another (p. 25). But on the other hand, Kohli also recognizes to some extent that this democracy is undermined by the same forces that are responsible for growth, which is an essential part of his social democracy. He recognizes that capital has a disproportionate amount of influence on polity and economy through its control over media and politicians (p. 52). Indeed, the rich control Parliament, where 300 members are millionaires (p. 55). Parliament hardly modifies decisions made by technocrats (p. 66). Policies that suit specific enterprises or industries are bought and sold via briefcase politics. Thus, social democracy depends on democracy, but the same process that produces growth also undermines democracy. This has implication for social democracy that Kohli does not consider. In Kohli's balance sheet, democracy is effective enough to make social democracy possible.

If Kohli thinks that social democracy is possible it is because of his very narrow—even bourgeois—view of democracy. He endorses growth; he praises India's high-growth record. This growth, as was discussed earlier, has come about, according to him, due to an increasing alliance between the state and business. Now, one aim of this alliance has been the suppression of labor rights. But Kohli does not think that this is a violation of democracy, the democracy of the poor, of workers. For him, election = democracy, more or less. That Maruti workers are beaten up and sent to jail so that the pro-business climate can be sustained has nothing to do with the violation of democratic rights, for Kohli, the social democrat. If growth is not benefiting the poor, the reasons are more politicist and subjective, and include a lack of commitment on the part of politicians and a lack of administrative capacity. What objective factors explain this *thinking*, this lack of *commitment or will and* lack of *political capacity*?

That Kohli, in his text, has directed attention to the increasing big business influence on the affairs of the state and to the undermining of democracy constitutes an important contribution. But to the extent that this criticism of the state is from the standpoint not of the working masses and their democratic rights, but from a standpoint according to which their life chances could be improved through state interventions *within capitalism* and from the standpoint of weaker sections of the private property-owning class, this criticism is severely limited. His view is part of a larger mode of thinking – 'egalitarian liberalism' (Callinicos, 2002:18),[197] which argues that substantive egalitarianism can be achieved without transcending the present order itself. The criticisms of the ideas in the book, which, once again, represents a wider tendency in left-bourgeois circles, point to two things. Intellectually: there is a need for more rigorous class-analysis of state and society. Politically: there is a need for democratically-organized mobilization of working masses aimed at establishing a genuinely democratic social system in South Asia, and internationally, which satisfies their material and cultural needs.

[197] Callinicos (2002).

PART 3: CRITIQUING CONTEMPORARY CAPITALIST SOCIETY AND ANTI-CAPITALIST POLITICS

Chapter 8

NEOLIBERALISM'S CLASS CHARACTER: CRITICAL VIEWS ON INDIA'S NEW ECONOMIC POLICY

Neoliberalism has different names in different geographical contexts. In the wake of the strikes in southern Europe against cuts in government funding, austerity is often synonymous with neoliberalism. In India, on the other hand, neoliberalism goes by the name of 'economic reforms' and the New Economic Policy (NEP). The views of proponents of neoliberalism have been widely published in India, including in its influential (and slightly progressive) *Economic Political Weekly*.[198] With the zeal of a politician trying to sell the reforms and the NEP to younger citizens (primarily university graduates), Bhagwati (2001), a Columbia University economics professor, conceptualizes reforms *qua* neoliberalism as representing 'a reversal of the anti-globalisation, anti-market, pro-public-enterprise attitudes and policies that produced our dismal growth performance [during the pre-1991 period]'. He says that these reforms are the most important factor in reducing poverty by increasing growth. His argument is that growth creates employment: it puts money in the hands of the government, which can provide health and other facilities for the poor, and it also provides incentive to the poor to invest in human capital. Datt and Ravallion say that 'the higher post-reform growth rates are delivering a steeper decline in poverty' (Datt and Ravallion, 2010:57). By raising living standards in urban areas, economic growth has had a positive effect on rural incomes (ibid.). The prime minister of India, who himself is an economist, talks about the need to encourage and revive the 'animal spirit' of the investors,[199] which will, in turn, promote welfare; the NEP is about this.

If neoliberalism—in other words, economic reform—is such a wonderful thing, why it is that in one survey, 'three-fourths of respondents who had any opinion on the subject say that the reforms benefit only the rich'? (Bardhan, 2005). Furthermore, why it is that people tend to vote out parties that pursue reforms mindlessly? This chapter seeks to conceptualize neoliberalism in the Indian context in terms of its multi-dimensionality and its contradictions.

---

[198]There is a massive amount of literature on the nature of the NEP, including its positive and negative effects. This paper does not aim to review this literature.

[199]The *Hindu* reports: '"Reverse the climate of pessimism … revive the animal spirit in the country's economy … Millions of our countrymen look up to the government to throw open channels for their progress, prosperity and welfare," Dr. [Manmohan] Singh told Finance Ministry officials after reviewing the state of the economy in a series of meeting during the day while stressing that reviving investor sentiment was on top of his priorities'. June 27, 2012.

The Bollywood movie—the 'dirty picture'—has been said to run on three things: entertainment, entertainment, and entertainment. The dirty picture of neoliberalism runs on three things, as well: class, class, and class. Indeed, neoliberalism must be seen as the restoration and reinforcement of class power (Harvey, 2005), specifically the class power that large owners of business have over the working masses in a situation where markets are less and less regulated and 'animal spirit' more and more encouraged. What is problematic about the NEP is not *this or that* aspect of it (e.g., the idea that it increases poverty and inequality). Rather, the *whole* 'policy' is the problem. So it requires a totalizing dialectical critique, one that situates its limited benefits in relation to its enormous costs and sees it from multiple vantage points.

This paper makes a number of observations on the multiple aspects of neoliberalism as a class project. No attempt is made to offer detailed empirical evidence for the statements made, nor are there extensive references in the existing literature on the topic. Although the arguments are about 'neoliberalism with Indian characteristics', they have wider applicability.

What Is NEP (Not)?

The New Economic Policy is not just a government *policy*, and it is neither entirely *new* nor merely *economic*. It basically represents the demands of the capitalist class, and more specifically, the demands of hegemonic fractions of the domestic and foreign-diasporic capitalist class at a particular stage in the development of Indian and global capitalism. This class now wants to—and with modern technological changes in transportation and communication, is *able* to—do business in a different manner than in the past. It wants the state to clear the way for this new way of doing things. India's yearly national budget more or less represents a wish-list of capitalist fractions represented by chambers of commerce, corporate lobbyists, and newspaper editors. Their wish-list gets a sympathetic hearing from the pro-market state managers, otherwise known as the 'sultans of reforms', who are CEOs occupying important positions within the state. The biggest and the most enthusiastic of the listeners is the current prime minister, Dr. Manmohan Singh, who, incidentally, has declared his respect for Thatcher, the co-architect of global neoliberalism along with Reagan. In a word, there is no shortage of intellectual support for the NEP. Much-needed support is provided by the opinion-makers of India's free media and so-called intellectuals (including its 'telectuals'—television intellectuals—and professors from imperialist countries who have been outsourced to India). No social–material practice can continue to operate without a corresponding discursive practice that justifies it.

Formally introduced in 1991, the NEP outlines the specific demands of the capitalist class for the state to create conditions where domestic and foreign capital can invest money to make a lot of money. The idea is to make money not only by using cheap natural resources like land, water, forests, and minerals, but also by using speculation and other non-productive means and by exploiting cheap skilled and unskilled labor. All existing barriers to money-making, says the NEP, should be removed and new facilitative conditions should be created. An important goal is to attract foreign capital and strengthen the position of Indian business in the fight for export markets and to obtain foreign technology. The Indian bourgeoisie seeks to transform India into a world power by making it a cheap labor office, a laboratory (for pharmaceutical and biotech companies, for example), and a factory for international capital. Some of the specific demands of business, as expressed politically by the NEP, include: the deregulation of private businesses; the privatization of government businesses; trade liberalization; granting permission to foreign capital to own businesses in India; tax cuts and other incentives for businesses; and the reduction or complete withdrawal of government benefits for the poor. The NEP, therefore, is the neoliberal program of the bourgeoisie first, and a government policy second.[200]

The NEP is certainly new, as its name suggests, but it is not as new as is commonly thought. All major interventions, including major anti-poverty policies since de-colonization, have been more or less about propping up a national capitalist regime (with some support from erstwhile 'socialist' countries), a regime that is a little protected from imperialism and a little free from the fetters of feudal remnants. Even in terms of actual spending, the Indian state *has been* a welfare state of the rich elite. Many of the resources in the hands of the state have been used for the propertied classes (in the form of various subsidies and cheap loans) and for wealthier, higher-income, more educated people.[201] According to the government's own estimates, in the mid-1990s (when the NEP was only a few years old), the central and state governments together gave out more than 10 per cent of the GDP in the form of explicit or implicit budgetary subsidies for 'nonmerit' goods and services (the latter largely accrue to the relatively rich) (Bardhan, 2005). The pre-1991 age, including the so-called Nehruvian age, was not exactly a golden age for the masses. Mass poverty and (petty) bureaucratic heavy-handedness were rampant. It is not that there is no absolute difference between the NEP and the pre-1991 regime. But the similarity between the two is not to be un-dialectically under-stressed. The NEP is similar to other past types of interventions, in terms of its basic class content.

The NEP is not merely about economic matters. This is because it must ensure political and ideological conditions for various accumulation strategies. 'Political conditions' in this case means state repression and judicial coercion (including the suppression of democratic rights, to be discussed later). 'Ideological conditions' here refers to the promotion of market fetishism in all spheres of everyday life, including our consciousness. Associated with market fetishism are the ideas of getting rich quickly by any means and of the market as the dominant method of helping the poor (hence the popularity of such things as self-help groups and micro-credit in the discourse of development, happily promoted by the state and civil society groups).[202]

---

200 This does not mean that the way in which capitalists' interests are reflected in the NEP can be *entirely* reduced to capital's interests. When these interests are mediated by the state, the autonomy of the state (including electoral compulsion in India) must be borne in mind. This is one reason why welfare policies are not entirely off the agenda of the neoliberal state. Harriss (2011) says: 'the neoliberal project in India is tempered by India's constitutional design and state tradition as well as by social movements... and popular democracy' (p. 128). This is true, as I have shown elsewhere. But the point to emphasize is this: the state does not have to spend every penny ensuring that capitalists freely make money in order to be called a neoliberal capitalist state. A neoliberal state does not have to be a state that spends nothing for the poor. Spending for the poor is potentially in the interest of the business world because it creates a market.

201 See the early work of Bardhan (1990) as well as Bardhan (2005). While I agree that state resources have been used to benefit the proprietary classes, I do not endorse Bardhan's analytical Marxist sympathies for the market economy, nor his viewing of state actors as a class.

202 Interestingly, the obsession with capitalist economic growth is such that a political party can engage in sectarian violence against minorities (e.g., the BJP in Gujurat), and still be more or less 'condoned' and indeed accepted if it promotes economic growth through pro-business policies. The ways in which sections of national and international business endorse Mr. Modi of the Hindu Right for the post of the top political job (prime

In summation, a dialectical conceptualization of the NEP and neoliberalism is needed: it must be sensitive to both the differences and similarities between the pre-1991 and post-1991 regimes, and to both the economic and the non-economic character of the NEP. Such a conceptualization must also see the governmental or policy aspect of the NEP as rooted in the class character of Indian society. The NEP is a policy *on behalf* of capital; it is therefore a policy *of* capital, *tout court*, mediated and implemented by the state. It is an error to think about neoliberalism merely as a governmental policy.[203] It is a class project.

Winners and Losers

Not only in terms of its underlying driving forces, but also in terms of its necessary consequences, the NEP is a class project: it produces an enormous amount of class inequality. India's neoliberalism has led to a small minority of winners and a very large majority of losers. It has vastly benefited the capitalist class, including those fractions that specialize in finances, IT, real estate, and natural resources, producing close to 70 dollar billionaires. It has placed a colossal amount of wealth—wealth produced by the sweat of the property-less masses—in the hands of a few.[204] A part of this wealth has been hidden away in overseas banks. A not-inconsiderable part is publicly displayed via pretentious lifestyles, which constitute one way in which the elite ideologically reinforce their class position by differentiating themselves from the majority. A wide variety of consumer items is indeed now available for those with money (approximately 200 million people in a country of 1200 million). The NEP has certainly brought with it some foreign technology and cheaper intermediate goods. It has also benefited some educated people employed in IT and related industries—including tech-coolies— thereby providing cheap labor to global capitalism. Many of these people tend to easily acquiesce to their own exploitation, despite the huge difference in remuneration between India and imperialist countries, and between their own remuneration and the earnings of ordinary souls. In spite of them being exploited by global capital, this stratum does enjoy a certain level of economic success, which has promoted a habit of conspicuous consumption among them and which is mobilized as an ideological prop for neoliberalism.

On the other hand, the NEP has heaped unspeakable miseries on the bottom 700–1000 million people in India, who include urban proletarians and semi-proletarians, a large number of urban small-scale business owners, and peasants. Neoliberalism has produced a massive amount of economic inequality, insecurity, unemployment and under-employment, casualization, informalization, greater labor exploitation, and lax or nonexistent implementation of protective factory acts. It has produced what Utsa Patnaik calls 'a republic of hunger' and what Jean Dreze calls 'a nutritional emergency'. It has produced a graveyard

ministership of India), the Mr Modi, who has been widely held responsible for the massacres of Muslims, says a lot about the 'mood' of the capitalists: as long as they can make money, they do not care about the secular or religious character of the state, because their main religion is money-making.

203 This error is not too dissimilar to the error of thinking about imperialism merely as a government policy, an error that Lenin pointed out in Kautsky.

204 As Patnaik (2010a) says: 'The State under neoliberalism … actively promotes an increase in the share of surplus value in the hands of domestic and foreign corporates as an essential component of its so-called "development strategy"'.

of people who have committed suicide (at a rate of two per hour)[205] because of their economic insecurity and their inability to pay the bills. This is happening not just in villages but also in formerly booming cities like Tirupur in South India.

On its own terms, the NEP is not a big success either. It has unleashed some entrepreneurial energy, the 'animal spirit' that Dr. Singh talks about. Yet India still accounts for only 2 per cent of the global economy and less than 1 per cent of world trade. Even in the IT sector, India remains a relatively minor player dependent on the technology and markets of the West. There is little sign that the average level of labor productivity in key sectors has improved relative to that in richer countries. India's capitalism remains one that is more based on formal subsumption of labor—a regime of exploitation based on long hours and low wages—than real subsumption of labor, which is based on technological changes and increasing labor productivity (Das, 2012b).

AGRARIAN NEOLIBERALISM

In poor countries such as India, there is a specific form of neoliberalism known as agrarian neoliberalism. This requires a special treatment, given that the vast majority of the workforce still depends on farming. Agrarian neoliberalism represents an internally contradictory logic: on the one hand, rural areas are *emphasized* as being attractive venues for big business activities; on the other hand, state investment in rural areas is *reduced*. Rural areas have become an arena for new forms of accumulation: buying peasants' land dirt cheap; contract farming; agribusiness selling seeds and other inputs to peasants at a high price; and patenting of peasants' knowledge. In terms of state neglect of rural areas, rural development expenditure as a percentage of the net national product has been decreasing.[206] Government subsidies for fertilizers, electricity, and other farm inputs, as well as investment in irrigation, have all been slashed. Access to cheap loans for farmers has been limited. Price supports to farmers have been reduced, and the Public Distribution System has been drastically curtailed.

Peasants are losing land to capitalist industrialization and land-speculation. Land ceiling laws are reversed because they are considered to be constraints on capital flows into farming. Peasants are being forced to leave their land because farming is not viable: the costs of cultivation are going up due to shrinking government support. These people are also adversely affected by the import of subsidized foreign farm goods. Highly indebted, many are driven to distress sales.

As Utsa Patnaik (2007) has admirably documented, food production and availability per capita is decreasing. This is in part because land is converted to non-food crops both by big companies and by smaller owners who do not have many alternative ways of earning money and who are therefore attracted to the prospect of making a little cash. This is a grave threat to food security. Also, in the areas where high-value farm products are produced (e.g., shrimps, flowers), intense exploitation of labor, land, and water happens in order to make the sector competitive in the global market. Declining investment in rural infrastructure (especially flood and irrigation control) is increasing vulnerability to such natural calamities as drought and floods. The role of the government in buying farm produce at a favorable rate from

[205] Sainath, a progressive journalist, has brilliantly highlighted this issue.
[206] That percentage dropped from 2.85% in 1993–94 to 1.9% in 2000–01 (Patnaik, 2007:155).

peasants is less and less important. With trade liberalization, farmers, especially those with limited amount of land and investible surplus, become more vulnerable, when prices fall; they become dependent on exploitative private traders (as in the pre-1991 times). Agrarian distress is creating a huge reserve army, a part of which is forced to migrate to cities. This, along with shrinking government support for workers reducing the already-meagre social wage, allows capital to raise the level of exploitation. That the NEP is producing increasing numbers of wealthy people, on the one hand, and thousands of millions of people whose basic needs (e.g., for food) remain singularly unsatisfied, on the other, speaks to the fact that neoliberalism is a class project.

Neoliberalism as a Spatial Project

The NEP as a capitalist class agenda is a spatial, scalar project. It is implemented through accumulation projects that involve massive restructuring of space relations, which produces spatial unevenness at multiple scales. It also involves institutions and actors at multiple scales: international, national, regional, and local.

The massive restructuring of space relations has two aspects. First of all, a new built environment is being produced in order to accelerate the movement of commodities at a cheaper cost between places in India and between India and the rest of the world, and to increase the pace of elite consumption. The transformation of space relations is revealed not only in the form of special economic zones and urban shopping malls, but also in the form of new roads, railway lines (including dedicated railway lines), airports, seaports, etc.[207] The second aspect of the restructuring of space relations in India is that in order to produce spaces like this and set up enterprises (e.g., hotels; manufacturing units) as well as construct housing for sale, slums are being cleared, and peasants and aboriginal people are being dispossessed of their land. Their land is required not only for residence but also for its natural resources, which are subjected to intense exploitation. Indeed, 'displacement has been an integral constitutive component of the process of development in India' (Vasudevan, 2008:41). Between the big bosses' right and the little people's right to be in a place, between these two equal rights, it is usually force that decides the matter. This force is often the brute force wielded by the private goons of big business, the moneybags, and the more legal force of the state (police, courts, etc.).

The production of space not only facilitates accumulation and money-making in the ways just noted, it is also an opportunity in itself to make money. This is because space—the economic landscape—is a commodity. What is called infrastructure is big business indeed. The production of space has an ideological moment to it as well. By constantly asserting that the country needs a large amount of money for infrastructure, the state justifies cuts in welfare expenditure as well as measures to court private capital through various incentives.

The NEP has also resulted in an enormous amount of unevenness between regions. This is because neoliberal investment, the main motive of which is profit-making, tends to be geographically concentrated, although the actual patterns of unevenness are not written in

[207] The class bias in the space transformation that constitutes road building is made visible in the fact that while millions of rupees are spent on high-speed roads, for example, the vast majority of villages with a population of 1000 or less are not even connected by a road. Obviously, people in these places do not have enough market power.

stone. A region that is backward today can thrive tomorrow. The fact that investment happens in a few cities or States, producing impressive glass buildings, gorgeous shopping malls, and islands of 'high-tech' firms, does not mean that all places in India can experience this: the process through which some places in the country become developed includes the process of most places not developing. Yet geographical differences are being put to ideological purpose—that is, to further the neoliberal agenda: a few places have achieved some economic development through neoliberal policies, and people are being told that *all* places can achieve this. Neoliberalism *is* a process of production of spatial inequalities and spatial displacements—indeed, of 'combined and uneven development'. A highly important manifestation of this unevenness is between rural and urban areas, with urban areas growing five times faster than rural areas, and with inequality between cities and villages rising in terms of nearly every aspect of life (e.g., education, health-care, etc.). Agriculture has more or less stagnated as public expenditure has dwindled and public resources are being diverted from it to infrastructure projects in the interest of big business. The socio-geographical face of the country outside the cities and their closely connected hinterlands is dismal; this is not, to deny the enormous unevenness between areas within cities (e.g., between gated communities and slums), but these are overall richer than rural areas.[208]

The patterns of uneven development both between cities and between States have interesting political dynamics. With regards to pro-business reforms, regional elites (in States and cities) have some power vis-à-vis the central government. These regionally based elites—comprised of alliances between politicians and local-regional businesses—compete with each other for external loans and domestic as well as foreign capital. Some States and cities get more investment than others, thus creating a new layer of uneven economic development on top of an already existing layer. When all places are equally neoliberal in their courting of capital, small differences in policy and other factors necessary for profitmaking become metamorphosed into large differences.

NEOLIBERALISM AS AN IMPERIALIST PROJECT

The NEP signifies imperialism. It is a part of the imperialist project. Neoliberalism in peripheral countries is a part of global neoliberalism, the history of which is connected to working-class struggle in the West and anti-colonial struggles in the periphery. More specifically, capitalism under the rule of financial capital has, since the 1970s, been seeking to withdraw many of the concessions (e.g., welfare benefits) it previously conceded to the working class of the advanced countries due to its struggles. And global big business is no more willing to concede some autonomy to the peripheral states and the national bourgeoisie of poor countries, bourgeoisie that it tolerated in the aftermath of anti-colonial struggles. From the perspective of global big business, the natural resources, markets, space (including the space to dump waste), and laboring bodies of these poorer countries cannot be entirely left in the hands of the national bourgeoisie to exploit: international capital must have relatively

[208] The cities have experienced neoliberalization in specific ways. As Banerjee-Guha writes, 'The consequences [of neoliberalization for cities] can be seen in the increasing focus on hyper forms and mega construction activities, increased speculation and expanded investment in land and real estate … , service sector, signature projects, mega cultural events and a reduced focus on the employment generating production process, affordable housing, and collective sharing of urban space and resources' (2009:105)

free (i.e., less constrained) and direct access to them. As it plays itself out in India, the NEP, which is both a medium for and an outcome of global neoliberalism, establishes a direct exploitative connection between the bourgeoisie (including its financial segments) of rich countries and India's poor masses to a degree that did not exist previously. An important aspect of neoliberalism is indeed 'the new determination to drain the resources of the periphery toward the center' (Duménil and Lévy, 2005:10) via the activities of international financial capital and other segments of international big business.

Such transfer of resources occurs when imperialist capital exploits the workers and peasants of India, a process that the NEP furthers. This imperialist exploitation is abetted by the states of imperialist countries as well as by India's pliant compradore[209] state, an exploitation that is epitomized by 'sultans' (monarchs) of reform like Dr. Singh, the current prime minister.[210] Not only this, but some of the Indian States are run under budgetary guidelines formulated by the American 'knowledge' firm McKinsey, the IMF, the World Bank, the international development agencies of the governments of advanced countries, and 'compradore' intellectuals and advisors bought off by these institutions. In many ways, and as is widely known, neoliberalism (embodied in privatization, cuts in government spending, etc.) was imposed by international institutions under the name of conditionalities for loans. In particular, the World Bank has been instrumental in pushing for the privatization of water-supply and electricity services, as well as other crucial public services, all in the name of efficiency and development. The same sorts of measures (e.g., austerity measures) have been undertaken in the imperialist countries themselves in the interest of their top '1%' and to the detriment of their own '99%'. Neoliberalism, signifying a new onslaught of capital on the toiling masses, is the thread that links the toiling masses of the world, although the masses in poorer countries are affected a lot more than those in richer countries.

Neoliberalism and Class Struggle

The NEP has been an arena of, and an object of, class struggle. This class struggle has been from above and from below. Given the NEP's devastating impacts, it is not surprising that a massive resistance has risen up against it. Since the 1990s, millions of people have gone on numerous strikes, including a nation-wide strike in February 2013. Some of the resistance has been against the venal, atrociously corrupt way in which the partnership between capital and the state has undemocratically milked public resources. Much of the resistance has been directly against privatization, liberalization, globalization, and reduction in state support for the poor and farmers. Because of the struggle from below (both real and potential), the state has sometimes slowed the pace of reforms slightly. This happens most frequently when a given reform will adversely affect the weaker members of the bourgeoisie, who cannot

[209] The word *compradore* is used in a loose sense in this paper: here it refers to the state managers and businesses in a peripheral country that enter into an alliance with the state and businesses of imperialist countries, an alliance in which the elements of the periphery are subordinate allies.

[210] In fact, the state apparatus is increasingly occupied by pro-market ideologues and neoliberal technocrats and indeed by businesspeople themselves. This signifies the neoliberalisation and technocratisation of the state apparatus, a distinct colonisation of the state by neoliberals. Kohli (2012) says that a distinct marker of the current epoch is the increasing and deepening alliance between state managers and the business class in India, an alliance that is responsible for growth with inequality. In earlier times, state managers were a little critical of the business class (Patnaik, 2010b).

compete in the global market. The state has also tried to provide some palliatives as a part of the neoliberal policy to ensure that reforms are not politically derailed by social unrest. Relative to the amount of damage caused by neoliberalism, there is too little actual support for the poor; note that the necessity for palliatives and the limits to these palliatives are both caused by neoliberalism.

The dominant neoliberal view is one of market idolatry: the poor should be sacrificed at the altar of the god of the market, the god of reforms, the god of growth. This god has more power than the numerous gods in India's holy land. This god will, in the long run, benefit 'the poor' and less well-off people, the ordinary people ('*aam admi*'). In the short term, while the poor are prostrating themselves before the market god, they get bruised laying on the hard surface, so they need some kind of band-aid. So-called employment guarantee schemes, like loan waivers for farmers and legislation guaranteeing access to food, are one such palliative measure. Finance Minister Chidambaram, like many others (e.g., Khatkhate, 2006), thinks that 'growth is the best antidote to poverty'; so, the Minister says, 'what is needed is not less, but more reforms' (that is to say, a higher dose of neoliberalism) (quoted in the *Hindu* on November 8, 2006).

The bourgeoisie needs 'growth' (that is, a massive increase in the money in its pocket in the shortest possible time). The political parties and the neoliberal state, both at the central and the provincial levels, promise to deliver this growth.[211] At each of the points in capital's circuit (M-C-C′-M′)[212], capital wants the state to help it make money, and quickly. This is the limit to how much and in what way the workers and peasants can benefit from palliatives. The idea that there is such a thing as neoliberalism with a human face—and the fact that neoliberalism has had to be *sold* to people— means that neoliberalism itself is inhumane and does not exist in the interest of the masses. Such an idea is essentially based on the lie that the basic interests of capital are compatible with the basic interests of the toiling masses of the country as a whole in a sustainable manner.

And where the numbing of consciousness through the official and academic-market–oriented propaganda, including the propaganda dealt out by finance ministers and other spokespersons of capital, fails; where the intoxication of the masses by the fetishism of seasonal festivals called 'elections' eases off;[213] where official bribing in the form of limited welfare is ineffective; and where, as a result, the masses *do* rise in revolt, the state has been using repression. This is class struggle from above. The state's aim is to clear away the barriers to the twin methods of accumulation: accumulation by dispossession and accumulation by exploitation (Das, 2012b). The dispossession, exploitation, and oppression of aboriginal people, all of which have been exacerbated by neoliberalism, have led to Maoist resistances in several hundred districts (Das, 2010). The Maoist threat is elevated to the biggest threat to the nation. It is then conveniently used as an excuse to suppress any democratically organized protest against neoliberalism. If this threat did not exist, some other similar thing would be invented.

---

211 For this service, politicians are compensated by businesses. Politicians use some of the money they get from businesses that benefit from neoliberal policies in order to produce trickery and deception (via, e.g., television air time, and bought news) and for bribery, all of which are necessary for obtaining votes and reproducing the political legitimacy of the neoliberal state.

212 This formula just says that money (M) is invested to buy commodities (e.g., raw materials; labor power) to produce new commodities (C′) which is sold for more money (M′) than invested.

213 Note that the majority of the masses think that reforms are pro-rich.

The capitalist class has also directly engaged in struggle from above by undermining the power of workers who strike against capital. Repression of striking Maruti workers is a case in point. Capital has repressed workers by hiring goons to hurt or kill them, by bribing union leaders, and by locking employees out. In recent years, personnel days lost due to lockouts are several times the number lost due to strikes. The courts also have ruled against the democratic right to strike. Between investors' rights to not invest and to withdraw investment as per their wishes, and workers' rights to withdraw their labor power, between these two equal rights, once again, it is force that decides. And force is being used more openly and more consistently under neoliberalism. In order to support the private property rights of big businesses whose accumulation strategies are destroying the livelihoods of millions and in order to protect the increasing inequality between the consuming-and-possessing class and the rest, the state is turning increasingly authoritarian. With this context in mind, I turn the discussion to the central government's current initiative on anti-terror laws.

NEOLIBERALISM AND THE LEFT

It is undeniably true that parties on the Left in India have put pressure on governments to implement certain pro-poor measures (e.g., public works) and to slow the pace of certain reforms. But overall, the forces of the Left[214] have virtually converted themselves into a conduit for the implementation of the NEP through ideological and administrative means. The parliamentary Left (as well as much of the 'unorganized Left')[215] has not provided a serious ideological critique of the NEP. Whatever critique the Left has is rather muted. It is limited because it takes place more or less from the standpoint of less economically competitive sections of the so-called progressive national bourgeoisie[216] (and a very small segment of the 'relatively well-paid' salaried working class, mainly unionized public sector workers). Not only that, but the critique is 'regulationist': it suggests that the solutions to the problems within the NEP lie solely in government regulation. The Left critique has not, generally speaking, looked at the NEP as being essentially a *capitalist* project, a project of the capitalist class, instead of seeing it as merely a new government policy that can be changed by changes in the government. The Left critique has not been conducted from the vantage point of the working class and poor peasants as comprising a bloc of anti-capitalist classes. It has therefore not been from the vantage point of the *transcendence* of capitalism. The Left is at

---

214 Unless otherwise noted, by 'Left', I am henceforward referring to the parliamentary Left as represented by the CPI and CPI-M.

215 This Left—like much of the academic Left—is informed by the spirit of civil society activism and micro-political resistance. The spectre of 'post-isms' (e.g., post-Marxism) haunts this Left. This petty bourgeois Leftism is allergic to proletarian socialism. Jameson and Eagleton's remark is useful here: 'any left politics that refuses Marxism—that historical horizon which, in Sartre's phrase, may be ignored not as yet transcended—is condemned to rehearse one or another variety of *pre*-Marxist radicalism' (Eagleton, 2009: 100; italics mine).

216 Interestingly, the following statement in the Economic and Political Weekly editorial of August 11, 2007, in the context of the discussion of the nuclear deal, says something about the class nature of Left critiquing of government policy that I am pointing to: 'The left is right in arguing that the [nuclear] deal is part of a larger web of relationships...[h]owever, this position of the left will not convince anybody, for until now it has formulated its arguments largely on the lines put out by *the domestic nuclear lobby* which has carried out a high-pitched campaign that the pact with the US will, in particular, place constraints on India's nuclear weapons programme.' (italics added). If the Left's critique of the nuclear deal had been a part of a comprehensive (=totalizing) critique of the devastating impacts on the toiling masses of the NEP as a class project, then that critique would have carried much greater weight.

the *pre*–democratic-revolution stage—that is, at *least* two stages removed from posing anti-capitalist, proletarian, revolutionary socialism as the goal. Indeed, it is this vision that directly influences the Left view of everything, including neoliberalism. Without revolutionary theory, it lacks revolutionary practice. One wonders: what is 'left' of the Left (ideology)?

Politically, the Left, which has been suffering from the 'parliamentary diseases',[217] has propped up and supported various bourgeois parties (e.g., Janata; Congress) from time to time, parties that have implemented neoliberalism. The Left has justified this support on two grounds: anti-imperialism (and anti-feudalism) and anti-communalism (to keep the Hindu fundamentalists out of power). The Left has, more or less, sought to limit the struggles of the working class to trade union struggles (i.e., bourgeois consciousness/politics in Lenin's words) and to electoral fights. The Left has sought to slow the pace of reforms (e.g., the opening of some sectors of the economy to international capital; the total privatization of profit-making state-owned businesses). But the Left does so 'not from the standpoint of developing a working class-led mass movement against capitalism' (Bardhan, 2005), nor as a part of an overall anti-capitalist agenda, but rather to defend weaker sections of the entrepreneurial class and to ensure the Indian bourgeois state retains some leverage to offset the pressure of foreign capital.[218]

The Left, on whose radar anti-capitalist, proletarian socialism does not yet exist because the Left is more interested in democratic changes *within* the capitalist system, has lent a pro-poor cover to various governments. This has allowed the governments of the day to administer the bitter pill of neoliberalism with a little sweetener—that is to say, to give the NEP a human face—and in a more consensual manner. *In practice,* then, the Left has virtually turned itself into a radical-nationalist fraction of the bourgeoisie. Its radical blusters and *theoretical*-sounding rhetorical flourishes cannot hide this.

At the provincial scale, where the organized parliamentary Left was and is in power, it has pursued the NEP and pro-big business measures.[219] One prominent State-level Left politician said to me once that 'we [i.e., the Left when it is in power in the States] need to establish industries at any cost and create a working class and make available consumer items before we think about other things'. Underlying this kind of Left politics is its loyal commitment to a capitalist society. When the Left was in power in Bengal, it embraced neoliberalism, arguing that it was following the model of 'socialist' China. The Left attacked 'the trade unions, saying that workers must learn discipline and forego strikes if West Bengal is to be able to secure investment' (Wickremasinghe and Jones, 2004). The Left-in-power has pursued neoliberalism at the provincial scale while sounding critical of it at the national scale.

---

217 Most of its energy is spent on elections rather than on extra-electoral mobilization of the masses and on raising the level of their class consciousness.

218 Bardhan (2005:4995) writes that the Leftists 'mainly represent the salaried class, particularly the public sector employees; almost all of the latter belong to the top quintile of the population (when the Left parties oppose pension reform or reform of the banking, insurance and civil aviation sectors, or reduction of subsidies to cooking gas or higher education or interest on savings certificates, the group they are pandering to is even a smaller fractile of the population)'.

219 Banerjee (2008:12-13) says: 'It was under … [Jyoti Basu's] leadership that the West Bengal Left Front government opened up the state's economy to private investors from outside, and the long-awaited Haldia petrochemical complex was brought to fruition as a public private sector joint venture…. Following this, in 1994 the CPI(M)-led Left Front government … adopted a new industrial policy which offered concessions to the magnates of the private sector and multinationals to set up industries in the state. …[in the process of pursuing neoliberal policies], the party ended up by robbing Peter to pay Paul—grabbing agricultural land (without paying adequate compensation to the farmers) and subsidising the investor industrialists by huge tax relief and other concessions that eat into the state exchequer '.

It has pursued neoliberalism ruthlessly, using both its control over trade unions and the false conception that the Left is pro-working class. Revealingly, when asked how his government would respond if a labor dispute arose against a foreign company operating in his State, the last Left Front Chief Minister said: 'Our involvement in trade unions is an advantage. The majority of workers are in support of this government. And we are trying to change their mindset. I tell them, look this is a new situation. We need FDI [foreign direct investments], we need infrastructure' (Dias, 2005).

And much of the non-parliamentary Left is non-threatening to neoliberal capital. This includes the Naxalite Left (which is influenced by versions of Maoism), the emergence of which was partly sparked by the weakness of the parliamentary Left and the aborted democratic revolution. It is no less responsible, however, for the current rot of the entire Left. Since their emergence in the late 1960s, the Naxalites have focused their activities on the oppressed peasantry and in more recent decades on the aboriginal people living in the most remote parts of India; they have also won some localized concessions (Das, 2010). This orientation is in keeping with the Maoists' nationalist and Stalinist perspective which declares the peasantry the principal revolutionary force (in contemporary India) and the coming Indian revolution to be a 'people's democratic', and not a socialist, revolution. From this perspective, the system of capitalist relations as such is not the enemy. On occasion the Maoists make ritualistic references to the working class, but in practice they are, hitherto, more or less disconnected from that class, which is the only class that has the potential to radically challenge neoliberalism. The Naxalite Left is not necessarily against capitalist accumulation as such; it does not even recognize that India is a dominantly capitalist social formation. Ironically, the politics of the state's fight against Maoism—which is ideologically steeped in class collaborationism and which itself is not too much of a threat to capitalist accumulation—is being used to remove all barriers to capitalist accumulation itself.

Concluding Comments

Neoliberalism is about changing the balance of class power in favor of the capitalist class. Neoliberalism is 'capitalism without Leftist illusions' (e.g., illusions that there can be such a thing as humane capitalism on a long-term basis). If this is true of rich countries, it is no less true of poor countries such as India. Neoliberalism across countries has some common attributes (5-Filho and Johnston, 2005).

The new economic policy such as that being implemented in India is a policy *on behalf* of capital. It is therefore a policy *of* capital, *tout court*, mediated and implemented by the state, at central and provincial scales. This paper has shown that India's NEP is more than a governmental policy. It is a programme of the bourgeoisie that promotes economic growth and bestows benefits to certain sections of the population, but has devastating impacts on the toiling masses. Indeed, this is what neoliberal capitalism generally does in the less developed world as a whole (Naruzzaman, 2005).

Neoliberalism in rural areas—agrarian neoliberalism—is particularly ruthless in its impacts. Neoliberalism is also a spatial project: it is implemented through the transformation of space relations and through this produces enormous spatial unevenness. Neoliberalism in India, like in the periphery as such, is also a part of the imperialist project, being implemented via burgeoning 'new compradore' elements both in the bourgeois world and outside. Given the adverse impacts of neoliberalism, it has inspired massive resistance from below, which has been countered by the state via a combination of unfathomable deception (i.e., that neoliberal growth is good for all), meagre concession, and heavy repression. Interestingly, in spite of offering some opposition, the Left has been, overall, a conduit through which neoliberalism has been delivered.

The specific demands that the new economic regime NEP articulates emanate from the ways in which capital seeks to connect to each term in Marx's (1977) general formula in *Capital 1* referred to earlier: M-C-C′-M′. Through various policies (e.g., low-interest loans; loan waivers; bailout packages), the neoliberal state promotes free markets and makes liquid investible resources (M) available to big business, often at below-market rates. The state makes commodities available in the form of cheap raw materials and cheap land (C), which have been obtained from people via primitive accumulation (or accumulation by dispossession). Through the liberalization of trade, the state makes foreign commodities available as well as intermediate goods. The state also helps capital access foreign markets. The non-implementation of a living wage drives wages below the cost of maintenance (i.e., the value of labor power). The state suppresses the right to strike and other democratic rights of workers. Factory acts that ensure workers' safety more or less remain unimplemented, in part because of the nefarious nexus of state officials and the business world. So the cost of production is kept at a low level. Capital's despotic rule in the labor process becomes even more despotic than before, a despotic rule that is strengthened by the ease with which capital can hire and fire labor. This makes for a heightened level of accumulation by exploitation.

Whether in India or the US, neoliberalism has had two kinds of success. One is political-economic and another is ideological. The political-economic success refers to the transfer of the burdens of the capitalist crisis (of profitability, etc.) on to the working class in a given place (a class fix), to areas other than the origin of the problems (a spatial fix), a more ruthless degradation and commodification of nature (an ecological fix), and to the direct political attack on unions (a political fix). The ideological success has come in two forms at least. One, as Harvey has argued (2005), while neoliberalism is supposed to be a system where the state is 'detached' from the market relations and where market relations are freer, all this is in the realm of ideas, and is therefore ideological. Neoliberal ideologues must be asked: how many trillions of dollars did the business class receive since 2008? By using this ideology, the state has legitimized two opposite tendencies: its very active interventions on behalf of the business class, and its withdrawal of the provision of limited welfare to the masses. The second form of the ideological success of neoliberalism is this: the critique of capitalism as such, of the *essence* as such, has been more or less diverted to the critique of the neoliberal *form* of capitalism (and to globalization, the geographical form of contemporary capitalism). Critique of *neoliberalism as capitalism* is not necessarily the same thing as the *critique of capitalism as neoliberalism*. The critique of the form has been divorced from, and has been prioritized over, the critique of the essence. Critique of capitalism as merely neoliberalism is the kind of critique, which seeks to find salvation in a capitalism, which is more regulated and more nationally-oriented, an issue I discuss in chapter 2 and which I return to the final Chapter. Given neoliberalism's multiple successes, it is an imperative that scholars scrutinize its genuine class character. Neoliberalism – whether as a process or not – is, like imperialism, an accumulation strategy of the capitalist class and its various competing fractions, a strategy that is articulated, and sought to be implemented, with varying success as a governmental policy.

Chapter 9

SCIENCE FOR PROFIT OR PEOPLE? A CRITIQUE OF THE STATE AND ITS RELATION TO THE DRUG COMPANIES IN THE USA

In July of last year (2012), the British multinational GlaxoSmithKline (GSK) was fined $3 billion for breaking the law and thus for putting patients at risk. This represents the biggest case of healthcare fraud in the U.S. history. Based in London and worth more than 110 billion dollars, it is one of the world's largest pharmaceutical companies. Its annual sales amount to 40 billion dollars. Its net profit is about 5 billion dollars. Critical reflections on this fraud case lead one to certain general principles operating in our unhealthy, profit-driven society.

THE PHARMACEUTICAL FRAUD CASE

The company bribed medical professionals (including psychiatrists) to prescribe medicines, often by paying for lavish dinners and luxury vacation trips (Morrow, 2012). It paid millions of dollars to doctors to attend, and speak at, meetings to promote the off-label uses of medicines. It encouraged the use of certain medicines for illnesses which were not approved in clinical tests. For example, Glaxo illegally promoted Paxil for treating depression in children from 1998 to 2003, even though this medicine was not approved for patients under 18. It also promoted Wellbutrin from 1999 through 2003 for weight-loss, sexual dysfunction, substance addictions and attention deficit hyperactivity disorder, although it was only approved for the treatment of major depression (Johnson, 2012). GSK paid huge sums of money to a doctor who hosted a popular radio show to promote a drug on his programme, in particular for unapproved uses (ibid.). At the drug promotion events, speakers received up to $2,500 for a one-hour presentation, earning almost 3 times more than they did working in their clinics in a day (Neville, 2012).

Like its competitors, GSK concealed the results of clinical studies. It provided false and incomplete information to the government about the safety of its medicines. When a GSK-funded doctor refused to remove safety concerns about the drug from an article he was writing, GSK removed his funding (Neville, 2012). The company funded fraudulent medical journal reports on its medicines. GSK also paid for articles on its drugs to appear in medical journals, and so-called independent doctors were hired by the company to promote the treatments.

Of course, GSK is not the only company which engages in fraud. Prior to the Glaxo settlement, the record-setting case involved Pfizer Inc., the world's biggest drug-maker. It paid the government $2.3 billion in 2009 in criminal and civil fines for improperly marketing 13 different drugs, including erectile-dysfunction drug Viagra and cholesterol fighter Lipitor, the top-selling drug in the world for years. Pfizer was accused of encouraging doctors to prescribe its drugs with free golf, massages and junkets to posh resorts (Neville, 2012).

These specific examples are a part of a wider unhealthy tendency of clinicians and patients alike being wooed by 'sophisticated advertising campaigns, [which are often'] disguised as education that promote expensive drugs of dubious efficacy' (Anderson, et al. 2005). These demonstrate several general principles at work in a capitalist society, the principles concerning the relationship among people's wellbeing, profit-motive and the state.

Pharmaceutical Companies and Capitalist Society

It is easy to see that our body-mind complex, which is a part of nature, has become an excellent means of profit-making; it has become an accumulation strategy.[220] This is a process that is effectively outside of social regulation, although it *appears* to be socially regulated. The business-world can virtually make anything and sell it: it is as if their profit *motive* creates the *usefulness* of the pills they sell.[221] Companies promote controversial disease states in order to sell its branded drugs which will apparently treat these states (Ebeling, 2011). Companies can influence the very medical diagnosis essential to a given disease being officially recognized as a disease (ibid.), and the whole process is a trade secret and therefore undemocratic.

A company can make any dangerous thing, any useless thing (without a real use-value), and make money out of it, in part through their control over both the production of images (advertisement, etc.). Resorting to fraudulent activities – engaging in sheer criminality -- is a way of cutting costs, and staying competitive in this almost-permanently crisis-ridden global economy. This is true about pharmaceutical companies as well as many other companies. Therefore, there can be no such thing as a clean capitalism, one without fraud, no matter how much governmental regulation by the state there is.

What is also interesting is the relation between capital and the state. Firstly, often the state agencies turn a blind eye to the criminal activities of drugs companies, and not just these companies (consider banks engaged in money-laundering). When the state – often under pressure from public protests -- does impose a little fine on the corrupt practices of the

[220] This strategy assumes that one's illness can be just treated by a pill. It is widely known than a large number of diseases (e.g. blood pressure, stroke, heart attack, diabetes, etc.) are often caused by the way people are forced to live and work: lack of proper nutrition, economic insecurity causing constant anxiety, lack of time for relaxing and for exercise and so on. These are associated with a society which is driven by the logic of money-making. This is indeed the stuff of social medicine (Anderson, et al, 2005). There is the further assumption that the medicines that are required to treat an illness must be produced and distributed for private profit.

[221] This also applies to the genetically engineered food items, whose long-terms impacts on the body-mind complex are not yet known; many scientists suspect that these impacts may not be benign indeed. Yet, companies producing genetically modified organisms are undeterred. Profit making at any cost, even through control over genes, is in the genes of these corporate citizens.

business world (drugs companies; banks involved in money-laundering), if this happens at all, the quantity of the fine is just a fraction of the annual revenue (which, for GSK, is close to $50 billion) (Wilson, 2011). The fine is also a very small fraction of the monies already made on the basis of the malpractices (such as selling a drug for which it should not be used). So, the fine is treated by companies merely as a cost of doing business. This, incidentally, means that it is not possibly a real cost because a large part of it, if not all of it, can be passed on to consumers. Paying fine is similar to the cost involved in paying workers or for technology. The fine could also be seen by them as what Marx would call a "necessary wastage" in the production process, akin to scrap iron in the metal industry. The token fine system shows that businesses can *buy* wrong-doing for a profit: they do wrong things, make money, and if caught, pay a little fine. In other words: the quantity of the fine is so limited that it is not really a fine that would stop malpractices. It is just a small quantitative deduction from the money already made. It makes no qualitative difference to the way the business world works. It is to be noted also that when caught engaged in illegal business activities, pharmaceutical companies such as GSK -- and indeed most other major companies – hardly face any criminal charges. The impunity of their managers is one aspect of the legal immunity provided to the entire ruling class, including those elements of it responsible for the financial crisis, which is adversely affecting working masses. When the state knowingly tolerates illegal activities of the business world, the boundaries between the state, which has a monopoly over legitimate coercion of various types, and civil society is increasingly blurred.

The business world paying a little fine for their wrongdoing needs to be contrasted to the state sending working masses to jail and/or physically harming them for their legitimate protests against injustice and deprivation, the protests which are increasingly being criminalized all over the world. One may consider the millions of people languishing in jails in all major countries of the world, 'democratic' or not. One may contrast their crimes, which often involve shop-lifting and such petty things and because of which millions of them languish in jails, to the criminal actions of companies of all kinds which are hazardous to the health and safety of all. We are made to think that law works the same way for all. This idea, this false consciousness, is precisely one of the ways in which the rule of capital -- not the rule of law -- works. The idea that society and the state are class-neutral is simply not true.

There is an interesting class dynamics here from another angle. The timid capitalist state that, on occasion, imposes a fine on corrupt businesses is itself corrupt (and criminal). It is itself not accountable to its suffering citizens, the bottom majority (if it is not the 90% as per the 'occupy' movement, but at least 60-70%). It gives away society's (natural) resources for almost free or throwaway prices to big companies. It withdraws funding for their welfare while giving away millions of dollars to parasitic bankers, in most undemocratic ways. The state takes from ordinary masses so many things, including often their only means of livelihood (land) and gives it to businesses. Powerful states illegally attack less powerful states who they and sections of the business class of the country they rule do not endorse. The political parties, which run the affairs of the state, blatantly buy votes and politicians in order to push through pro-business legislations against the interest of ordinary working people. The list of state's corrupt and illegal conduct all over the world is almost limitless. Given this, the state cannot possibly have enough "moral" courage to adequately punish the businesses for the crime (such as that of being unaccountable) it itself commits.

Besides, will a deterrent-causing fine not discourage (foreign) investment? This is what spokespersons of capital working in/for the governments ask. The state will do anything to make sure that the moneyed class, the propertied class, makes investment and makes enough money out of its investment, its property. But it will hardly do anything to make sure that working masses can put to use the only property they have (i.e., their labor power) to earn a decent dignified living: think about millions of under- and unemployed men and women. Millions of people, even now, work as bonded laborers, like slaves, and employers make money off their unfreedom, which is *il*legal, which is not as per the rule of law. Big business and the state, no matter which party or coalition of parties manages its affairs, belong to the same family. The business of fining businesses signifies a little internal battle within the family. The state and capital are two arms of a single body, the body of the alienated social relation. It is a spectacle. Like other companies, pharmaceutical companies are citizens. They have the right to make profit. Ordinary citizens -- who have almost nothing but their power to work -- have a right to live with dignity and a sense of safety. Between these two equal rights, it is the right of the first kind of citizens, the pharmaceutical companies in this case, that wins.

What drugs companies do has very serious implications for the health of ordinary working people, whose economic ability to fight diseases, including those which are byproducts of drugs taken, is being compromised due to corporatization and privatization of health care. Imagine taking a medicine for an illness one may not have. Imagine taking a wrong medicine for an illness one does not suffer from. Our health depends on these companies, their profit. By making us unhealthy, by making us even die slowly (due to various side effects of medicines, including unapproved medicines), if they can make money, so be it. The business of business is money-making. It is not health-making. One may ask: why is our health in the hands of the profit-seeking companies which often benefit from scientific research in publicly funded institutions?

When asked why drug companies do what they do – make excessive amount of money often in ways that are not legal – they say that the drug business is risky and that the money they are making reflects that: society is paying for the risk. Drug companies face many types of risk (Spilker, 1998). When they invest in discovering new drugs, they face risk (discovery risk). After all, the several years of investment may not result in a new drug. Even after a drug is discovered, it may not reach the market and become commercially viable (development risk). Even if it reaches the market, not enough of it may be sold (marketing risk). To the extent that this is true, the question is this: if drug companies indeed face these and other types of risk, why is the risk not socialized then? Why indeed is the production-distribution of drugs not socialized? Why does society not remove the production and distribution of drugs from the 'risky' sphere of private profit-making? Why should these 'citizens' be allowed to meet their risk *at the expense* of the general public?

The pharmaceutical industry is one of the largest and most profitable in the world (Fisher, 2003). What happens within this industry has wider implications. In particular, malpractices within this industry are potentially responsible for creating an environment in which people tend to trust science less. Motivated by profit-seeking, these companies do invest money in research. They seem to be 'producing' and disseminating scientific ideas (e.g., the idea that a drug x will produce effect y, when in reality this is not the case). Increasingly, clinical research is being funded by pharma dollars (Anderson et al., 2005). This means that they control the knowledge about medicines and the production of the medicines themselves, and this is done in the profit interest. The practice of science—and practitioners of it—has been subordinated to business practice. This subordination of science to profit results in suffering of millions, as the malpractices of medicine companies such as GSK indicate. This potentially leads to the distrust of science, which in turn contributes to idealist and social-constructionist thinking, as demonstrated by, for example, anti-science postmodernists, whom Meera Nanda, Alan Sokal and others have been rightly critical of. The idealists and social constructionists equate science *with* the use that science is put to (under capitalism). They fail to imagine that science -- discovery of things and mechanisms that exist independently of the observing mind by going underneath the world of appearances -- is possible and necessary, and that science *does not have to be* subordinated to profit-making but can be subordinated to the satisfaction of human needs.

There has been opposition to the criminal and corrupt conduct of drugs companies. Is this enough? It is not that the working masses in cities and villages, in poorer and richer countries should not protest against the malpractices on the part of drug companies and other companies. They should. But these protests can only be a part of the fight against these companies' control over human health and replace this with a system of democratic control over our resources and our health, nationally and internationally.

Chapter 10

The State, the Business World and Death of Ordinary Working People in the US: Where Does the Problem Lie?

When we examine the world from a place-perspective and dialectically, we see relations of similarity and difference. That is, we see that different things happen in different places, and that there is also an underlying process that not only binds together what happens in the different places in question, but also connects these places to the system of which they are a part.

In a single week in April 2013, two places in the US experienced similar events: both places were rocked by deadly explosions that killed, maimed, and traumatized people. Both places were transformed into or looked like war zones. But the state responded differently to each event.

On April 15, bombs at the world-famous Boston Marathon killed three people and injured 170 in a city of more than a million. The historic and liberal-minded city was forced into a 24-hour lockdown by a combined force of over 9,000 security personnel, imposing a martial-law-like condition. Workers went without pay or services. Homes were raided without warrants. What was in place was what Agamben (2005) would call a 'state of exception.'

Just two days later, another explosion happened. It was at a fertilizer plant in West, Texas, a small town with fewer than 3000 people. 14 people were killed and over 200 injured. Numerous homes and buildings were destroyed or damaged.

Both places suffered terrible tragedies, but there are differences. The extent of the damage, including the number of people killed or maimed, is much greater in West, Texas, than in Boston, both in absolute terms and relative to their populations. Yet the state apparatus did not raid the home of the fertilizer plant's owner, nor did it attempt to arrest him. This is despite the fact that the plant's bosses have committed criminal negligence. Why? Whereas politicians grilled top intelligence officials about possible information-sharing failures in the Boston case, similar soul-searching did not happen in the Texas case.[222] Interestingly, at least seven different state- and national-scale regulatory agencies were tasked with overseeing the fertilizer company, and that while two federal level agencies did not

---

[222] Elk, Mike. 'Texas Explosion: Gov't Shared Info for Anti-Terrorism, But Not Workplace Safety', http://inthesetimes.com.

know that potentially dangerous amounts of ammonium nitrate were stored on the site, at least three state agencies *did* know that the plant had a large stockpile of ammonium nitrate but did not share this information with the relevant federal agencies. Why this discrepancy in the use of state power to discipline and punish? What does this discrepancy reveal and hide? And what do these places within the US reveal about what the state does outside its formal borders? That is, what do these places reveal about a state that seeks to annihilate space—namely, the distance between itself and its enemy-others—by using its power both to kill and to know about others?

Further, while millions of words and lines were written and spoken about the Boston bombing in the media relatively, comparatively little media space was given to the Texas killing. Why such a difference, and that too in a society, whose ruling elite goes to war in the name of democracy and free speech? What does this 'discrepancy' reveal and what does this hide? And what do these places inside the country reveal about what the state does outside its formal (paper) borders.

The Texas Explosion: Its Broader Historical-Geographical Context

Let us first recap a few details about the Texas explosion, based on what little information the media have made available. The plant illegally stored a large amount of liquid and granular fertilizers (anhydrous ammonia and ammonium nitrate), which, under certain conditions (e.g., when set on fire), can cause explosions.[223] The blast at the plant shook the earth, punctuating the 'timeless' calm of the idyllic 'West-comma-Texas'. A huge fireball rolled through the town of West, showering burning debris and shrapnel over a five-block radius.[224] The intensity of the blast was comparable to an earthquake of 2.1 on the Richter scale, creating a crater more than 10 feet deep and 90 feet wide. Some people thought that 'a nuclear bomb went off.'[225] As many as 75 homes and buildings were destroyed, including the local high school and a 50-unit apartment complex. The poorer residents may become homeless. The surviving members of the community are suffering from not only physical injuries but also emotional ones. According to estimates by the Insurance Council of Texas, the explosion caused more than $100 million in damage.[226]

The US industrial disasters have a long history indeed. The West Fertilizer explosion, which is one of the worst industrial disasters in many years, happened just a day after the 66th anniversary of the Texas City disaster, which is said to be the worst industrial accident in US history.[227] Just over a century ago, a deadly fire swept through a blouse factory in Manhattan, killing 146 garment workers, most of them immigrant women. The Triangle factory owners,

---

223 Fountain, Henry. 'Fertilizers Meet Fire, With Disastrous Consequences', NYT, http://www.nytimes.com/2013/04/23/science/fertilizers-meet-fire-with-disastrous-consequences.html?_r=0.

224 Caroll, Rory. 'Mass casualties feared after explosion in Texas fertiliser plant', http://www.guardian.co.uk/world/2013/apr/18/texas-explosion-fertiliser-plant-blast.

225 Ibid.

226 Robbins, Danny and Josh Lederman. 'Obama Consoles Families, Survivors of Texas Blast', http://swampland.time.com/2013/04/25/obama-consoles-families-survivors-of-texas-blast/.

227 The same day as the West Fertilizer explosion, which forced the evacuation of the entire town, a fire at an oil refinery in Beaumont, Texas, injured five workers [reference].

who had locked their employees inside for fear of theft, were acquitted of criminal charges, but the disaster led to the first real workplace safety laws, beginning in New York State, and much later, to the establishment of the Occupational Safety and Health Administration by President Richard Nixon in 1970. Three years before the April 2013 explosion, four major industrial accidents had happened: the Massey Energy Upper Big Branch mine explosion killed 29 miners, the biggest mining accident since the Mannington explosion that killed 78 miners 40 years before; the Deepwater Horizon oil rig explosion in the Gulf of Mexico killed 11 workers (and caused one of the largest environmental catastrophes in history); a Connecticut power plant explosion killed five; and a refinery explosion in Washington state killed seven workers.

The Texas industrial disaster is one of thousands of such 'accidents' that take place annually in the US, and indeed worldwide.[228] In this blessed country of opportunity, every year, on average, over 4,500 workers are slaughtered in industrial accidents and nearly 4 million people are injured at work. As many as 13 US workers leave home for work every day and do not return.[229]

WHY DID TEXAS HAPPEN? WHY, INDEED, DO INDUSTRIAL DISASTERS HAPPEN?

The Texas incident was overdetermined, like any event: it had *multiple* reasons. There is, in fact, a hierarchy of reasons. It is the reason at the top of this hierarchy (the class character of the system, including its profit motive), which is discussed last, that colors the other reasons.

The Company's Negligence

The company lied. The plant had on site 2,700 tonnes of ammonium nitrate. The town itself, you may recall, had a population of 2,700; that's one tonne per person! This was 100 times the amount of chemical fertilizer used in the Oklahoma City bombing in another April, in the year 1995. The total amount is 1,350 times the amount that would require a facility to report its stockpile to the Department of Homeland Security.[230] The company willfully suppressed this information. This is a criminal offence. Unaware of the substances they were dealing with, the firemen sprayed water, which in this case only exacerbated the fires. If the company had reported what chemicals were there, evacuation would have been easier, better, and faster.

Not only did the company lie, it also cut corners, putting the safety of the workers and the community at risk. It 'avoided spending the money for safety mechanisms, and the fire

[228] A few days after the disaster in Texas, Bangladesh experienced one of its—and one of the world's—worst industrial disasters: a building that housed five garment factories that supplied cheap products to western markets collapsed, killing more than 350, many of them women. Not only this, but the terrible tragedy in a chemical plant owned by an American company in India's Bhopal is still in our collective memory.

[229] 'When your workplace is the terrorist', http://stillhavetoprotest.wordpress.com/category/uncategorized/

[230] Goodman, Amy. 'The West, Texas, explosion shows the deadly effect of profit before safety', http://www.guardian.co.uk/commentisfree/2013/apr/25/west-texas-explosion-deadly-profit-safety.

department didn't train their employees properly, or have the right equipment.' [231] The plant has indeed been known for several violations of existing laws; for example, its ammonia tanks were not properly labeled.[232]

Inadequate Law and Inadequate Law Enforcement

It is not enough to say that the company lied or cut corners. One must also ask what conditions allowed it to do what it did. We are talking about the *US* state, not an ordinary state. If the US state wants to know or do something, it does. Anything, anywhere, with respect to anyone. Or almost. It is ignorant to say that the state merely *happened* to be ignorant about the negligence of this plant and other, similar plants. What companies such as the one in West, Texas do cannot be isolated from a) what the state does and how, or b) what it prefers not to do, a) and b) being two sides of the same coin. In other words, what the company did cannot be isolated from the two facts of weak laws and their inadequate enforcement.

Let us deal with the weak law enforcement: the relevant state apparatuses that can discipline and punish companies are ill-funded and ill-staffed. This is a time-worn strategy of capital. It was true about Marx's England (which he talks about in *Capital, Vol. 1*) *as it is now* (in poor and rich countries alike). The strategy: to set up an institution to look after the workers in order to appear responsible, but not to provide adequate funding to it.

Consider the Occupational Safety and Health Administration (OSHA). Like many similar organizations, it was established partly in response to working-class struggles and with some support from the then Democratic party (see Harvey, 1996:338-339), and thanks to the hard work of many of its employees, it has saved the lives of more than 451,000 workers. However, this organization has been sapped of its energy. OSHA's last visit to the Texas plant was in 1985. Why so few inspections? The agencies such as OSHA have are under-staffed and under-funded.

Some 4,500 are killed each year in industrial accidents in the US, and the state spends $550 million a year on workplace safety,[233]half as much as it spends protecting fish and wildlife. Do humans have the same moral and material worth as these non-humans, or are we to obliterate such a banal binary?

Under the current funding cut proposals, OSHA will have its budget cut by 8.2%, amounting to about $50m. This is under Obama, who blocked a bill in 2006 to make chemical plants safer—the Obama who, many people think, can be pushed to do more for workers and the environment.[234] OSHA covers 7–8 million workplaces in the US but has only between 2,000 and 2200 inspectors nationwide. It can inspect a given plant once every 129 to 131

231 Mitchell, Greg. 'Famed EPA Whistleblower Hits Media Coverage of 'Criminal' Texas Plant Explosion', http://www.thenation.com/blog/173985/famed-epa-whistleblower-hits-media-coverage-criminal-texas-plant-explosion#.

232 Dart, Tom and Richard Luscombe. 'Texas explosion: residents of West shocked by devastation', http://www.guardian.co.uk/world/2013/apr/18/texas-fertiliser-plant-explosion-devastates-town.

233 Clinton, Elizabeth. 'A corporate-made catastrophe', http://www.viewpointonline.net/a-corporate-made-catastrophe-elizabeth-clinton.html; accessed April 26

234 In 1977, OSHA had 37 inspectors for every million workers. Today it has only 22, a reduction of more than 40 percent. As a result, OSHA has all but abandoned regular inspections of work sites (wsws.org)

years. In Texas, which has even fewer inspectors than the national average, it might take even longer for federal inspectors to visit every workplace.

As the following figure (constructed from available data) shows[235], while the rate of safety-related workplace incidents increased between 2010 and 2012, the number of investigations has decreased. Hence, the percentage of incidents that are investigated (shown in brackets) has also decreased. It would appear that businesses have virtual impunity.

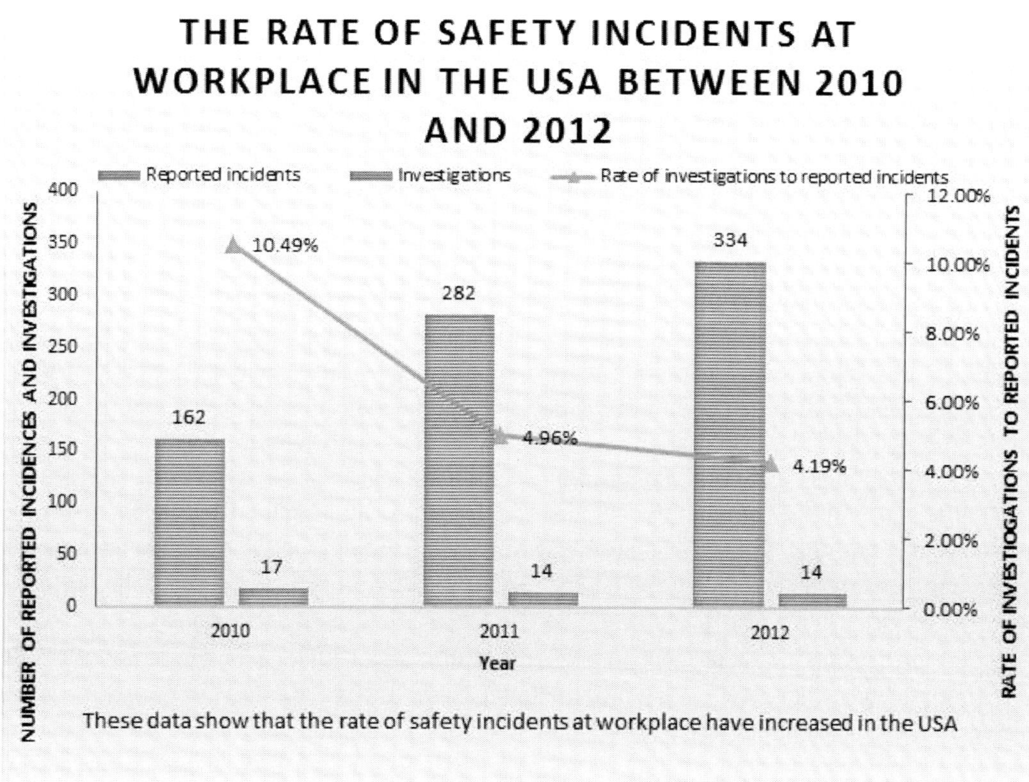

Let us locate the Texas disaster in a wider perspective, outside of which it cannot be understood properly. The democratically elected US governments of both the big business parties illegally kill and maim innocent people *abroad*, largely to create favorable long-term conditions for big businesses, and they often do this on the basis of lies. Take, for example, the lie that this or that government is hiding weapons of mass destruction. Hence, there is a political climate of lies in which those who control the economic lever of society (i.e., companies) also lie and in which governments have limited moral legitimacy to challenge such lies. The US governments of different times have been and are complicit in thousands of workers being killed *at home*, including those killed due to unsafe working conditions (recall that the number is 13 every day). What the US does abroad and what it does at home are similar. They are also connected. Consider this: 'Although Americans were 270 times more

235 'How Regulation Could Have Helped Prevent Texas Plant Explosion: Mike Elk Discusses with Chris Hayes', http://inthesetimes.com/video/14893/how_regulation_could_have_helped_prevent_texas_plant_explosion_mike_elk_dis/; accessed April 27, 2013.

likely to die a workplace accident than a terrorist attack in 2011, the Department of Homeland Security's budget that year was $47 billion, while OSHA's budget was only $558 million.'[236] Illegal, incessant, and imperialist wars deplete the coffers. The state's priorities are clear, and they contradict those of ordinary citizens, who need economic security, decent jobs, healthcare, etc.

Not only are the relevant law-enforcing apparatuses weak, but the laws themselves are weak. For example, criminal penalties under the OSHA law are very weak. Fines are a pittance, and can be reduced upon bargaining between companies and the state. Paying a little fine here and there is just part of the cost of doing business. When OSHA inspected the Texas plant in 1985, it fined the company for safety violations. And the amount was $30. Yes, $30. This is said to be a mere 3% of what it could have fined.[237] Even when a worker dies in a factory, the fines are too small—less than $10,000—to make companies invest in workers' safety. Besides, if a few die, there are plenty in the reserve army of laborers, both at the national scale (e.g., in small towns; in the poor neighborhoods of central cities) and globally (e.g., low-cost immigrant workers).

One may ask: why did the workers and the community not do anything?[238] Note that OSHA typically inspects a business *only after* it receives a complaint from a worker. Fearing retaliation from employers, workers often do not complain. The situation is worse in non-unionized places and worksites in rural areas, such as the plant in question, which is located in the proud 'right-to-work state' (read: 'right to super-exploit state')—a state that lures businesses from other states with its business-friendly climate.

Politicians will disagree that the amount of oversight is inadequate. Rick Perry, governor of Texas, has said that '[t]hrough their elected officials [people] clearly send the message of their comfort with the amount of oversight.' So democracy protects the people, the ordinary working masses? Perry also recently touted the lax regulatory environment in Texas while trying to lure businesses there from states like California and Illinois.[239] He is not alone. If *state*-level agencies have such a soft attitude to business, it would be futile to ask why zoning in West, Texas was not in place to stop houses and other buildings from being located near a chemical plant. Laws to protect workers and communities are weak or deficient at *all* scales.

Subordinating the Human Need for Safety to Profit

The causes of the disaster are many, but they are not equally important. The bottom line is this: we live in a society where profit – need for profit -- subordinates human needs,[240]

---

[236] Elk, Mike. 'Texas Explosion: Gov't Shared Info for Anti-Terrorism, But Not Workplace Safety', http://inthesetimes.com; accessed April 26, 2013.

[237] 'Transparency Thursday: As the Debris Settles, Answers from the West Fertilizer Co. Plant Explosion', http://normativenarratives.com/2013/04/25/transparency-thursday-as-the-debris-settles-answers-from-the-texas-fertilizer-plant/. Also note that: even if the company had paid $1000, it would not be much.

[238] A local resident actually complained about the smell of chemicals, which prompted an investigation.

[239] Goodman, Amy. 'The West, Texas, explosion shows the deadly effect of profit before safety', http://www.guardian.co.uk/commentisfree/2013/apr/25/west-texas-explosion-deadly-profit-safety; accessed April 26.

[240] One can argue that the need for profit of (the corporate citizen) is as significant as the need for human beings – ordinary citizens -- for food and shelter, etc. Both have the right to satisfy their needs. When that is the case, it is force that decides which need – whose need -- will be satisfied. This force is the force of capital – class

including the need for safety, to itself. It is this that underlies what given companies do to remain competitive and that also sets limits on what the state does. The criminal negligence of companies such as the one in Texas cannot be satisfactorily explained in terms of weak law or weak law enforcement (or indeed in terms of the above-average level of greediness of a given owner). Rather, government policies more or less reflect business interests, especially given the declining influence of working class power. The nature of laws and enforcement may explain why some companies in some places at certain times do what they do. That nature cannot, however, explain why all companies generally pursue profit at the expense of workers' safety (and, indeed, of the ecological health of our planet), any more than the prices of commodities being high or low can explain the true nature of their production, outside of the theory of value.[241] Explaining industrial disasters in terms of neoliberal deregulation is to assume that a better, pro-worker government is possible and that it could adequately and permanently solve the problem at hand—that the interests of ordinary people and those of capital can be somewhat compatible. It is a massive theoretical and political mistake to treat neoliberalism merely as a *governmental* policy (as discussed in Chapter 8).

The profit motive subordinates the political system to itself, more or less. That is why Obama of the Democratic party could say of Boston that 'any responsible individuals, any responsible groups will feel the full weight of justice.' On the other hand, when it came to individuals bearing the full weight of justice for the explosion in Texas, he could say nothing.[242] Why is there no manhunt when a company is criminally responsible for killing people? Why are corporate crimes and violence, both symbolic and material, not serious enough to meet the 'full weight of justice'? Why are companies greeted with non-prosecution agreements and self-reporting clauses? The answer: the state must protect the system of profit-making and the private ownership of wealth which is being produced by ordinary people. This happens at the expense of the right of an ordinary working person to a decent life. As O'Connor, executive director of the National Council for Occupational Safety and Health, said, 'As companies ... emphasize profits over safety, workers pay the ultimate price.'[243]

CONCLUSION: CORPORATE TERRORISM—WHAT IS TO BE DONE?

The bosses at the West plant—and at all plants where such disasters happen—deserve the blame for the 'accident' and the resulting loss of life, as do politicians and officials obsessed

power which businesses have by virtue of property ownership; and this force is also the force of the state which protects and backs up class force. Without these forms of force, the need for profit cannot be satisfied. It is in fact not a real need. Money itself cannot be eaten or lived in or worn. And food, clothes and shelters can be produced without the need for profit, as these things do not have to take the form of commodities for sale for a profit. The idea of a corporate need for profit is an entirely artificial need, that emerges out of the current class-society, although it appears as a universal need.

[241] Note that the imperative to produce more at lower cost and to make a profit is creating a need for chemicals used in farming, and the explosion in the West, Texas chemical fertilizer plant cannot be considered in isolation from this fact.

[242] Mokhiber, Russell. 'The Full Weight of Justice: Corporate Terrorism in West Texas', http://www.counterpunch.org/2013/04/19/corporate-violence-in-west-texas/

[243] Goodman, Amy. 'The West, Texas, explosion shows the deadly effect of profit before safety', http://www.guardian.co.uk/commentisfree/2013/apr/25/west-texas-explosion-deadly-profit-safety; accessed April 26.

with the deregulation of business. And the system, which subordinates people's lives to the profit-imperative, is to be blamed as well. It is the imperative to reduce costs and increase profits that the state must defend, at any cost. The disaster in Texas has to be located on a broader imaginative/conceptual map.

Both the inaction in Texas and the over-action in Boston are expressions of one thing: the capitalistic—and indeed imperialistic—character of the American state. The Texas and Boston cases must be seen in their wider international context. Businesses have the right to exploit, and this the state must respect and defend. Ordinary citizens have the right to fulfilling and safe working (and living) conditions. Between these two equal rights, it is the force that decides. Domestically, it is, ultimately, the force of the state. Internationally, it is the force of the imperialist states such as the US. The US state as a 'super-imperialist' state reinforces conditions for businesses making (super-)profits in the global periphery, and it has to make sure other states—those in the periphery—do not deviate from the true path of salvation.[244] This is behind America's imperialist wars. Ideologically, it would be difficult for it to protect workers' rights at home while crushing these same rights abroad. Having spent billions on imperialist wars in the ultimate interest of big businesses and having given said businesses tax and other concessions, the US is in any case 'short of' money to fund regulatory agencies at home. Also, the businesses at home have to obey the law of value (the law of competition) increasingly operating internationally.[245] If the cost of doing business is raised in Texas or in America due to effective regulation, will Texan and American businesses, whom the state must generally protect, not go bankrupt or move to another place with less regulation?

It is not surprising that a huge amount of money is spent on the so-called fight against terror. Some of the effect of that spending was seen in the huge mobilization of forces and weapons in Boston. As the anger against austerity and unemployment in cities and rural towns in the US grows, and as the consequences of the business–state alliance are played out as they were in West town, the state is compelled to reveal to its own citizens its naked strength. The Boston spectacle of the state of exception was indeed just that. Can one believe that the safety of the people was the reason for the state having taken action in Boston, when it does not care to prevent the thousands of workplace deaths, such as those in Texas, that happen every year? Ordinary people face the terror of profit more often and more intensely than the terror of some people fighting imperialism and militarism in misguided ways. And the fight against terror is really a fight against anyone who is fundamentally opposed to profit-making. *Where* that 'anyone' is located, whether in the US or abroad, is ultimately immaterial.

So *what is to be done*? The answer lies in the multi-tiered explanation of disasters such as the one in West, Texas. Action for changing the situation is necessary at every level of the explanatory interpretation offered here of these disasters. Such action must include a democratically organized intellectual-political struggle of the masses through parties and popular workers' councils in workplaces and communities. These organized groups must hold accountable politicians and companies who commit crimes against ordinary working people, and must push for better wages, for better regulation of work-places, and for the workers'

[244] See Wood, Ellen. 2003. *The Empire of Capital*, Verso, London

[245] That is why Amin (2010) talks about *the law of globalized value*. It is, of course, a challenge to think about logics of capitalism internationally while avoiding 'third worldism'.

right to see business accounts—including in rural places like West. Because there are severe limits to what can be achieved merely though such struggles,[246] such struggles for rcforms must be a part of—and must happen with the overall theoretical-political perspective of—a much broader multi-scalar class-struggle to establish democracy in the workplace and in every other part of society. That would be a socio-ecologically just society, where human needs and nature would not be subordinated to profit-making and imperialist aggression, nor to bureaucratism ruling in the name of the people.

[246]These limits exist because of the private ownership of property, capitalist competition and the class-character of the state.

Chapter 11

WHY ARE SO-CALLED RADICAL MOVEMENTS NOT AS RADICAL AS THEY APPEAR? A CRITIQUE OF THE MAOIST MOVEMENT IN INDIA

Social movements can aim for reforms within a system. They can also aim for revolution. Reform and revolution can lie on a continuum of political movement/activity. Reformist activities are not necessarily opposed to revolutionary activities.[247] But there is something special about revolutionary activities, because revolution signifies the masses entering politics, it signifies masses being actively involved in the process: and that is why there is nothing more politically charged than revolutionary activities, or the activities that aim at a revolution.

There is a large amount of literature in social sciences on social movements in rural/agrarian contexts and in society at large (Paige, 1975; Mohanty, 1977; Draper, 1977; Wolford, 2004; Miller, 2000). Research in social sciences on revolutionary movement has raised issues about leadership and organization. This means that joining protests, organizing meetings for and of the masses, and distributing flyers are among the activities that activists (and activist-scholars) engage in. But one cannot think about revolutionary movement, indeed, any political movement, without the framing ideas, i.e., the theory of society and of radical social change. Revolution requires ideas with which we critically interpret and explain the world with a view to change it. Importance of theory led Marx to say that: theory acts like a material force when it grips the masses, suggesting that there is a reciprocal relation between society and (critical) ideas about it. An academic activist who seeks to contribute to a movement may contribute to the development of an appropriate theory to guide that movement. This theory decisively identifies the problems and points to the barriers to their determined resolution. It also identifies the resources to be mobilized: for example, which classes will contribute to the revolutionary movement?

Scholars of social or political movements, whether or not they are active in these, must remain critical of the movements. And a critical assessment of a revolutionary movement must include a critical assessment of its theory of revolution: whether its theory is revolutionary. In particular, what is the theory of society, including its mode of production

---

[247] See Luxemburg's famous *Reform or Revolution* (1900). http://www.marxists.org/archive/luxemburg/1900/reform-revolution/

and the state, that a revolutionary movement possesses? The Maoist movement provides the particular context for my thinking about revolution. [248] And class-critique and geography, in particular, scale and spatial variation, are at the heart of my thinking about it.

The Maoist Movement in India

First let me briefly present a historical-geographical context of the movement. It started in the late 1960s. It became known as the Naxalite movement. The name 'Naxalite' comes from the name of the region where it originated: the Naxalbari subdivision of Darjeeling district of India's West Bengal province, a district which is incidentally world-famous for tea. To lead the movement, a political party -- CPI(ML) -- was formed in 1969 to coordinate localised struggles into a mass movement. In post-Naxalbari times, the Naxalite movement split into some 40-50 Marxist-Leninist groups, locked in a perpetual fraternal fight for the expansion of their areas of influence. All ML groups owe their origin to events in Naxalbari and are guided by their interpretation(s) of Maoism (which they find to be an advance in Marxism). The M-L movement is divided mainly on the basis of their tactical approach to parliamentary/extra-electoral politics. Some almost exclusively focus on armed struggle and are, more or less, underground[249]; while others [e.g., CPI(ML)] Liberation) use a combination of both underground and over-ground methods and even participate in elections (Banerjee, 1999: 203-4).[250] Although the movement has weakened in its area of origin, it has spread to newer areas since the 1960s. It exists, to some degree of intensity, in a quarter of India's 600 districts, covering 40% of the country's geographical area. The armed struggle of a faction of the Naxalite movement (known as CPI-Maoist) has led the political establishment to describe the movement as the largest internal security threat to the country.

The Naxalite movement is considered by many – especially, the sympathizers and supporters -- as very progressive and radical. One sympathizer claims that most of the progressive trends in social activism today in different parts of the country (e.g., pro-poor

[248] My views on this have undergone three stages of development (listed as 1, 2 and 3). 1. When I was working on my doctoral dissertation on the role of the state in the production of uneven development in the mid-1990s, I had a theory of political economy, which was, without my knowledge, not inconsistent with the theory of society which the Maoist ideologues subscribe to. 2. In early 2000s, I started researching the Maoist movement itself. And I had a somewhat positive view about it: I thought that the movement had people in it who love their country, and who are self-sacrificing and courageous, and that the movement was working to alleviate people's suffering in specific localities. Now, in the process of researching the Maoist movement, I also started conducting some more theoretical work on how to conceptualize capitalism itself and capitalist (uneven) development in relation to class struggle, in the age of new imperialism (Das, 2012b). This work led me to critique my earlier theory of capitalism. 3. With this, I also started questioning the Maoist movement itself and my earlier somewhat-favorable views about it. In other words, as my own theoretical understanding of capitalism changed, and as I consequently became *self-critical*, I became increasingly *critical of the Maoist movement* itself. And I have remained so. I still believe that the movement has lots of self-sacrificing and courageous people who hate to see so much poverty and authoritarianism in a liberal democracy such as India. But I think that the movement is a very problematic adventure. I think so not from the standpoint of the state, and capital and the landed classes, but from the standpoint of the vast majority of the population, the working masses. And geography, in particular, scale and spatial variation, is an important part of my criticism of the theoretical basis of the Maoist movement.

[249] CPI (Maoist) has spread itself from the Telengana region of Andhra Pradesh to the tribal-dominated districts of adjoining Maharashtra, Chhatishgarh, Jharkhand, and Orissa.

[250] Liberation has its bases primarily in Bihar and pockets of influence in Uttar Pradesh, West Bengal, Assam, Tamilnadu and Punjab and Orissa.

rhetoric and policy of the government; the growth of voluntary organisations working among the 'subaltern') can be traced indirectly to the issues raised by, or associated with, the Naxalite movement in the 1960s and the 1970s (Banerjee, 2002). Another commentator says that for the first time in post-independence India, the movement asserted the demands and conditions of the poor and landless peasantry and of rural areas in general 'at the centre of national consciousness' (Kamat, 2002:11). The uprising in Naxalbari 'captured the imagination of radicals far beyond the locale within which it took place' (Jalal, 1995: 213).

Marx regularly made a distinction between appearance and reality. The Maoist movement *appears* to be radical and progressive. The appearance is not entirely false. After all, they have campaigned for poor aboriginal people's economic and political rights; they have disciplined many oppressive landlords, money-lenders, government officials and politicians who have hurt the poor. They have built small dams for the villagers. They have provided mobile hospital facility in some areas, and so on. Where domestic or foreign big business is seeking to control the natural resources (e.g., minerals; land), Naxalites, in some places, mobilize the aboriginal peoples against the land grab and against the destruction of their environment by capitalist development (see Kujur, 2006; Roy, 2011). But this progressive image is also ideological: that the movement is progressive and radical is only partially true. It is not really an anti-systemic movement in the real sense. Why? The main reason is their faulty theory of society.

Maoists'/Naxalites' Theory of Class Relations

The Maoists believe that India, like the less developed world in general, is semi-feudal, and not dominantly capitalist. The word semi-feudal is used often synonymously as feudal and sometimes as a kind of hybrid relation, which is more feudal and less capitalist. Any sort of extra-economic coercion in economic relations is automatically seen as a sign of feudalism. According to one of the important parties, which are guided by Maoism (which also goes by the name of 'Marxism-Leninism'), the Indian society is characterised by 'the stubborn remnants of feudalism in production relations and value systems' (CPML-Liberation).[251] In terms of production relations, the stubborn feudal remnants are 'bondage, usury and other forms of tied relations'. And, these remnants 'have been adopted by the capitalist landlords and kulaks for extraction of absolute surplus value', and are therefore reproduced 'in new forms'.[252] 'Thus, the semi-feudal 'extra-economic' coercion is *an essential part* of newly expanding capitalist relations, which hinders the *free* development of *capitalist* forces among the peasantry' [italics mine]. Also, in terms of politics, 'These 'feudal survivals ... [also] act

[251] Such survivals – Althusser (2005) -- not only ensure the availability of cheap labor power and raw materials for both Indian big capital and imperialism, but also the persistence of casteist ideas/practices, intolerable level of patriarchal prejudice, rabid communal fanaticism and barbarity in different spheres of life.

[252] According to Maoists/Naxalites, although 'commercialisation in Indian agriculture is now more or less generalised, [yet] majority of the poor and middle peasants are still trapped in subsistence or near-subsistence farming, including those who take a part or whole of their produce to the market for the sake of exchanging it for consumption goods.' There are various problems this formulation. The nature of dominant class relations in a country is to be determined by the dominant form of the surplus product being produced. Even if small producers can be seen as producing some surplus, the surplus based on the use of wage-labor is the dominant form of surplus product in more or less all countries, including India. This will especially be the case in India because agriculture accounts for a small part (barely 20%) of total GDP. I do recognize that GDP figures and percentages may not reflect class-categories.

as the biggest stumbling block to any real democratic awakening of the Indian people.' '[T]he principal contradiction [is] between feudal remnants and the broad Indian masses'. 'The Party, therefore, characterises the Indian society as semi-feudal'. [CPI-ML programme]'. This means, the current 'stage of our revolution [is] the stage of people's democratic revolution with agrarian revolution as its axis.' [ibid].[253] 'Only a successful People's Democratic Revolution i.e., New Democratic Revolution and the establishment of People's Democratic Dictatorship of the workers, peasants, the middle classes and national bourgeoisie under the leadership of the working class can lead to the liberation of our people from all exploitation and the dictatorship of the reactionary ruling classes and pave the way for building Socialism and Communism in our country, the ultimate aim of our Party'.

In other words, the Naxalite/Maoist theory as a variant of Stalinism, believes in a two-stage theory of revolution: a democratic revolution first, and a socialist revolution to be considered sometime in the distant future. There is a temporal gap between the stages, which is indeterminate in length, and during which capitalism will be stabilized: productive forces will be developed, and democratization enhanced, including in government, and in gender, caste and ethnicity relations.

AN ASSESSMENT

To their credit, Naxalites/Maoists have paid serious attention to gender and caste relations. Many of them have given their lives for this cause. But while emphasising these, they conflate these non-class relations with class relations. Oppressive caste and gender relations (in the economic sphere) are seen by them as necessarily indicative of some kind of feudalism. That capitalism itself can make good use of these relations is not given serious consideration. More importantly, they regard what are really capitalist relations at a low level of development of productive forces as some form of feudal relations of exploitation. Thus what is a question of capitalist class relation is mistakenly conflated with a given level – high level – of the development of productive forces. If there is no economically advanced capitalism, therefore there is no capitalism, there is no capitalist social relation of production see Das 2012b for a detailed argument). Here the question of geography, of scale, is important: under pressure from regional, national and international markets, property owners in some places, specifically at the local scale, make use of extra economic coercion (e.g., use of bonded labour, caste oppression, etc.) to cut costs and neutralize any nascent opposition on

[253] 'Though the primary aim of this democratic revolution will be to abolish all feudal remnants and the concomitant autocratic and bureaucratic distortions in the polity, it will necessarily have several socialist aspects as well. Beyond creating conditions for a decisive victory of democratic revolution, the struggle against big capital will also pave the way for an uninterrupted transition from the democratic to the socialist stage of revolution.' [CPIML Liberation.]. On wonders what the social aspects are? And, how can the struggle be uninterrupted if the working class shares its state power with significant fractions of the property-owning class? Monopolies develop out of and are deeply connect to so-called nationalist sections, who produce commodities on order from monopolies. Why will the nationalist section of the capitalist class allow the working class to put a halt to – or effectively slow -- its accumulation logic being fully and freely manifested? Why would it even let the working class rule if it knew that at some point in time, the working class would go against them (the nationalist sections)? And are the so-called national elements of the capitalist class not connected to the monopolies (as contractors, as manufacturers of parts, and so on), so is it politically (conceptually) significant to make the kind of distinction between the two fractions that the Naxalite movement (and the like) are making, the kind of distinction which is sought to be put to political use?

the part of labour to what I call accumulation by exploitation. These property owners are capitalists, not semi-feudals. They are a part of the capitalist system which is *itself* the biggest threat to democracy and development, and this is the case irrespective of whether there are feudal relations in some areas (and this may be true in some localities, especially where commodification has not been widespread). A revolutionary movement worth the name, in the contemporary world, can only be uncompromisingly anti-capitalist, in theory and practice.

To be radical is to go to the root of the matter. The root of the matter – the root of the major socio-economic problems (mass poverty; economic backwardness, growing authoritarianism, persistence of gender and caste relations, and so on) is the set of class relations of capitalism, at multiple scales. But the Naxalite movement is not a threat to the capitalist system as such, to the capitalists as such. A radical, effective threat to the capitalist property relations is ruled out by its adherence to the theory that India is not yet a fully-functioning capitalism, that it is a semi-feudal country. The Naxalite movement does not recognize that capitalism as *the dominant mode* of people's existence exists. To the extent that the capitalist class is touched (affected), the movement merely provides some kind of resistance against accumulation by dispossession or primitive accumulation (i.e., against some elements of the capitalist class undemocratically trying to grab resource commons, traditionally held by aboriginal people and other oppressed people). A part of their protest against mining capitalists taking away people's land is the idea that they can do things – i.e., control capitalist businesses -- a little better, in a more people friendly way. Even Roy, an enthusiastic supporter of Naxalites, and who believes in going beyond communism and capitalism, thinks that Naxalites' industrialization policy is 'woolly' (2012: 210). And I must say that the movement's theory is in good company. More specifically, I see indeed some kind of similarity/affinity between the Maoist theory, and Harvey's (2005) theory of accumulation by dispossession, which is highly problematic and which is influenced by[254] and has influenced a large number of scholars and activists. Like Harvey, they emphasize accumulation by dispossession at the expense of accumulation by exploitation, i.e., the class relation of *capitalism itself* (for a further discussion on Harvey's theory, see chapter 5 on labour freedom). Thus effectively, the Naxalites now fight for a bourgeois society cleared of vestiges of feudalism and a society without excessive amount of primitive accumulation, a society where there is not too much concentration of capitalists' wealth. They struggle for an authentic system of (liberal) democracy, one without autocratic and bureaucratic distortions, before any fight against capitalist relations as such can begin.[255] It is a fight, which belongs to

[254] One of the scholars who has influenced Harvey's empirical world with respect to the periphery is Arundhati Roy. Roy has written widely, usefully, and sympathetically about issues surrounding dispossession and authoritarianism, including in areas where Naxalites are active, but she is one who rejects a consistent class-analysis and its political implications.

[255] According to CPIML(Liberation), 'Indian society is marked by four main contradictions -- the contradiction between imperialism and Indian nation, that between feudalism and the broad masses of the people, between big capital and the Indian people, the working class in particular, and the contradiction among various sections of the ruling classes. ... [The] *principal* contradiction [is] between feudal remnants and the broad Indian masses, for the feudal remnants constitute the biggest stumbling block on the road to free and rapid development of productive forces in the country. *This determines the stage of our revolution – the stage of people's democratic revolution with agrarian revolution as its axis. [The]* primary aim of this democratic revolution will be to abolish all feudal remnants and the concomitant autocratic and bureaucratic distortions in the polity ... [http:// cpiml.org/8th_ congress/partyprogramme.html; italics added).

The analysis of another major Naxalite stream -- CPIML (New Democracy) -- is almost exactly the same. It quite clearly expresses its two-stage theory: 'The Indian Revolution, taken as a whole, passes through *two distinct stages* of historical development, i.e., the people's democratic and the socialist revolution. ...How rapidly the

the family of fights, fights against excessism and appearances that I discuss briefly in chapter 2.

It is true that society is characterised by combined and uneven development, that modern and archaic forms (dead weight of the past) can co-exist in some localities. At the local scale, capitalists can and do make use of extra-economic coercion, but seen at the national scale, things are different. The nature of a society, whether in India or in Canada, the USA, or the Philippines or Peru, can only be, and must be, determined at the national scale (and within a global perspective). Politically, this is because at the national scale is class power is translated to, and expressed in, state power, which protects and reproduces capitalist class relations, the social power of capital, at the *national* scale. It is at *this* level that any resistance against the class system to be called class struggle proper has to happen. Also, economically, the law of value fully operates at progressively larger spatial scale, national scale, and international scale. What determines the nature of society is what happens in terms of class dynamics at the national scale – i.e., whether property- owners hiring labour for a wage in order to make money can normally go out of business if they do not cut costs. The so-called feudal remnants, feudal relations here and there, at the local scale, *cannot* determine the nature of society as such, and therefore the stage of revolution and political struggle against that society.

Political Implications of Faulty Theory

The fact that the movement is not systemically anti-capitalist, that it is not radically against the capitalist system as such and that it even mistakenly assumes that political hegemony of the working class can coexist with economic supremacy of national capitalist class, is manifested in several inter-related ways.

One is the wrong identification of political resources of the movement: i.e., over-reliance on peasants and under-stress on the proletarians who only have the power to stop the production of capitalist form of wealth. Peasants, for the movement, become the revolutionary class, with rhetorical lip service paid to proletariat. But the problem is that while peasants can be a revolutionary force (and especially, against feudal elements and imperialism and in the fight for land), peasants are not a homogenous class. There are both bourgeois and proletarian elements within it (although proletarian tendencies are overwhelming now). So it cannot lead and take an independent role. When the push comes to shove (during revolutionary times), they either choose the proletarians or the bourgeoisie – all this is ignored. But this is all staple food in the theory and history of anti-capitalist revolution.

Having changed his original view of the democratic dictatorship of workers and peasants, which was very problematic (as Trotsky pointed out), Lenin (1917) said this: "No one, no force, can overthrow the bourgeois counter-revolutionaries except the revolutionary

socialist revolution will be completed will depend on the degree of our strength, the strength of the conscious and organized proletariat, the unity and organization of the Indian toilers under the hegemony of the proletariat and on the strength of the world socialist movement'. And who will participate in the first stage of the revolution? 'The people's democratic revolution under the leadership of the working class will establish a democratic dictatorship of the working class, the peasantry, the urban petty bourgeoisie and the *national bourgeoisie* under the leadership of the working majority of the Indian people'. The new, people's democratic state will ensure the '*Protection of Industry and trade of national bourgeoisie* (http://www.cpimlnd.org/party-documents; italics added).

proletariat. Now, after the experience of July 1917, it is the revolutionary proletariat that must independently take over state power. Without that the victory of the revolution is impossible. The only solution is for power to be in the hands of the proletariat, and for the latter to be supported by the poor peasants or semi-proletarians'.[256]

Because the proletariat is not the main revolutionary force, at least in practice, this is empirically seen in the geography of the movement. There are two aspects to this criticism being made here. One is that the movement suffers from: an over-reliance on the rural areas and consequently by an under-emphasis on urban areas which represent concentrated form of capitalist power. Further, and in terms of rural areas themselves, the movement is not particularly powerful in the areas of strong agrarian capitalism. It is generally confined to areas where the development of capitalist relations of exploitation is relatively stunted. A certain segment of the Naxalite movement (CPI Maoist) is almost totally confined to the areas demographically dominated by the aboriginal peoples (who constitute less than 10% of the total population of the country). This means that the movement is weakly integrated into the class struggle of the non-agrarian working class based in urban areas. The most oppressed/exploited social groups may not necessarily be the most revolutionary, may not have the ability to lead a revolution and establish a new society.

Many sections of the Maoist-inspired Left have a complete distrust of bourgeois parliamentary system. While for the mainstream Left, winning seats is the main emphasis, for several Maoist Left segments, any talk of elections is equated to revisionism. It is one thing to desire that the liberal bourgeois democratic system is obsolete. But in reality it is there. And it is futile to ignore the fact that the system does offer some limited – albeit very limited -- possibilities for exposing the patently undemocratic practices of the state, the ruling classes (domestic and foreign). It is futile to ignore the fact that the system offers limited opportunities for educating the masses about the limits to what is possible within the electoral system and about alternative anti-capitalist, anti-feudal programmes. To participate in the parliament is not the same as wanting to increase the seats in it. That the liberal democratic process provides some political space for pursuing people's causes is a factor yet to be fully recognized in the Naxalite political discourse (Mohanty, 2006). There are ample opportunities to lead the masses around various immediate demands, demands for a living wage, etc. and for such things as publicly provided 'schools, electricity, water and health centres' (Bhatia, 2006: 3181). But most of the Naxalite groups do not wish to engage with the present government except as an enemy' (Bhatia, 2006: 3181). This is because Naxalite leaders assume that their *theoretical* knowledge about the state (what it can and cannot do) is shared by the masses. This is a serious epistemological lapse. Democratic mass movements are necessary in struggling, within an overall revolutionary framework, to get concessions from the state and the propertied classes.[257] They are also necessary for building solidarity and promoting class-consciousness among the exploited classes who must emerge as agents of their self-emancipation *in the process of* fighting for these concessions at multiple scales. It is not enough that Naxalite leaders and ideologues themselves know that the state (and the ruling classes) cannot meet the radical-democratic needs and demands of the poor. To paraphrase Marx's second famous *Thesis on Feuerbach* (Marx and Engels, 1977: 13),

[256] https://www.marxists.org/archive/lenin/works/1917/jul/15.htm

[257] One may also consider the objective and subjective barriers to the extent to which sick, hungry, absolutely illiterate peasants can actively and immediately participate in an ideologically-driven organized mass movement for self-emancipation, in spite of their favourable class-instincts?

whether the state and the ruling classes can meet the radical demands of the exploited classes cannot be (just) a '*scholastic* question'.[258] It is, much rather, 'a *practical* question': it must be resolved in practice, i.e., through their own struggles, within an overall revolutionary perspective, for their radical demands.

For a section of the Naxalite Left, use of violence against the property owners and police is generally written into its script. This is partly because in the Naxalite theory, extra-economic force as the basis for exploitation is stressed, and because, in many areas of their operation, the movement does indeed encounter regular extra-economic coercion on the part of the propertied class. In these areas, bourgeois state apparatus, and associated formal separation between the economic and the political, are almost non-existent. It is as if police, and even much civilian administration, are on the payroll of the propertied. Under these conditions, one section of the Naxalite Left ('People's War Group) believes that '[A]rmed Agrarian Revolution is the only path for achieving people's democracy i.e., new democracy, in our country' The state's response has been partly economic (giving some concessions, carrying out developmental work). It has also been militaristic. The Naxalites' armed action is being used by the state as a justification for killing/harming not only Naxalite supporters and leaders[259], but also progressive people outside, and independent of, the Naxalite movement; many in the latter group are potentially supporters of the exploited masses.[260] Between 2003 and 2012 only, 8498 people have been killed in the conflict between Naxalites and the state, including 4961 civilians, 1840 security personnel, and 1707 Naxalites. The vast majority of those killed are civilians or at least those who are not directly connected to the conflict.[261]

To the extent that a section of the Naxalite Left focuses on military struggle, this fact is self-limiting. The stress on violence can dilute the emphasis on democratic, class-based, political-ideological education and organization of the masses, the opportunities for which do exist. As Lenin (1978:11) said in *Revolutionary Adventurism*: '*without* the working people all bombs are powerless, patently powerless'. Political power of the masses to challenge the whole capitalist system does not come from the Maoist 'barrel of the gun'. Nor does it come from 'spontaneous consciousness' (of peasants, etc.). Lack of a rigorous theory of society discussed earlier – or lack of belief in the need for conscious theory of society and movement – is manifested in the admiration for spontaneity (spontaneous outbursts of masses' anger against exploitative property owners). Spontaneity is a reaction to desperate conditions needing some urgent change. But revolutionary consciousness -- which aims at destroying relics of capital's pre-history and transcending the capitalist system along with undemocratic and imperialist ways in which that system operates – has to be *actively* worked for on the basis of a) Marxist theory of the capitalist system and b) attendant political struggles and organizations.

---

[258] Marxists have made the theoretical argument that: the state will not cross some well-defined limits in terms of meeting the demands of exploited classes (Das, 1996). Those who are not convinced by this *theoretical* answer may find the answer in and through practice (=struggle). It is interesting that feminists and anti-casteist thinkers and activists believe that the state is not as inflexible as Marxists think because it can meet a variety of *their* demands.

[259] I am not saying that if the Naxalite armed outfit did not exist, the state would not use violence against the masses fighting for justice in a peaceful manner. It is just that the Naxalite use of force makes it relatively easier for the state to justify any use of force against the masses fighting for their rights, including those fighting within the Naxalite areas.

[260] They are killed by landlord armies supported by mainstream political parties. They are also killed by state's military forces or by state-sponsored civilian militias.

[261] http://www.satp.org/satporgtp/countries/india/maoist/data_sheets/fatalitiesnaxalmha.htm

CONCLUSION

The fine human qualities such as revolutionary patriotism in an oppressed nation, a sense of hope, the spirit of self-sacrifice, and courage (both to criticize the powers that be and to be involved in an appropriate political practice), the qualities that people, including myself, often associate with the movement or indeed any serious social justice movement, will not bear much fruit, if the basic theory of society that drives the movement is faulty. A radical, progressive, Marxist movement is a class-based movement. It helps transform the consciousness of exploited classes and mobilizes them to translate the potentiality of their class power -- the power they have by virtue of being producers of wealth (value) and by virtue of being the numerical majority (majority citizens) -- into actual class power. A radical party enhances the effectivity of class power which exists by virtue of the class structure. A radical party helps the exploited classes conquer state power and uses that power to destroy the class power of the propertied and begin the process of genuine democratization of economy, polity, family, and culture. It strikes at the root of the system of inequality. In a society where capitalism is the dominant mode of production, a truly radical party is one that must aim at destroying (and not re-regulating) capitalist class relations as well as all other forms of class relations, as a part of a national and international movement. A radical party believes in the necessity and possibility of *self-empowerment* of the exploited classes. 'The time of surprise attacks, of revolution carried through by small conscious minorities at the head of masses lacking consciousness is past'.[262] One reason for this is that unlike in the past revolutions, the dominated classes are the majority, aspiring to control the affairs of the new society. The Maoists' ideological-political focus on what they call feudalism will continue to keep millions of toiling people effectively outside of their influence,[263] whose lives are adversely impacted by the bourgeoisie, including its so-called 'national' fraction, which is inextricably connected to the monopoly fraction and its imperialist backers.[264] Even if a society has a significant amount of pre-capitalist relations, it does not at all follow that a bloc of four classes *including* the national capitalist class, can solve its problems. Any coalition with the bourgeoisie (and we see plenty of coalition between Naxalites and bourgeois parties at the sub-national scale) can only result in revolutionary disaster. This has happened in history throughout the world. Capitalism is deeply connected to pre-capitalist remnants and to caste-, gender- and race oppression in specific places, and businesses always make use of authoritarian-undemocratic practices to make money, so to completely remove these relations and bring about genuine democracy requires a multi-scalar uninterrupted struggle against *the capitalist system itself*, at the national and international scale. To the extent that the concrete nature of capitalism varies from place to place (in some areas property owners may use undemocratic methods than in other areas), the actual tactic of mobilization may change accordingly. But the theory of society, which is sought to be revolutionized, is a different matter. All that glitters is not gold. All movements that appear radical are not really radical.

---

[262] http://www.marxists.org/archive/marx/works/1850/class-struggles-france/intro.htm

[263] These comprise the vast reserve army of laborers in rural areas (including those with small pieces of land) and in urban slums. This reserve army raises the level of exploitation of the currently employed through the mechanisms of low wages and overwork, despotically imposed by capital, and this reduces employment opportunities of those who are a part of the reserve army, as Marx argued in chapter 25 of *Capital* volume 1. What follows is that those who are employed *and* those who are not are both impacted by the capitalist system.

[264] The 'national' faction will be a part of their people's democratic state.

Chapter 12

PROTEST POLITICS IN THE WORLD: A MARXIST CRITIQUE

The world is experiencing at least three kinds of crisis. There is, of course, an economic crisis, and a consequent livelihood crisis. There is an ecological crisis. In this context, apart from the intractable climate change issue, the crisis of the Japan's nuclear industry is one of the latest worries. And, finally, there is a crisis of leadership of the masses, which can potentially address these crises. All countries, including major capitalist democracies such as the US and India as well as the countries experiencing the phenomenon of Arab Springs, are facing these crises, to varying degrees.

Underlying the first two crises is the profit-system. Much has been written about how the structurally determined 'greed' – the endless desire for accumulation for the sake of accumulation -- of the financial elite contributed to the US mortgage crisis and consequently the financial crisis itself. This crisis is not the first. It will not be the last in the capitalist world. Some people are saying that another meltdown in the housing market in the US is coming. Crisis is permanent in capitalism. Massive unemployment and austerity measures on the one hand and extremely high level of concentration of wealth in the hands of the financial elite, and indeed top corporations, on the other are the immediate outcomes of the crisis. Millions of people in the richest countries of the world – close to 30 millions in the US only -- are food-insecure. The level of unemployment in the rich countries is colossal. Close to million people are un- or under-employed in the US alone. The US has the highest rate of child poverty in the advanced world. In the years when the US was experiencing its highest level of prosperity, one in five was in poverty. The situation in the poorer countries is much worse: millions experience food insecurity, unemployment, and similar problems. When society's resources are concentrated in the hands of an elite and when these resources are used for making profit for this elite, then unemployment, poverty and all other social problems are the definite and expected consequences. Besides, advanced countries such as the US have not yet fully recovered from the 2008 financial crisis, and because of the dependence of emerging economies on them, their own economic growth is slowing down.

And then there is an ecological crisis. The profit-driven character of the economic growth process that is behind the economic crisis also underlies the massive ecological crisis. The Japanese nuclear disaster is the latest manifestation of the ecological crisis. Japan is using a nuclear technology that is 30-40 years old. Such an obsolete technology is used to cut costs and increase profits of the (US-based) nuclear companies. These are a part of the global network of nuclear companies that lobby for publicly-subsidized private investment in nuclear power in major countries. They played a significant role in the so-called US-India strategic partnership, an imperialist framework.[265]

It is arguable that while the profit system underlies both economic and ecological crisis (and the two are not un-connected), this system will not go just because it is crisis-prone (unless the planet's ecological system itself collapses under the 'profit burden'). Human agency – the agency of the working masses -- is necessary for establishing a truly democratic system. But there is a crisis in this sphere as well. It is this crisis that will be discussed briefly in this chapter.

WORLD-WIDE PROTEST POLITICS

Thousands of millions of people want to change things. But this wanting is often, more or less, limited to: 'protest politics'. This refers to the campaigns on the part of marginalized people (e.g., rural people, aboriginal people; urban youth) against companies setting up industries displacing ordinary people, against this or that case of excess in the system, this or that unfair policy of the government, this or that case of corruption. The quality of democracy would be poorer without these protests. These are necessary. But they are deficient, as mentioned in chapter 2. Let us explore why and what can be done.

Take the case of Arab Springs. The proletarians (including in the Suez Canal area and in various cities) and the youth have fought valiantly against the authoritarian regimes in North Africa, which were/are also regimes of high inflation, neoliberal cuts, low wages, poverty and misery. Egypt, an epicenter of Arab Springs, was a model neoliberal state, which listened to – obeyed -- imperialist institutions such as World Bank in implementing the 'economic reforms'. The western imperialists had propped up, and/or were cutting lucrative deals with, these regimes. In imperialist countries themselves, workers have appeared on the streets in thousands to protest the suppression of democratic rights (e.g., right to bargain over wages and working conditions). They have been on the street against austerity, the proximate cause of which is the economic crisis: having given trillions of dollars to capitalist companies to bail them out, their governments are forcing the workers to pay the bill. On March 26, 2011 half a million people, the vast majority of whom are workers, marched in London to protest the social cuts in the UK. This may easily be the second largest protest in the country's history. Protests have also taken place in Japan against the Japanese nuclear disaster, as well as against austerity measures in Europe. In the world, 2011 will go down as a year of mass struggle.

The North African situation at the global scale and the story of the regular struggles of the masses in every country indicate that proletarians do fight for their rights. They are not passive, as some on the Left – the so-called 'postmodern Left' -- suggest. The history of

[265] To implement such a partnership, India's pro-business prime minister even staked his job; and for this, votes were perhaps bought and sold in India's famous talking-shop (the Parliament), a place which has been immensely successful not in terms of helping the masses (workers and poor peasants) but in dis-arming them politically, enthralling them with the fetishism of the vote.

human society – in terms of macro-scale events and processes -- is always a history of struggle against injustice on the part of direct producers.

But struggle is one thing. Success is another. Have people won any significant democratic freedom? Have they won any significant improvement in their economic conditions, without which the significant democratic freedom, even if it were to arrive, has limited worth? No. Indeed, in North Africa, because the masses fought and because the imperialists thought that their fighting could take a radical turn, they were crushed under the wheels of an imperialist war, shamelessly justified on the basis of humanitarian aid. The imperialist governments have all of a sudden found billions of dollars for the unjust war when they have been saying that they have no money for welfare and to create jobs for the unemployed. The region has only seen one form of authoritarian regime or another.

The fight for democratic freedoms cannot be successful without the fight for democracy being a part of the fight for a society without exploitative private property relations. Why? First of all, even if masses fight for democracy, democratic rights may not be granted because un-democratic practices and relations are used by capitalism. This is more so when capitalism – in imperialized countries -- is at a lower level of development of productive forces. Indeed, how many Third World *capitalist* countries have even liberal *democracies*? Secondly, even if some democratic freedoms are granted and maintained due to an intense pressure of the masses, they can be withdrawn anytime the masses turn more vigilant and more militant. Consider India's case in the 1970s under Indira Gandhi, the emergency. There are also mini-emergencies (at sub-national scales, including in aboriginal areas) countless times in India (and in other poor countries): when masses fight for their social rights (e.g., for land, for a decent wage, etc.) in the democratic and peaceful way, repressive measures are often launched. Even in advanced capitalist countries, workers' right to bargain are being crushed, and various forms of civic freedom are being limited. The Snowden affair is a testimony to this. Thirdly, what is the record in terms of actual practice of liberal democracy? In such liberal democracies like the US or even India, what percentage of parliamentarians can present a vision on behalf of the workers and poor farmers/peasants, a vision that goes against big companies and big landowners (or agri-business)? In such liberal democracies, how many people from working class and poor peasant type backgrounds can fight in national and provincial elections and win? These are not inconsequential questions to ask: we need to seriously consider the severe limits that capitalism puts in front of the realization of even basic democratic rights, and how capitalism undermines any fight for democratic rights. Liberal-democracy is a *form* of *capitalist* rule. The form is not unimportant either from the standpoint of workers or businesses. But as soon as the *form* hurts the *real* content (money-making and the political hegemony and stability necessary for money-making), the form will be gotten rid of or severely deformed/weakened. A state of exception is just down the corner.

Even the so-called opposition groups, as in North Africa, with whom the imperialists tie up, are just that: as in any other country with a semblance of democracy, these opposition groups merely oppose the current ways in which the booty of the nation – the blood and sweat of the workers and poor peasants – are divided between different fractions of the national property-owning class and between them and the imperialists. Indeed, these opposition groups have an agenda which is no less neoliberal, no less capitalist than the current agenda of the government they are trying to overthrow. If things were otherwise, the imperialists would not want to support these groups. The aim of the imperialists is clearly to put in place a regime (with or without the Gaddafis or the Mubaraks), which will be more subservient to them. Their aim is to signal that they will not tolerate any oppositional politics going beyond a change of the current *political* character of the regime, i.e., it will not allow revolutionary politics (politics of class) to take root.

As long as workers and the youth remain tied to this or that bourgeois or petty-bourgeois party-formation/movement, as long as they lack a truly combined vision, i.e., a vision that seeks both democracy and a system that does not privilege profit-making at the expense of human needs -- and this is what I mean by the crisis of revolutionary leadership -- the chances of success in achieving even democratic freedom are rather limited, as are the chances of success in addressing common economic needs of the ordinary people. Not that some success here and there will not happen. Not that the system will never allow a two-party or multi-party-system. Not that an industrialization project based on peasants' dispossession will not be withdrawn here and there in the face of a fight. But such occasional and localized concessions are more likely to contribute to the reproduction of the global system itself, unless the politics of opposition is guided, in theory and in practice, by a proletarian anti-capitalist revolutionary agenda. The politics of opposition to *aspects* of the system is not the same as the politics of opposition to the system itself, to the totality, as such.

So, there *is* protest politics everywhere in the world (e.g., protests against environmental degradation, child labor, racial prejudice, trafficking, discrimination against women, and so on). There is indeed little indication that the protests which are occurring everywhere are being seen, in theory and practice, as parts of *a system* of political-intellectual campaigns against *a common*, or the central, target (i.e., use of society's resources for limitless private gain), aiming to completely get rid of that system. Protest politics 'represents new forms of political subjectivity' (Newman, 2007:166), one that is of 'a heterogeneous mass', and not of class, not the proletarians (p.171). Indeed, solidly informed by poststructuralism (p178), it goes beyond 'class paradigms of Marxism'; it demands through, some form of collective action, certain economic reforms, it includes cultural politics of identity, and it embraces anarchism. Much of so-called critical intellectual work comes out of this context.

NEED FOR RADICAL THEORY

In opposition to the ideas underlying protest politics which does not and cannot fundamentally challenge the system (as well as to the *more openly* free-market ideologies), there is a need for an intransigent, radical, theory that lays bare the unbending and unyielding character of the current system of economic and political power relations and at the same time charts the possibilities of reforms, the reforms as a part of the broader project of transcendence of the system. Such a theory must recognize this: concessions are possible to obtain but seen in a proper time-space perspective, every little concession given now and here is taken back there or in another point in time. The temporal and spatial life of the system is much larger than individuals' and groups'. The theory must also recognize that nearly every material concession that hurts the ruling class is used ideologically to produce consent in the minds of people to the system, consent to the idea that 'the system can be reformed, so please be patient'. Notice the contradiction: the system teaches *patience*, but it itself is based on an incessant or *impatient* process of money-making. Masses are told that they need to sacrifice their current satisfaction of needs at the altar of the profit-driven market-system, which will deliver good things in the future. Liminality is for the masses, not for the moneybags. The system is bathed with a passion, with 'revolutionary' impatience, impatient to make as much money (even illegally) in as less time as possible. There is no corresponding revolutionary 'impatience' or urgency on the part of the 'leadership' of the oppressed, however. Underlying the contradiction mentioned above is a deep hiatus between the system's concept of time and that of the oppressed. For the system (or, more correctly, the 1% or the 10% which rules it): things have to happen quickly, money has to be made quickly, 'labor reforms' will have to be passed quickly which will allow companies to fire employees freely, and so on. For the oppressed-majority, the idea, more or less, is 'postponism': that we can wait to be fed better; that we can wait to see a completely new world, and that all we can do now is to ask for some reforms. This is the idea propagated by most of the unions and Left parties. Notice also another contradiction: between *greed* of the 1% and *asceticism* of the 99%. The 1% seeks to make as much money as it can and satisfy its most diverse needs for luxuries. And the bottom 99%, or even the bottom 70%? It has to be satisfied with less, with small concessions.

The postponism of the majority and its asceticism are not un-connected with how the political-intellectual leaders who seek to speak on behalf of the majority theorize the system, how they think about the main contradiction underlying the various forms of the crisis the world is facing. I have indicated some of the inadequacies in chapter 1. It should suffice to say that: underlying the belief that we can fight for a change here and there is a deeply philosophical inclination towards a combination of empiricism, presentism and reformism/opportunism. A little visible evidence of some concession here, at the present moment, is used to *theoretically* mean that the system can deliver significant concessions *always*. And therefore what we see -- the system being able to deliver some concessions, some progressive legislation -- is mistakenly taken by many to be what is real, i.e., what is fundamentally true about the system. So a truly radical critique of the system, with its radical vision for the future, is blunted, and this has adverse implications for practice.

Underlying many of the campaigns (protest political activities) is this belief in the potential reformability of the system for the good of all in the long run. We forget that: when, for example, a wage increase is won in one place, it may come at the expense of workers elsewhere, or it may come at the expense of worker's solidarity *in situ* (a little wage increase can be granted on the ground that workers cannot go on a strike or form an independent union). A theory of wage cannot rule out wage increase. Even when wage increase happens at a larger scale than in a few companies or locally, i.e., even if it happens, say, nationally, we must understand two things. First, as Marx remarks in *Capital vol. 1*, it 'only means, in fact, that the length and weight of the golden chain the wage-worker has already forged for himself, allow of a relaxation of the tension of it', that we reproduce ourselves as slightly better-fed slaves who help the property owners accumulate their wealth. Second, the increase in wages 'can never reach the point at which it would threaten the system itself'. The system sets the limit on how good our life can be. As soon as the rise in wages interferes with the normal rate of profit making at a given time, wages start falling. 'The rise of wages therefore is confined within limits that not only leave intact the foundations of the capitalistic system, but also secure its reproduction on a progressive scale.' After winning some wage increase due to both favourable circumstances of accumulation (e.g., nationally and regionally based process of accumulation) and a certain degree of unionization, American workers in the auto-industry are now forced to sell themselves for almost half the wage they were used to receive.

What is needed at the moment is an adequate theory; the principles that can guide such a theory are discussed earlier, and especially in chapters 1-2. At the minimum, and in the context of the multiple crises the humanity is facing, such a theory must recognize *what is present* (e.g., class exploitation; imperialism; oppression of women, racial minorities and aboriginal peoples, profit-driven ecological destruction; gross commercialization of all spheres of human life including culture and social relations; and state authoritarianism). The theory must recognize what is present at various levels (i.e., levels of structural mechanisms and empirical events, as Roy Bhaskar has stressed, or in terms of essence/content and form). Only this sort of recognition of the present can escape from empiricism (the idea that what is visibly seen is real). This theory must also recognize *what is absent.* Now what is absent must be seen at two levels. First, in terms of future, it refers to the opposite of what is present, i.e., to the satisfaction of humanity's material-cultural and political needs; it refers to the need for collective democratic control over our lives, our planet, our bodies, our culture. In other words, what is absent is: the humanity's majority being able to satisfy its needs and to control its affairs. Second, what is absent refers also to revolutionary politics: the massive democratic organizations of the masses (including their more class-conscious elements) intellectually and politically, the organizations that are democratically guided by a revolutionary leadership of the masses, in different parts of the world and at multiple geographical scales. Both politically conscious masses and a revolutionary leadership are necessary to get to the future from the present.

The theory – the theory-as-critique -- must acknowledge *explanatorily* that what is present is the main cause of what is absent. The theory must therefore recognize *politically* that what is 'absent' has to be presented and what is present has to be absented. And this theorization has to be performed at multiple scales, and most specifically, nationally and internationally, and with a sensitivity towards the longer time scale at which the system's tendencies, the mechanisms, operate. Is there a whole lot in between these absenting and presenting practices, in the longer term? Dialectically seen, has the humanity created a possibility for anything really significant between individualist control and collective control, between making money for the sake of money (even fictitious money) and the satisfaction of democratically-defined human needs?

The fight for concessions – including democratization of the government -- is enormously worth it. It is worth it to the extent that it increases the fighting power of the poor-majority for the ultimate absenting of the present. Surely, someone who has not eaten for days cannot be expected to fight against a law that bans abortion rights or right to form a union. Immediate relief is important. Concessions are also worth fighting for if the process of fighting inculcates awareness among the masses that there are strong limits to what is possible to gain within the system and if they impart to the masses the political and intellectual skills necessary to fight (and to manage a different future world).[266] Intellectually, progressives can assess the significance of the fight for reforms on these (and perhaps other similar) grounds. Politically, they can encourage reforms on these and other similar grounds (and of course, the pursuit of reforms must happen through proper organizational means to bear the fruits). But these intellectual and political tasks presuppose the following recognition: the need for the fight for concessions in/from the system is informed by a proper *theory* of the system itself

[266]Consider how NYC occupiers set up public libraries, public health-care system, public eating-places, and so on. That the occupy movement could not have wider impact is a different issue.

and the strategy to transcend it altogether. To theorize the system is to unpack its logic of operation, the mechanisms and tendencies, including tendencies to change.

We should remember that we live in a world where wealth is produced for money making, where we will feed ourselves as long as we feed the system with money through our labor[267], where we work as long as we live and live as long as we work. In the current arrangements, our everyday activities as a species are not directly geared towards the satisfaction of our manifold needs as humans. Therefore, when concessions are given, it is not necessarily because the system 'wants' to satisfy our needs. Much rather it is because the system is – or managers of it are -- a little fearful of the masses (turning more revolutionary): lest they will demand an alternative system, which will be controlled by them, and by the logic of human need. Sometimes even the ultra-rich can ask to be taxed a little, or taxed a little more than they usually are, or they ask for being regulated a little by the government. All this self-abnegation – self-negation -- happens purely because of their fear of possible ultimate 'negation of negation' (expropriation of the expropriators). This temporary self-denial on the part of the ruling elite happens because of their anxiety about *their* future, not about *ours*. In other words, concessions are *given* by the elite to keep the system going so that the product of masses' work can continue to be *taken* away from them. Concession-giving is really the opposite of what it appears to be. It is not giving. It is taking. Everything stands on its head in this modern class-divided world. False ideas are created in people's minds. Concessions are a small part of the system. The system determines – sets limit on (in the language of Raymond Williams) -- the manner, the form, the magnitude, the timing and spacing of the concessions. Concessions are not an indicator of the goodness of the system or of the fact that it is a legitimate one. A few benefits wrung from the system – even when these benefits are given in a context of the fear of the masses turning more revolutionary -- do not change much the fundamental character of the system, which needs to incessantly make money, any more than a few pieces of falling hair make a person bald. Such is the law of quantity and quality in dialectics. And there have been fewer and fewer of these benefits anyway in the recent past. The question is: what is to be done about this crisis of the politics of the working masses? Before addressing this, we should know: what is *not* to be done about the crisis of the revolutionary leadership?

WHAT IS NOT TO BE DONE?

Let's return to the concept of 'the crisis of the revolutionary leadership'. A crisis is more than a problem. It is a problem which needs to be *urgently* addressed. This urgency lies in the fact that: the current leadership (in the form of various Left parties and trade unions) of the workers and semi-proletarians is not as effective as it should, and the new leadership is not yet fully born at a large enough scale in a politically effective manner. A leadership is necessary which will: analyze the objective conditions in the world and explain the nature of the crises to be fixed and it must offer up a solution by using that explanation.

[267] Business owners by delaying gratification and by investing do not create wealth. Where did they get the wealth in the first place, one may ask? And yes, many business owners do contribute to production by doing some work, but does their income reflect that contribution or does it reflect the fact that they own the property? Owning is not working.

As far as the Left is concerned, the lack of appropriate government regulation is often an explanation of the world's problems, so it is thought that an alliance with some sections of the bourgeoisie (especially, the economically weaker sections) will result in better regulations. More pressure on the system, outside of any vision for transcending the system, is what is said to be necessary. This partly explains – or at least, justifies -- the rise of neoliberalism as an object of theoretical critique and as a tool in the hands of protest politics: it forgets that a better-regulated capitalism – a capitalism which is not neoliberal, one which is less regulated by market forces than by non-market forces -- is still capitalism. And given the global nature of capitalism, it is often practically difficult to regulate it within national borders by mechanisms that are based within those borders. Therefore, and as stressed in chapter 2, all the forces which merely fight against neoliberalization as a social form – or indeed, against globalization as a geographical form -- of capitalism *in abstraction from* the real content of capitalism (its exploitative class character, which has not changed since its birth) *cannot* assume revolutionary leadership, although fights against neoliberalization and globalization *are* crucial starting points. Many critics of neoliberalism and indeed of capitalism would like the latter to be regulated and kept in check by non-state forces (NGOs; local communities). This would not do either, in part because NGOs themselves depend on the state and/or capitalists for their existence. NGO-ization is the bottom-up aspect of neoliberalization, as Petras (1997) has argued: their origin lies partly in the need to clear up the mess created by neoliberal capitalism and to keep a lid on the anger of the poor. In other words, a leadership is *not* revolutionary (it cannot lead the masses to transcend the system and establish an alternative humane democratic system based on the logic human need), if it is rooted in a vision of social democracy of any type (some problems of social democracy are discussed further in chapter 7).

There are still others who believe that capitalism can be regulated, and the problems of poverty and the environmental degradation, etc. can be addressed by, the working class unions – or indeed by their bureaucracy. The union bureaucracy – in part, given its economism -- has often been deeply complicit in the reproduction of capitalism (and in the context of advanced countries, of imperialism). In the USA recently, the union bureaucracy said to the government in a province (Wisconsin) that: 'we will agree to the cuts you are suggesting but allow us to exist and collect union dues'. Well, if you agree to the class-onslaught on the working class launched by the ruling class, what is the point of remaining as unions? Given its income and privilege (e.g., access to administration, company bosses), the union bureaucracy is a class-like force which does not, and cannot have, the interest of the working class, *unless*, the unions are directly controlled by rank-and-file workers in democratically organized committees in factories, offices, on farms and in neighbourhoods. So neither the state, nor NGOs, nor the existing union bureaucracy can solve the massive problems facing the working class and poor peasants of the world. They are *not* revolutionary. And, as argued in chapter 11 on Maoism, a revolutionary leadership cannot be one either that confines its theoretical and political work to a fight against feudal remnants or caste/racial oppression and against imperial domination, then b) rest and allow capitalism to stabilize, and c) possibly plan an anti-capitalist struggle in the indeterminate future (when perhaps productive forces have developed to a 'high' level inside a country).

So, What is to be Done?

The Root of the Problems is Capitalism

Who/what *is* revolutionary then? A person or a group of persons or an organization is capable of taking up the role of a revolutionary leadership when it absolutely asserts: that capitalism is a system, which works at local, regional, national and, most fundamentally, international scales, and which is the most fundamental cause of most important socio-ecological problems, that capitalism must be replaced for us to truly begin to address the world problems nationally and internationally, that it can only be overthrown by the class that produces surplus value (i.e., proletarians), in an alliance with other working masses and with semi-proletarians (e.g., poor peasants in agrarian economies), and that this fight against capitalism must be coordinated not only nationally but also internationally, and that all the bigger or smaller fights against this or that aspect of capitalist and 'non-capitalist' injustice must be inter-linked and become parts of the project of establishing a democratic society beyond capitalism.

Necessity of Uninterrupted Multi-Scalar Struggle

The revolutionary leadership must accept that: capitalism is a system that not only makes use of, and subordinates, various types of relations and processes which pre-date capitalism (e.g., gender and caste relations; various feudal type remnants; extreme forms of inequality in land distribution) and various forms of political authoritarianism, but also it makes use of national domination. In contemporary, neoliberal, times, the latter takes the form of domination of poorer countries by such institutions as the World Bank. This is the stuff of new-imperialism. Therefore, the revolutionary leadership must accept that to successfully fight against undemocratic practices, feudal remnants, and imperial domination, it must fight against capitalism as well.

A revolutionary leadership is therefore one that mobilizes and unites geographically and socially fragmented class-forces to fight for achieving various democratic tasks, including the resolution of the agrarian question (including extreme inequality in the land distribution) in many parts of the less developed world. The leadership will, on the basis of these struggles, launches an attack on capitalism itself in an uninterrupted fashion and nationally and internationally. But a leadership whose vision is confined to merely democratic tasks cannot fully achieve the democratic tasks (because the bourgeoisie will not allow it to), nor can it fight against the bourgeoisie. This is what Trotsky and Lenin realized and asserted based on the historical analysis of Russian revolutions and the world situation. In addition, a revolutionary leadership must accept that socialism cannot be achieved within the confine of a country or a world-region, let alone within a province of a country (e.g., West Bengal or Kerala or California or Porto Alegre), although anti-capitalist struggle can and must start at all scales and in as many places/countries as possible.

Political Nature of Revolutionary Leadership and Radical Needs

The revolutionary leadership is one which must mobilize people to enable their entry into the public political process and must help them shed their reliance on experts such as union bureaucracy, law-makers, lawyers, professors, journalists and so on, and must mobilize the working class *independently* and not *attach* them to petty bourgeois and bourgeois formations (e.g., democratic party of the US or labor party/government of the UK). A revolutionary leadership identifies proletarians (or at least the more class-conscious elements among them) as the leader of the revolution and mobilizes them, fully keeping in view the lessons of history. It must be based on the idea that the process of revolutionary change – mobilizing people to fight to end the system – is also a process of the slow transformation of the masses into new human beings who will defend and look after the system in a democratic and humane way. As Karl Marx put it, 'Revolution is necessary not only because the ruling class cannot be overthrown in any other way, but because only in a revolution can the class overthrowing it rid itself of all the muck of ages and fit itself to found society anew'.

The leadership mobilizes the masses through a party that is adequately centralized and whose affairs are conducted in the most democratic manner including by being open to internal and external criticisms. The leadership launches class struggle, in the most democratic manner the system allows it to, and inside and outside the state institutions such as the parliament, but it does not have an obsession to win seats in the parliament through various deals with petty bourgeois and bourgeois parties. It has no illusions about the parliamentary road to socialism. It mobilizes proletarian and semi-proletarian forces around day-to-day issues that affect them, including neoliberal cuts. It mobilizes these forces to demand the fulfillment of 'radical needs'[268]. Radical needs (or demands), as mentioned several times earlier, are the real needs (or demands) of the masses, not the needs which the system says it can afford to meet, or which it can objectively meet. So, the revolutionary leadership mobilizes people around the demand for the fulfillment of the following rights to ensure that their radical needs are met: the right to employment (including the right to land and other farm inputs for poor peasants in agrarian economies), a living wage, a reduced working day and leisure, decent and affordable housing, high-quality health-care and education as well as culture (films, televisions programmes, music, museums, and the like not controlled by big business and its politicians). These rights also include the right to decent financial support for the elderly and the disabled; and the right to a healthy and safe environment at work and in neighborhoods. In the specific context of the global periphery and in its rural areas, the revolutionary leadership mobilizes middle and poor peasants around their specific needs: land distribution, and state-provision of means of production, complete freedom from landlord, usurious and mercantile exploitation. The revolutionary leadership also fights for the defense of democratic rights, including those of minorities and aboriginal populations. And it fights against militarism and war, imperial domination and peripheral countries entering into global strategic partnerships with imperialist countries. The revolutionary leadership must put the agenda of workers' democratic control over landed and financial aristocrats and over major capitalist monopolies as immediate steps necessary to satisfy the fulfillment of the social needs of the masses, especially those monopolies which control the production of things and services (e.g., food items and seeds, medicines, houses,

[268] Note that Heller (1976) defines radical needs differently than I do here.

clothes, utilities, etc.) without which radical needs cannot be met and people cannot live like humans.

The revolutionary leadership must mobilize the working masses based on a *socialist* agenda, a part of which is, as just mentioned, a fight for the achievement of the democratic and national tasks as well as the tasks necessary to save the ecological health of the planet on a most urgent basis.[269] The aim of this mobilization will be socialism – a democratic humane control over world's resources to be used democratically to satisfy human needs in an ecologically sustainable manner – and not a better regulated, more humane, more democratic, capitalism without feudal remnants and foreign intervention.

Role of Theory and Education

As classical revolutionaries have said, the time of revolution comes when the existing ruling class cannot rule in the way it has been ruling and when the masses do not want to live the way they have been living and would like to be on the public scene to force a change. The revolutionary leadership must demonstrate its sheer collective intellectual power to be able to anticipate revolutionary crisis caused by the conflict between production forces and relations at the world scale, prepare for the revolution and lead and sustain the revolution, all based on the objective analysis of objective conditions at the global scale, not necessarily inside a country.

The Marxist Left, in the global periphery or elsewhere, must first launch a massive theoretical education on the dominant role of *capitalism* as such, i.e., the dominant role of capitalist economic, political and ideological systems. A minimum requirement for this to happen is also widespread comradely and polite discussion of various Left and communist party views on capitalism and anti-capitalism in as *non-sectarian* a manner as politically and intellectually possible. The logic of class exploitation and domination and associated profit-drive unites the warring competing fractions of the business class and monopolies, partly via the state and partly via their own associations and networks. At a concrete level, the capitalist class is divided economically and politically, but when faced with a common enemy, the whole class tends to unite. The 'anti-capitalist' forces appear not to have learnt this lesson: the logic of anti-capitalism – the logic of the imperative to completely transcend capitalism -- has not united the anti-capitalist forces, and which is one reason the capitalist logic continues to exist in the way it does.

Capitalism is a totalizing and global system. The force that can fight it has to fight capitalism as a global system and has to fight every way in which capitalism impacts us, including the ways in which it makes use of pre- and non-capitalist processes. A fundamental theoretical requirement for a leadership to assume revolutionary status is first be convinced, and to convince others, that it is capitalism that is the problem, and that it is capitalism that must be replaced. Revolution is an incessant struggle against *all* forms of class relations and at all scales of the global society. It requires revolutionary, radical, ideas. These ideas – these critical ideas -- must grip the minds of the masses. Only a revolutionary leadership can contribute to the production and dissemination of these critical ideas. Critique needs a

[269]If a few more Russian and Japanese type nuclear disasters happen, we may not be around to even talk about capitalism and anti-capitalism.

material medium. The revolutionary leadership and organization are an important medium. The masses are the ultimate medium.

Whether this can happen will determine how long we will continue to experience barbarism in many forms such as massive destruction of livelihood, land-dispossession, intensified level of exploitation on the farms, in factories and offices, massive ecological disasters, unheard-of levels of income inequality, and heightened and widespread level of alienation, eternal threat of imperialist wars, and so on. The choice is once again: continuing barbarism or a future society which is truly caring and humane and thoroughly democratic in all spheres of life.[270]

[270] One word for this society is socialism.

WORKS CITED

Agamben, Giorgio. 2005. *The State of Exception*, The University of Chicago Press, Chicago

Althusser, L. (2001). *Lenin and Philosophy and Other Essays*. New York: Monthly Review Press.

Althusser, L (2005). *For Marx*. London: Verso.

Amin, S. 2010. *The Law of Worldwide Value*, New York: Monthly Review Press.

Anderson, M., Smith, L. & Sidel, V. (2005). "What is Social Medicine?", *Monthly Review*. Vol. 56, No. 8; http://monthlyreview.org/2005/01/01/what-is-social-medicine.

Arthur, C. 2002. *The New Dialectic and Marx's Capital*, Leiden: Brill.

Aston, T. and Philipin, C. 1987. *The Brenner Debate*, Cambridge: Cambridge University Press.

Bagchi, A. K. (1995). Dialectics of Indian Planning: from Compromise to Democratic Decentralization and Threat of Disarray. In. T.V. Sathyamurthy (Ed.). *Industry and Agriculture in India since Independence*. (pp. 46-95). Delhi: Oxford University Press.

Banaji, J. (1999). "Metamorphoses of Agrarian Capitalism", *Economic and Political Weekly*. Vol. 34, No.40.

Banaji, J. (2010). *Theory as History*, Leiden: Brill

Bandyopadhyay, D. (1995). Reactions on Land Reforms in India since Independence. In T.V. Sathyamurthy (Ed.). *Industry and Agriculture in India since Independence*. (p. 325). Delhi: Oxford University Press.

Bardhan, P. (1999). *The Political Economy of Development in India*. Oxford: Blackwell.

Bardhan, P. (2005). 'Nature of Opposition to Economic Reforms in India', *Economic and Political Weekly*. Vol. XL, No. 48.

Baru, S. (1995). Continuity and change in Indian Industrial Policy. In T.V. Sathyamurthy (Ed.). *Industry and Agriculture in India since Independence*. (p. 24). Delhi: Oxford University Press.

Basu, K. (1996). The impact of structural adjustment on social sector expenditure: evidence from Indian States. In C.H. Hanumantha & H. Linnemann. *Economic Reforms and Poverty Alleviation in India* (pp. 228–54). New Delhi: Sage Publications.

Bensaid, D. 2002. *Marx for Our Times*, London: Verso.

Benton, T. & Craib, I. (2011). *Philosophy of Social Science*. New York: Palgrave.

Bhaduri, A. (1983). *The Economic Structure of a Backward Agriculture*. London: Academic Press.

Bhaduri, A. (1993). *Unconventional Economic Essays: Selected Papers of Amit Bhaduri*. Delhi: Oxford University Press.

Bhagwati, J. (2001). "Growth, Poverty and Reforms", *Economic and Political Weekly*. Vol. XXXVI, No. 18.

Brass, T. (1995a). "Old Conservatism in *'New' Clothes*", *Journal of Peasant Studies. Vol. 22, No. 3,* pp. *516-540.*
Brass, T. (1995b). "Reply to Utsa Patnaik: If the Cap Fits…", *International Review of Social History*, Vol. 40, No. 1, pp. 93-117
Brass, T. (1999). *Towards a Comparative Political Economy of Unfree Labour: Case Studies and Debates.* London: Frank Cass Publishers.
Brass, T. (2008). "Capitalism and bonded labor in India: Reinterpreting recent (Re-) Interpretations", *Journal of Peasant Studies.* Vol. 35, No. 2, pp. 177-248.
Brass, T. (2011). *Labour Regime Change in the 21st Century: Unfreedom, Capitalism and Primitive Accumulation.* Leiden: Koninklijke Brill NV.
Brenner, R. (1977). "The Origins of Capitalist Development: A Critique of Neo-Smithian Marxism", *New Left Review.* No. 104, pp. 25-92.
Brenner, R. (1986). The Social Basis of Economic Development. In J. Roemer (Ed.), *Analytical Marxism.* Cambridge: Cambridge University Press.
Boyd, R., Gaspar, P. & Trout, J.D. (Eds.). (1991). *The Philosophy of Science.* Cambridge, Mass: The MIT Press.
Burkett, P. (1999). *Marx and Nature.* New York: Palgrave.
Butler, J. (2002). What is Critique: An essay on Foucault's Virtue. In D. Ingram (Ed.), *The Political: Readings in Continental Philosophy.* London: Basil Blackwell.
Byres. T. (1994). The State and Development. In T. Byres (Ed.), *The State and Development Planning in India.* Oxford: Oxford University Press.
Byres, T.J. (1995). "Political Economy, the Agrarian Question and the Comparative Method", *The Journal of Peasant Studies.* Vol.22, No.4, pp.561-580.
Callinicos, A. (1988). *Making History: Agency, Structure and Change in Social Theory.* New York: Cornell University Press.
Callinicos, A. (2002). *Equality*, Cambridge: Polity Press.
Callinicos, A. (2006). *The Resources of Critique.* London: Polity.
Caporaso, J.A. & Levine, D.P. (1992). *Theories of Political Economy.* Cambridge: University Press.
Castree, N. and Braun, B. 2001. *Social Nature: Theory, Practice and Politics*, Oxford: Blackwell.
Chaudhuri, P. (1995). Economic Planning in India. In T.V. Sathyamurthy (Ed.). *Industry and Agriculture in India since Independence.* (p. 110). Delhi: Oxford University Press.
Chayanov, A.V. (1966). *The Theory of Peasant Economy.* D. Thorner, B. Kerblay & R.E.F. Smith (Eds.). Homewood, IL: The American Economic Association.
Chibber, V. (2013). *Postcolonial Theory and the Spectre of Capital.* London: Verso.
Clarke, S. (Ed.). (1991). *The State Debate.* New York: St Martin's Press.
Collier, A. (1994). *Critical Realism: An Introduction to Roy Bhaskar's Philosophy*, London: Verso.
Das, R.J. (1995). "Poverty and Agrarian Social Structure – A Case-Study in Rural India", *Dialectical Anthropology.* Vol. 20, No. 2, pp. 169-192.
Das, R.J. (1996). "State Theories: A Critical Analysis", *Science & Society.* Vol. 60, No.1, pp. 27-57.
Das, R.J. (1998). "The Social and Spatial Character of the Indian State", *Political Geography.* Vol. 17, No. 7, pp. 787-808.
Das, R.J. (1999a). "Politicism and Idealism in State Theory", *Science and Society.* Vol. 63, No. 1, pp. 97-104.
Das, R.J. (1999b). "The Spatiality of Class and State Power: The Case of Indian Land Reforms", *Environment and Planning A.* Vol.31, No. 12, pp. 2103-2126.

Das, R.J. (2001a). "The Political Economy of India", *New Political Economy*. Vol. 6, No. 1, pp. 103-117.
Das, R.J. (2001b). 'Class, Capitalism and Agrarian Transition: A Review and Critique of Some Recent Arguments', *Journal of Peasant Studies*, Vol 29:1, pp. 155-174.
Das, R.J. (2010). Radical Peasant Movements and Rural Distress in India: A Study of the Naxalite Movement. In W. Ahmad, A. Kundu & R. Peet (Eds.). *India's New Economic Policy*. (Pp. 281-306). Routledge, New York.
Das, R.J. (2012a). Why Must Social Science be Critical, and why Must Doing Social Science be Difficult? *Radical Notes*. http://radicalnotes.com/2012/11/03
Das, R.J. (2012b). "Forms of Subsumption of Labour under Capital, Class Struggle and Uneven Development", *Review of Radical Political Economics*. Vol. 44, No. 2, pp. 178-200.
Das, R.J. (2012c). "From Labour Geography to Class Geography: Reasserting the Marxist Theory of Class", *Human Geography*. Vol. 5, No. 1, pp. 19-35.
Das, R.J. 2013. 'Capitalism and Regime Change in the (Globalizing) World of Labour', *Journal of Contemporary Asia*, 43:4, 709-723.
Datt, G. and Ravallion, M. (2010, February, 13). "Shining for the Poor Too", *Economic and Political Weekly*. Vol. XLV, No. 7.
Davidson, R. 2012. *The motional life of your brain*, London: Hudson Street Press.
de Boer, K. and Sonderegger, R. (eds.). 2012. *Conceptions of Critique in Modern and Contemporary Philosophy*, Basingstoke: Palgrave Macmillan.
Derks, A. (2010). "Bonded Labour in Southeast Asia", *Asian Journal of Social Science*. Vol. 38, No. 6, pp. 839-852.
Desai, A.R. (Ed.). (1986). *Agrarian Struggles in India after Independence*. Delhi: Oxford University Press.
Desai, A. (1987). "Rural Development and Human Rights in Independent India", *Economic and Political Weekly*. Vol. 22, No. 31, pp. 1291-1296.
Dias, W. (2005, September 29). One-Day General Strike in India Exposes Need for Socialist-Internationalist Strategy. *World Socialist Web Site*. Retrieved from http://www.wsws.org/en/articles/2005/09/indi-s29.html
Dowd, D. 2002. *Understanding Capitalism*, London: Pluto Press.
Draper, H. 1977. *Karl Marx's theory of revolution: state and bureaucracy*, Monthly Review Press, New York
Drèze, J. & Sen, A. (1995). *India: Economic Development and Social Opportunity*. Oxford: University Press.
Duménil, G. & Lévy, D. (2005). The Neoliberal (Counter-) Revolution. In A. Saad-Filho and D. Johnston (Eds.). *Neoliberalism: A Critical Reader*. (p. 9-19). London: Pluto Press.
Dumont, R. with M. Mazoyer. (1973). *Socialisms and Development*, New York: Praeger.
Dyer, G. (1996). "Output per Acre and Size of Holding: The Logic of Peasant Agriculture under Semi-feudalism", *The Journal of Peasant Studies*. Vol.24, Nos. 1-2, pp.102-131.
Eagleton, T. (1991). *Ideology*. London: Verso.
Eagleton, T. (2009) (1991). *Walter Benjamin or Towards a Revolutionary Criticism*, London: Verso.
Eagleton, T. (2012). *Why Marx was right?*, New Haven: Yale University Press.
Ebeling, M. (2011). "Get with the Program!: Pharmaceutical Marketing, Symptom Checklists and Self-Diagnosis", *Social science and Medicine*. Vol. 73, No. 6, pp. 825-832.
Fisher, M. (2003). "Physicians and the Pharmaceutical Industry - a Dysfunctional Relationship", *Perspectives in Biology and Medicine*. Vol. 46, No. 2, pp. 254-272.
Foley, B. 1985. 'The politics of deconstruction', in R. Davis and R. Schleiffer eds. *Rhetoric and Form: Deconstruction at Yale*, Norman: Oklahoma University Press.

Foster, J.P. (2000). *Marx's Ecology: Materialism and Nature*. New York: Monthly Review Press.

Foucault, M. (1997). What is Critique? In S. Lotringer. (Pp. 41-82). *The Politics of Truth*. Los Angeles: Semiotext(e).

Fracchia, J. (2008). "Capitalist Labour Process and the Body in Pain: The Corporeal Depths of Marx's Concept of Immiserization", *Historical Materialism*. Vol. 16, No. 4, pp. 35-66.

Geras, N. (1987). "Post-Marxism", *New Left Review*. No. 163, pp. 4082.

Gibson-Graham, J.K. (2006). *The End of Capitalism (as we know it): A Feminist Critique of Political Economy*. Minneapolis: University of Minnesota Press.

Gimenez, M. and L. Vogel (2005). 'Marxist--Feminist Thought Today', *Science & Society* 69(1): 5-10

Goodman, D. & Watts, M. (Eds.). (1997). *Globalising Food: Agrarian Questions and Global Restructuring*. London: Routledge.

Goodman, D. & Watts, M. (1997). Agrarian Questions: Global Appetite, Local Metabolism: Nature, Culture, and Industry in Fin-de-siècle Agro-food Systems. In D. Goodman and M. Watts *Globalising Food: Agrarian Questions and Global Restructuring*. London: Routledge.

Gupta, S.P. (1996). Recent Economic Reforms in India and their Impact on the Poor and Vulnerable. In C.H. Hanumantha Rao & H. Linnemann (Eds.). *Economic Reforms and Poverty Alleviation in India*. (pp. 146-147). New Delhi: Sage Publications.

Harman, C and Brenner, R. (2006). 'The origins of capitalism', International socialism, http://www.isj.org.uk/index.php4?id=219

Harriss, J. (1992). "Does the Depressor Still Work? Agrarian Structure and Development in India: A Review of Evidence and Argument", *Journal of Peasant Studies*. Vol. 19, No. 2, pp.189-227.

Harriss, J. (2011). How Far have India's Economic Reforms been "Guided by Compassion and Justice"? Social policy in the neoliberal Era. In S. Ruparelia, S. Reddy, J. Harriss, & S. Corbridge (Eds.). (pp. 127-140). *Understanding India's New Political Economy: A Great Transformation?*. New York: Routledge.

Harvey, D. (1985). *Urbanization of Capital*. Baltimore: John Hopkins University Press.

Harvey, D. (1996). *Justice, Nature and the geography of difference*, Blackwell, Oxford.

Harvey, D. (2003). *The New Imperialism*. Oxford: Oxford University Press.

Harvey, D. (2005). *A Brief History of Neoliberalism*. New York: Oxford University Press.

Harvey, D. (2007). *The Limits to Capital*, London: Verso.

Harvey, D. (2010). *The Enigma of Capital and Crises of Capitalism*, Oxford: Oxford University.

Heller, A. 1976. *The Theory of Need in Marx*, London: Allison & Busby.

Heller, P. 2000. *The Labour of Development: Workers and the Transformation of Capitalism in Kerala, India*, by Patrick Heller. Ithaca, NY: Cornell University Press.

Hilton, R. (Ed.). (1976). *The Transition from Feudalism to Capitalism*. London: New Left Books.

Hoffman, J. (1975). *Marxism and the Theory of Praxis: A Critique of Some New Versions of Old Fallacies*. New York: International Publishers.

Hoffman, J. (1988). *State, Power, and Democracy: Contentious Concepts in Practical Political Theory*. New York: St. Martin's Press.

Hoffman, J. (1995). *Beyond the State: An Introductory Critique*. Cambridge: Polity Press.

Jessop, B. (1990). *State Theory: Putting the Capitalist State in its Place*. (pp.161-162). Cambridge: Polity Press.

Johnson, L. A. (2012, July 3). GlaxoSmithKline to pay $3B for health fraud. *Guardian*. Retrieved from http://www.theguardian.com/world/feedarticle/10317876

Kautsky, K. (1988).*The Agrarian Question*. 2 Vols. London: Zwan Publications.
Keat, R. & Urry, J. (2012). *Social Theory as Science*. London: Routledge.
Khatkhate, D. (2006). "Indian Economic Reform, A Philosopher's Stone", *Economic and Political Weekly*.
Kincaid, H. (1996). *Philosophical Foundations of the Social Sciences*. Cambridge: Cambridge University Press.
Kliman, A. 2007. *Reclaiming Marx's 'Capital'*, Lanham: Lexington books.
Kolchin, P. (1987). *Unfree Labour: American Slavery and Russian Serfdom*. Massachusetts: Harvard University Press.
Kohli, A. (2012). *Poverty amid plenty in the new India*. Delhi: Cambridge University Press.
Kumar, A. (2008). "Dissonance between Economic Reforms and Democracy", *Economic and Political Weekly*. Vol. XLIII, No. 1.
Kurien, C.T. (1994). *Global Capitalism and the Indian Economy*. New Delhi: Orient Longman.
Laclau, E. & Mouffe, C. (2014). *Hegemony and Socialist Strategy*, 2nd Edition. London: Verso.
Laibman, D. 1992. *Value, technical change, and crisis: Explorations in Marxist economic theory*, Armonk, New York: Sharpe
Laibman, D. 2007. *Deep history: a Study in Social Evolution and Human Potential*, Albany: State University of New York press.
Lebowitz, M. 2003. *Beyond Capital: Marx's Political Economy of the Working class*, Basingstoke: Palgrave.
Lenin, V. (1899). *The Development of Capitalism in Russia*. Moscow: Progress Publishers.
Lenin, V. *Materialism and empirio-criticism*, Collected Works vol 14, Moscow: Progress Publishers.
Lenin, V. (1917). *The state and Revolution: The Experience of 1848-51. Available from* : http://www.marxists.org/archive/lenin/works/1917/staterev/ch02.htm
Lenin. (1964). The Dual Power. In *Lenin Collected Works*. (Vol. 24, pp. 38-41). Available from: https://www.marxists.org/archive/lenin/works/1917/apr/09.htm
Lenin, V. (1965). *Collected Works*, Vol. 28. London: Lawrence and Wishart.
Lenin, V. 1974 (1917). The Tasks of the Proletariat in the Present Revolution. In *Collected Works*, Vol. 24. London: Lawrence and Wishart.
Lenin, V. 1978. *Revolutionary Adventurism*, Progress Publishers, Moscow.
McNally, D. 2006. *Another world is possible: Globalization and anti-capitalism*, Winnipeg: Arbeiter Ring Publishing.
Mao, T. (1937). *On Practice: On the Relation Between Knowledge and Practice, Between Knowing and Doing*. Available from: http://www.marxists.org/reference/archive/mao/selected-works/volume-1/mswv1_16.htm
Markovic, M. (1983). 'The idea of critique in social theory', http://www.marxists.org/archive/markovic/1983/critique.htm
Martin, N. (2009). "The Political Economy of Bonded Labour in the Pakistani Punjab", *Contributions to Indian Sociology*. Vol. 43, No. 1, pp. 35-59.
Marx, K. (1845). *German Ideology*. Available from: http://www.marxists.org/archive/marx/works/1845/german-ideology/ch01b.htm
Marx, K. (1857). *Grundrisse*. Available from: http://www.marxists.org/archive/marx/works/1857/grundrisse/ch03.htm
Marx, K. (1859). *A Preface to the Critique of Political Economy*. Available from: http://www.marxists.org/archive/marx/works/1859/critique-pol-economy/preface-abs.htm
Marx, K. (1973). *Surveys from Exile: Political Writings*, Vol. 2. London: Penguin Books. P. 138.

Marx, K. (1976). *Wage-labor and Capital & Value, Price and Profit*, New York: International Publishers.
Marx, K. (1977). *Capital Volume 1*. New York: Vintage.
Marx, K. (1981). *Capital Volume 3*. New York: Penguin.
Marx, K. and Engels, F. 1977. *Selected Writings*, Oxford: Oxford University Press.
McNally, D. 2006. *Another world is possible*, Winnipeg: Arbeiter Ring Publishing.
Menard, R. (2001). *Migrants, Servants and Slaves: Unfree Labor in Colonial British America*. Aldershot: Ashgate.
Migdal, J. (2001). *The State in Society*. Cambridge: Cambridge University Press.
Miliband, R. (1977). *Marxism and Politics*. Oxford: Oxford University Press.
Miller, B. (2000). *Geography and social movements*, University of Minnesota Press, Minneapolis.
Mohanty, M. (1977). *Revolutionary violence: a study of the Maoist movement in India*, Allied, New Delhi.
Montero, R. (2011). "Free and Unfree Labour in the Colonial Andes in the Sixteenth and Seventeenth Centuries", *International Review of social History*. Vol. 56, No. 19, pp. 297-318.
Morrow, W. (2012, July 5). Pharmaceutical Giant GlaxoSmithKline fined $3 Billion. *World Socialist Web Site*. Retrieved from http://www.wsws.org/en/articles/2012/07/glax-j05.html
Nanda, M. (1995). "Transnationalization of the Third World State and the Undoing of the Green Revolution", *Economic and Political Weekly*. Vol.30, No.4.
Naruzzaman, M. (2005). "Economic Liberalization and Poverty in the Developing Countries", *Journal of Contemporary Asia*. Vol. 35, No. 1, pp. 109-127.
Nayyar, R. (1996). New Initiatives for Poverty Alleviation in Rural India. In: C. H. Hanumantha Rao & H. Linnemann (Eds.). *Economic Reforms and Poverty Alleviation in India*. (pp. 175, 188). New Delhi: Sage Publications.
Newman, S. (2007). *Unstable universalities: Poststructuralism and radical politics*, Manchester: Manchester university Press.
Neville, S. (2012, July 3). GlaxoSmithKline Fined $3bn after Bribing Doctors to Increase Drugs Sales. *Guardian*. http://www.theguardian.com/business/2012/jul/03/glaxosmithkline-fined-bribing-doctors-pharmaceuticals
Ollman, B. (2003). *Dance of the dialectic*, Urbana: University of Illinois Press.
Paige, J. 1975. *Agrarian revolution*, Free Press, New York.
Panitch, L. (1997). 'The socialist register 1997 preface', *Socialist register*, Winnipeg: Fernwood.
Paolucci, P. (2007). *Marx's Scientific Dialectics*, Chicago: Haymarket.
Patnaik, P. (2010). "A Left Approach to Development", *Economic and Political Weekly*. Vol. XLV, No. 30.
Patnaik, P. (2010b). "The State under Neoliberalism". *MR Zine*. Retrieved from: http://mrzine.monthlyreview.org/ 2010/ patnaik100810.html
Patnaik, U. (Ed.). (1990). *Agrarian Relations: The Mode of Production Debate*. Oxford: Oxford University Press.
Patnaik, U. (1999). *The Long Transition: Essays on Political Economy*, New Delhi: Tulika Press.
Patnaik, U. (2007). *The Republic of Hunger*. Gurgaon: Three Essays Collective.
Patnaik, U. & Hasan, Z. (1995). Aspects of the Farmers Movement in Uttar Pradash in the Context of Uneven Capitalist Development in Indian Agriculture. In. T.V. Sathyamurthy (Ed.). *Industry and Agriculture in India since Independence*. (Pp. 274-279, 287). Delhi: Oxford University Press.

Petras, J. (1997). 'Imperialism and NGOs in Latin America', *Monthly Review*, vol. 49:7, https://monthlyreview.org/1997/12/01/imperialism-and-ngos-in-latin-america

Przeworski, A.. (1985). *Capitalism and Social Democracy*, Cambridge: Cambridge University Press.

Raj, K.N., Amartya Sen, and C.H. Hanumantha Rao (eds.). (1988), *Dharm Narain: Studies on Indian Agriculture*, Delhi: Oxford University Press.

Rao, C. H. & Linnemann, H. (Eds.). (1996). *Economic Reforms and Poverty Alleviation in India.* New Delhi: Sage Publications.

Rees, J. (1998). *The Algebra of revolution*, Milton Park: Routledge.

Rosenau, P. (1991). *Post-Modernism and the Social Sciences: Insights, Inroads, and Intrusions*. Princeton: Princeton University Press.

Rudolph, L. I. & Rudolph, S. H. (1987). *In Pursuit of Lakshmi: The Political Economy of the Indian State.* Chicago: University of Chicago Press.

Saad-Filho, A. and Johnston, D. eds. (2005). *Neoliberalism: A Critical Reader*, London: Pluto.

Sathyamurthy, T.V. (Ed.). (1995a). *Industry and Agriculture in India since Independence.* Oxford: Oxford University Press.

Sathyamurthy, T.V. (1995b). Introduction. In T.V. Sathyamurthy (Ed.). *Industry and Agriculture in India since Independence* (pp. 27, 31). Delhi: Oxford University Press.

Sayer, A. (1992). *Method in Social Science: A Realist Approach*. London: Routledge.

Science & Society. (2006). *Rethinking Marx and history*, Vol 70:2.

Sen, A.K., 1981, *Poverty and Famines: An Essay on Entitlement and Deprivation*, Delhi: Oxford University Press.

Shiva, V. (2014). 'Small is really beautiful', *Deccan Chronicle*, January 1.

Sinha, B and Pushpendra. (2000). *Land Reforms in India – Vol. 5*, New Delhi: Sage

Skocpol, T. (1985). Bringing the State Back In. In E. D. Rueschemeyer & T. Skocpol (Eds.), *Bringing the State Back In.* Cambridge: Cambridge University Press.

Smith, M. (2010). *Global Capitalism in Crisis: Karl Marx and the Decay of the Profit System.* Halifax and Winnipeg: Fernwood Publishing.

Sokal, A. and Bricmont, J. (1998). *Fashionable Nonsense: Postmodern Intellectuals' Abuse of Science.* New York: Picador.

Spilker, B. (1998). "Reducing Pharmaceutical Risk", *Drug News and perspectives.* Vol. 11, No. 6, pp. 325-330.

Srivastava, R. (1995). India's Uneven Development and its Implications for Political Processes: an Analysis of Some Recent Trends. In. T.V. Sathyamurthy (Ed.). *Industry and Agriculture in India since Independence.* (p. 233). Delhi: Oxford University Press.

Sumit, R. (1995). "Liberalization" and the Indian Economy: Myth and Reality. In: T.V. Sathyamurthy (Ed.). *Industry and Agriculture in India since Independence.* (pp. 138-139). Delhi: Oxford University Press.

Sutton, J. (1996). *Recent Marxian Theory*, Albany, NY: SUNY Press.

Sweezy, P. (1976). 'A Critique', in Hilton [1976].

Tharamangalam, J. (1981). *Agrarian Class Conflict: The Political Mobilization of AgriculturalLaborers in Kuttanad, South India*, Vancouver and London: University of British Colombia Press.

Therborn, G. 2008. *From Marxism to Post-Marxism*. London: Verso.

Thorner, D. (ed.). (1996). *Ecological and Agrarian Regions of South Asia circa 1930*, Karachi: Oxford University Press.

Timpanaro, S. (1980). *Materialism*, London: Verso.

Trotsky, L. (1939a). *Marxism in our Time.* Available from: http://www.marxists.org/archive/trotsky/1939/04/marxism.htm

Trotsky, L. (1939b). *The ABC of materialist dialectics*, http://www.marxists.org/archive/trotsky/1939/12/abc.htm
Trotsky, L. (1995) (1973). *In Defense of Marx*. New York: Pathfinder.
Trotsky, L. (1973) (2011). *Problems of Everyday Life*, Atlanta: Pathfinder.
Van Stuijvenberg, P.A. (1996). Structural Adjustment in India - What about Poverty Alleviation? In C.H. Hanumantha Rao & H. Linnemann (Eds.). *Economic Reforms and Poverty Alleviation in India*. (P. 52). New Delhi: Sage Publications.
Varshney, A.. (1995). *Democracy, Development and the Countryside: Urban-rural Struggles in India*, Cambridge: Cambridge University Press.
Varshney, A. (1998). *Democracy, Development and the Countryside: Urban-Rural Struggles in India.* Cambridge: University Press.
Vasudevan, R. (2008, March 15). "Accumulation by Dispossession in India", *Economic and Political Weekly*. Vol. XLIII, No. 11.
Veblen, T. 1904. *The Theory of Business Enterprise*, Transaction Publishers.
Vogel, L. (2014). *Marxism and the Oppression of Women: Toward a Unitary Theory*. Chicago: Haymarket.
Wickremasinghe, N. & K. Jones. (2004, May 13). India: Stalinists to Promote Congress Power Bid. *World Socialist Web Site*. Retrieved from http://www.wsws.org/en/articles/2004/05/ind-m13.html
Williams, R. (1976). *Keywords*. New York: Oxford University Press.
Wilson, D. (2011, November 3). Glaxo Settles Cases With U.S. for $3 Billion. *New York Times*. http://www.nytimes.com/2011/11/04/business/glaxo-to-pay-3-billion-in-avandia-settlement.html?_r=0
Wolford, W. (2004). 'This land is ours now: spatial imaginaries and the struggle for land in Brazil, *Annals of the Association of American Geographers*, 94:2, 409-424.
Wood, E. (1986). *The Retreat from Class: A New 'True' Socialism*. London: Verso.
Wood, E. (1999). *The Origin of capitalism*, Monthly Review.
Wood, E. (2003). *The Empire of Capital*. Delhi: Leftword.
Wright, E. (1978). *Class, Crisis and the State*. London: New Left Books.
Wright, E. ed. (2005). *Approaches to Class Analysis*, Cambridge: Cambridge University Press.
Wolff, R. and Resnick, S. (2012). *Contending Economic Theories*, Cambridge: MIT press.
Zizek, S. (2009). *The Parallax view*, Cambridge: MIT press.

ACKNOWLEDGMENTS

I would like to gratefully acknowledge the permission to draw upon previously published materials from the following journals published by Routledge. Chapters 4-6 heavily draw on articles published, respectively, in *New Political Economy*, *Journal of Contemporary Asia*, and *Journal of Peasant Studies*.

Chapter 3 is a revised version of an article published in *Science& Society*. I am thankful to David Laibman, the editor of the journal, for granting me permission to use the material in this book.

AUTHOR'S CONTACT INFORMATION

Dr. Raju J. Das
Associate Professor
Faculty of Graduate Studies
York University
Ross Building 431
Toronto, Canada, M3J 1P3
Telephone: 1-905-417-4652
E-mail: rajudas@yorku.ca

INDEX

D

E

K

L

M

N

O

T

U

V

W

Z